SharePoint 2010

Branding in Practice,
A Guide For Web Developers

Yaroslav Pentsarskyy

ISBN: 1460908732

ISBN-13: 9781460908730

Library of Congress Control Number: 2011902184

INTRODUCTION

SharePoint 2010 is an exciting new release of already well-established platform. SharePoint has evolved dramatically over the years: from intranet and collaboration sites to public Internet content management system supporting complex scenarios and deployments. As any other content management system, SharePoint allows extending its functionality and supports a variety of options and approaches. There is a vast amount of resources on how you can develop custom components for SharePoint 2010. When it comes to branding, it's a different story. There are few accepted approaches on how to implement branding in SharePoint and very few guides on how to approach branding tasks as a whole and integrate them into the solution development process. Branding is a feature which your customer (external or internal) has agreed to pay for, and that feature has to be incorporated in the proper way into the rest of the solution.

This book is meant to help you apply your existing branding skills to the SharePoint world in the best possible way.

We'll explore how to brand collaboration sites as well as publishing sites. We'll also see how you can brand sites that are hosted not only on a dedicated server but on a shared infrastructure in a cloud—which promises to be a very popular scenario.

I hope you will enjoy the read and keep in touch with all the SharePoint branding trends using my blog: www.sharemuch.com.

WHOM THIS BOOK IS FOR

This book is meant for web developers or user interface developers who already know CSS, JavaScript, and HTML to a fair extent. You also have to be familiar with some of the concepts in SharePoint and .NET; in other words, you have to know how to perform basic functions in SharePoint. This book will bridge anything else you will need to successfully apply your existing branding skills to the SharePoint world.

Although on a small project you might have overlapping responsibilities to develop back-end features and perform branding, this book assumes you perform only branding functions, and we'll try to stay away from .NET development topics. On a typical project, your teammates in charge of .NET development will create some of the artifacts for you, and in some other cases it'll be assumed you have to create them. I believe you'll feel more confident knowing a few extra things about SharePoint development artifacts so you're ready for either scenario.

Here are the three objectives that this book is trying to achieve:

- *Get you familiar with branding scenarios and various approaches to those scenarios.*

  When you're beginning with SharePoint 2010 branding, you need a clear direction on how to proceed with development; once you're confident on how to get started, you can pick from various approaches applicable to your case. This book is structured to give you typical branding scenarios so you're clear on what's applicable in your case and what are the exact steps to get there.

- *Give you a real code with all of the steps you need to do to run it.*

   We've all been there. You have a technical problem, you find the solution someone has posted online, you put it together...it doesn't work. The last thing you want to see is a sample that's broken. This book comes with references to downloadable solution files that have been compiled and tested.

- *Get you thinking about what else you can do with features described and scenarios used.*

   Since I assume you already have prior CSS, JavaScript, and HTML knowledge, this book tries to give you handy tips on how to take your solution one step further by applying your existing knowledge to SharePoint 2010. Throughout each sample, you will find pointers that will get you thinking how else you could use features discussed.

With this set of objectives, I really do hope you will find this book easy and intuitive to navigate and not just something you could read online from a blog post. It will take a bit of time to get completely familiar with things, but my goal is to help you get there fast and be confident your approach has a sound architecture and is something you will be proud of.

With that, I hope you have fun reading this book, and if you want to give me your feedback, visit my blog and drop me a note: www.sharemuch.com.

ABOUT THE AUTHOR

Yaroslav Pentsarskyy has been architecting and implementing SharePoint solutions since its 2003 release. Yaroslav has extensive .NET and SharePoint development experience working with medium-sized businesses, nonprofits, and government organizations.

As a recipient of the Microsoft Most Valuable Professional (MVP) 2009 and 2010 Award, Yaroslav is also a developer audience leader for VanSPUG (Vancouver SharePoint Usergroup) and actively contributes to local and not-so-local technical communities by presenting at technology events and sharing his findings in his almost-daily blog: www.sharemuch.com.

Outside of work, Yaroslav enjoys travelling and maintains a growing list of "places-to-visit".

ACKNOWLEDGMENTS

My thanks extend to local and worldwide usergroup leaders with whom I have been involved over the last few years. Your involvement in the community helps people tremendously. Please keep doing what you're doing.

I also would like to mention and thank all of the bloggers out there who share their ideas online. It takes a lot of effort and dedication to post all of those tips on your blogs almost every day. Without those posts we wouldn't have such a great community.

BOOK SOURCE CODE

This book comes with a source code for each chapter. As you go through the book, you will see many examples and source codes. The source codes in the book are for you to follow the flow of the logic that is referenced, not to type it out into your Visual Studio. If you would like to see actual examples in action, download the corresponding chapter source code that is ready for you to compile and use. The source code samples assume you're running the system with:

- Microsoft SharePoint Server 2010 installed.
- Visual Studio 2010 Professional or higher installed.
- PowerShell enabled.
- Sufficient account permissions to access SharePoint 2010 Central Administration and Service Applications.

At the time of my writing this book, Microsoft provided for download a *2010 Information Worker Demonstration and Evaluation Virtual Machine (RTM)*. You will find it just by searching the name above. It's a great starting resource, especially if you don't have the necessary time to install SharePoint 2010 with most of its components. By downloading the virtual machine above, you will save time and can get started with some of the samples in the book right away.

Also, all source codes can be downloaded from the "Downloads" section at www.sharemuch.com. Below is the source code index for each sample:

CHAPTER 2

Visual Studio 2010 solution structure for the branding project

CHAPTER 3

Creating basic themes
Creating complex themes in Visual Studio 2010
Working with compile time directives in SharePoint style sheets
Structure of collaboration Masterpage
Dynamically discovering granular components of the masterpage
Setting alternative Masterpage for collaboration sites

CHAPTER 4

Publishing Masterpage structure
Modifying Masterpage on the SharePoint 2010 publishing site
Setting custom style sheets for the SharePoint 2010 publishing site
Customizing administrative UI and modal dialogs

CHAPTER 5

Applying common design artifacts and settings on existing specialized sites

CHAPTER 6

Customizing search center look and feel
Adding new metadata to your search results view
Adding graphic representation of item ratings to your search results

CHAPTER 7

Getting started with third-party UI components integration
Replacing SharePoint out-of-the-box menu control with third-party components

CHAPTER 8

Publishing page layout structure
Getting started with creating custom SharePoint pages
Provisioning several pages with one module
Rendering additional page-specific metadata during page edit
Provisioning page content to your pages programmatically
Custom web parts and their role in SharePoint branding
Branding specific instances of out-of-the-box web parts
Provisioning web parts directly to page layouts

CHAPTER 9

Applying branding to SharePoint list views
Making changes to list view and list item detail view using XSL
Defining list view look and feel in your custom list schema
Creating custom list item detail forms
Conditionally displaying user interface elements in SharePoint list forms
Dynamically changing SharePoint 2010 list form rendering templates
Branding aggregated content within lists and rollups

CHAPTER 10

Working with external SharePoint 2010 web service calls
Working with internal SharePoint 2010 web service calls
Using JQuery and additional extensions to enhance interaction of SharePoint forms
Working with custom web services in SharePoint 2010

CHAPTER 11

Creating basic SharePoint ribbon controls
Creating a flyout anchor on your ribbon
Working with large ribbon JavaScript files
Working with ribbon groups and tabs
Creating site-level ribbon tabs
Determining the state of ribbon tabs and hiding ribbon
Working with SharePoint application pages and their relation to ribbon
Opening modal windows upon ribbon control clicked

TABLE OF CONTENTS

Introduction v

Whom This Book is For. vii

About the Author. ix

Book Source Code xiii

Chapter 1 Getting Things Set Up. 1

Setting up your development virtual machine 2
Recommended tools for SharePoint user interface
development 4

**Chapter 2 General Overview of SharePoint 2010 Branding; What's
Where and Why?.** 9

SharePoint 2010 collaboration sites 10
SharePoint 2010 publishing sites 14
SharePoint 2010 specialized sites 19
Setting up Visual Studio solution structure
for the branding project 22

Chapter 3 Customizing SharePoint 2010 Collaboration Sites 31

Creating basic themes 32
Creating complex themes in Visual Studio 2010 34

Working with compile time directives in
SharePoint style sheets. 40
What collaboration Masterpage is all about. 44
Setting alternative Masterpage for collaboration sites 61
Dynamically discovering granular components of the
masterpage and branding a typical site 67

Chapter 4 Customizing SharePoint 2010 Publishing Sites **79**

What publishing Masterpage is all about. 79
Modifying Masterpage on the SharePoint 2010 publishing site 93
Setting custom style sheets for the SharePoint 2010
publishing site 99
Customizing administrative UI and modal dialogs 104

Chapter 5 Customizing SharePoint 2010 Specialized Sites **109**

Applying common design artifacts and settings on existing
specialized sites 120

Chapter 6 Extending Search Look and Feel **127**

Customizing search center look and feel. 128
Adding new metadata to your search results view. 137
Adding graphic representation of item ratings
to your search results 144

**Chapter 7 Integrating Third-Party UI Components
into SharePoint** **151**

Getting started with third-party UI components integration . .152
Replacing SharePoint out-of-the-box menu control
with third-party components 155

**Chapter 8 Getting Started with and Branding SharePoint Publishing
and Custom Pages** **163**

What publishing page layout is all about. 164
Getting started with creating custom SharePoint pages. 175

Provisioning several pages with one module. 181
Rendering additional page-specific metadata
during page edit 185
Provisioning page content to your pages programmatically 192
Custom web parts and their role in SharePoint branding 196
Branding specific instances of out-of-the-box web parts . . . 200
Provisioning web parts directly to page layouts 204

Chapter 9 Changing the Look of SharePoint Forms 211

Applying branding to SharePoint list views. 211
Making changes to list view and list item
detail view using XSL 214
Defining list view look and feel in your custom list schema . . .219
Creating custom list item detail forms. 224
Conditionally displaying user interface
elements in SharePoint list forms 230
Dynamically changing SharePoint 2010
list form rendering templates 236
Branding aggregated content within lists and rollups 238

**Chapter 10 Client-Side Interaction with External and Local Web
Services 247**

Working with external SharePoint 2010 web service calls . . . 248
Working with internal SharePoint 2010 web service calls 252
Using JQuery and additional extensions to enhance
interaction of SharePoint forms 256
Working with custom web services in SharePoint 2010 266

**Chapter 11 Creating SharePoint 2010 Ribbon Components and
Managing Existing Ribbon Elements 275**

Creating basic SharePoint ribbon controls. 275
Creating a flyout anchor on your ribbon 278
What if your ribbon JavaScript is too large for one file? 281
Working with ribbon groups and tabs. 284
Creating site-level ribbon tabs. 288
Determining the state of ribbon tabs and hiding ribbon 291

Where is SharePoint out-of-the-box ribbon defined? 293
Working with SharePoint application pages
and their relation to ribbon. 295
Opening modal windows upon ribbon control clicked 298

...Etc.. 305

CHAPTER 1

Getting Things Set Up

Before we get started with SharePoint 2010 branding, I want to make sure we both are on the same page as to how things are set up and that you're looking on the same screen I am writing about. Since in many examples of this book we're going to be working with SharePoint 2010 professional development tools like Visual Studio and advanced user tools like SharePoint Designer, I am not going to assume you have an infrastructure team which has the development environment set up for you. Instead, we're going to use a virtual machine you can download online called *2010 Information Worker Demonstration and Evaluation Virtual Machine (RTM)*. If you search for the above virtual machine, you will find an archived version of the system which has typical intranet and Internet infrastructure set up. It also has professional development tools which we're going to use here.

Providing you're going to use a computer which supports virtualization technology and running Windows 7 or Windows 2008 Server R2, you can attach the downloaded virtual machine image to your computer and use it to run scenarios we outline in this book. Remember, the virtual machine you will download is not a development environment you can use on a day-to-day basis. There are some limitations on the site you will download this machine from, including a time limitation after which the virtual machine will expire. However, it's a perfect environment for consistent demos which you will be able to get started on right away. For production development, I recommend getting a similar environment set up using your own tools.

Setting up your development virtual machine

In this section I would like to cover the basics of importing the virtual machine you will either download from the source I provided or any other source. I assume you will be running your host operating system as Windows Server 2008 R2. Feel free to validate and follow more detailed instructions on setting up your machine with the source which is going to provide it for you. In here I will outline some of the most typical basics.

Your host system will need:

- Windows Server 2008 R2 with the Hyper-V role enabled (see technet **Hyper-V** for more details).

- Drive Formatting: NTFS; also ensure your drive is uncompressed.

- Processor: Intel VT or AMD-V capable.

- RAM: 8 GB or more recommended; you can try running it with 6 GB but the performance is not going to be the best.

- Hard disk space required for install: 50 GB.

Once you have downloaded and extracted the virtual machines:

- Install the Hyper-V role on your Windows Server 2008 R2 host.

- Open Hyper-V Manager.

- Under Actions, click **Virtual Network Manager....**

- Choose **New virtual network** (under **Virtual Networks** pane).

- Choose **Internal** from the type list, click **Add**.

- Enter **Internal** as a name and click **OK**.

- Under **Actions**, click **Import Virtual Machine**.

- **Browse** to locate the folder where your virtual machine package is.

- Click **Import**—the import status will appear in the **Operations** column.

- Select the imported virtual machine and click **Settings** in the right pane of the Hyper-V Manager.

- Here you can select the amount of RAM and other settings you would like to assign to your virtual machine.

- Also, confirm the **Network Adapter** is connected to the **Internal** network.

- Click **OK** and start the newly added virtual machine.

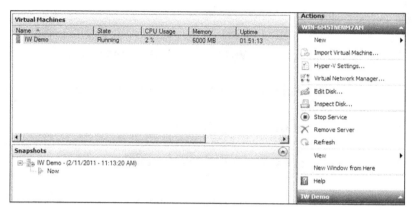

Figure 1-1 Virtual machine running in Windows 2008 Server R2 environment.

This will get you started from the technical standpoint.

Recommended tools for SharePoint user interface development

Apart from the out-of-the-box tools you may have in your development virtual machine, I recommend a few useful (community and other free) tools which will help your development process significantly. You can download them right into your development environment.

1. Latest version of Mozilla Firefox with Firebug plug-in. I can't imagine anyone doing user interface development without Firebug; it's too bad that it doesn't run on all of the other browsers. Many other browsers have their own developer toolbars (which you can normally call up by pressing F12) but the richness of features you get with Firebug, in my opinion, is greater. I do, however, recommend downloading other browsers, especially if you're branding SharePoint for the web, to ensure your customizations run smoothly in as many browsers as a large percentage of your visitors use.

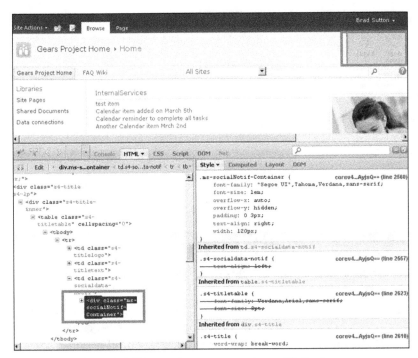

Figure 1-2 Discovering page markup with Firebug.

2. Notepad++ is a great tool which you can download. Essentially it's a developer version of a text editor. It's quite useful if you want to edit an ASPX or XML (or any other format) document without editing it in Visual Studio. If gives you some nice features and is very fast. It also recognizes markup of very many languages, so it's easier to read CSS or JavaScript in it.

3. CKS: Development Tools Edition is a specific extension to Visual Studio 2010 which can be downloaded online. The extension package can be installed using standard Visual Studio UI; the process is explained on the site where you download the package. CKS Dev significantly helps with the development process for SharePoint 2010 in Visual Studio 2010. You get templates for various branding and back-end artifacts, which saves time. In this book I will not assume you're running CKS Dev, and if you are, be sure to read the documentation on the tool to see how a few things we have done manually here can be speeded up.

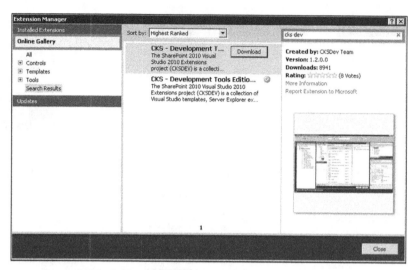

Figure 1-3 Installing CKS Dev as a Visual Studio 2010 extension.

As I go through the chapters, I will mention a few other community resources you can use in your development. SharePoint has many free and community components which have been developed by community leads. I recommend checking once in a while at www.codeplex.com and searching for "SharePoint"—you will be surprised how many great tools are there.

CHAPTER 2

General Overview of SharePoint 2010 Branding; What's Where and Why?

SharePoint 2010 branding doesn't have a single answer to it. SharePoint started as a simple application meant to allow users to author content and host it on the intranet. There are many blogging platforms out there that allow doing just that. Over time SharePoint has evolved to support better scalability so you can have the same functionality in environments with larger user bases. This called for a little bit more complex architecture of the product. Obviously large user bases called for back-end features allowing the managing of higher volumes. As things progressed and stabilized, SharePoint started to grow to support various industries and user scenarios. When most organizations used SharePoint for the intranet, some started to use it to host their public sites; others used it as a platform for custom applications. In this release, which has been around for a while now, SharePoint has definitely evolved into a platform on which developers build their custom applications as well as utilize variety of tools and templates to build sites and workspaces which do not require development.

This one paragraph above giving an overview of SharePoint will hopefully help you understand why things are the way they are in SharePoint. Since you have been doing user interface development and possibly web development before, you probably got used to some platfroms. That's why it's important to keep an open mind when working with SharePoint and understand how things have evolved. In some cases you will notice that it will require more work to perform certain tasks than you used to. When this happens, things are likely to be set up this way to accommodate more complex deployments and scalability, and your scenario is caught in the middle between high and medium complexity. Various scenarios call for different templates. Instances of sites are created based on those templates, and, depending on how different they are, you might have a few templates to create a solution consisting of several sites.

Typical SharePoint implementation consists of a variety of sites based on the site templates. A site template defines what features will be available on the instance of the site. The features we're speaking of are not just functionality, but also branding and other components of the site. Those features make up the template functionality, look, and feel. SharePoint 2010 has a variety of existing templates which typical corporate sites are usually based on. If you're tasked with the branding of an existing SharePoint 2010 site, this doesn't mean you have to create new templates; you can leverage artifacts responsible for the branding of the site and transform your existing site into a completely new look and feel. In this chapter we will go over the main out-of-the-box site templates and take a look at what artifacts contribute to site branding.

SharePoint 2010 collaboration sites

SharePoint, in its early design, was meant for pure collaboration and intranet scenarios. SharePoint 2010 has many out-of-the-box site templates to support collaboration. Collaboration site templates are mainly focused on collaborative features and have standard, basic design. Sites based on the collaboration site templates are not meant for Internet site scenarios but purely for intranet. This also means that branding for the collaboration site is somewhat limited and different from the templates, which will be used for Internet sites which we discuss further.

Let's take a look at one of the basic collaboration sites—a team site.

Navigate to the instance of collaboration site, in case of our virtual environment its URL is http://intranet.contoso.com.

To create a new instance of collaboration site:

1. From existing SharePoint site, click **Site Actions** -> **New Site**.
2. Under **Filter by**, select **Collaboration**.
3. Pick **Team site** from the list of options.
4. Give your site a title and URL and click **Create**.

After the site has been created, you will see it similar to the below:

Figure 2-1 The look of the newly created team site home page.

The three areas you see highlighted are the:

Header—This exposes the top navigation controls and the title of the site. You also see the controls that allow management of the site, such as the **Site Actions** menu and ribbon tabs. Those controls will only appear if the user has valid permissions to edit the page or manage the site.

Left Navigation—The items that appear in this control can be managed from the administrative UI and by default those will automatically populate, depending on the lists and document libraries present on the site.

Content section—This section is dedicated to the content of the site. By default, some of the content is already preloaded so that users of a team site have something to start with. This content can be edited providing the user has sufficient permission to modify the page.

The layout of the page in the figure above is defined by the out-of-the-box Masterpage.

The Masterpage is a file that defines the header of the page and a few other elements you see on the page. Masterpages drive the look and feel of each page layout that uses it. Custom and out-of-the-box Masterpages reside in the Masterpage gallery. To access the gallery from SharePoint UI:

1. Ensure you're logged in to the site with sufficient permissions to manage it. In our demo environment you would log in as **contoso\administrator**; the password will be provided on the site where you downloaded the virtual machine image.
2. From the home page of existing **Team Site** instance, http:// intranet.contoso.com, click **Site Actions->Site Settings**.
3. Under **Galleries** click **Masterpages**.

By default, SharePoint 2010 comes with three out-of-the-box Masterpages:

1. Default.master.
2. Minimal.master.
3. v4.master.

SharePoint 2010 team site uses *v4.master*. By default there is no user interface inside site administration to change the Masterpage the site is using.

That's not very flexible, you might say—and you are right. Collaboration sites, as we will establish even further, don't have the richness of UI customization, but there are few ways you can still leverage the look and feel.

1. Click **Site Actions->Site Settings**.
2. Under **Look and Feel** click **Tree View**.
3. Uncheck **Enable Quick Launch** and click **OK**.

This will remove the quick launch options for site users.

Now, from the **Look and Feel** section of **Site Settings**, click **Top Link Bar**. This setting will allow you to create a top menu for the site. The information entered here will be saved in the SharePoint database and rolled up in the user controls defined in the Masterpage Team Site and will allow you to edit the page:

Let's navigate to the home page of the site and edit it:

1. **Site Actions->Edit Page**.
2. Place the cursor below the welcome text on the page.
3. From the ribbon click **Insert->Existing List**.
4. From the **Web Parts** list, pick **Calendar**.
5. Save the page by using ribbon controls.

Take note of how your page looks, including the calendar.

Let's take a look at how you can modify site colors:

1. Click **Site Actions->Site Settings**.
2. Under **Look and Feel** click **Site Theme**.

The site theme user interface you see below allows you to choose colors and fonts that will be used on the site. Select any theme of your choice and click **Apply** to see how your team site changes its look.

Take note of the changes you see to links and the calendar web part you have added.

Themes are essential to branding of SharePoint 2010 collaboration sites.

In the next chapter we will take a look how you can create your own simple themes and incorporate your custom CSS into the theme allowing not just to change colors and fonts, but to define your own styles.

SharePoint 2010 publishing sites

More and more, SharePoint has been evolving as a content management system allowing for complex authoring scenarios and workflows. SharePoint 2007 and 2010 have been used as platforms for many Internet sites and this trend is growing even more. The capabilities that make SharePoint 2010 a great platform for Internet sites are part of the SharePoint publishing template. The SharePoint publishing site template includes, among other functionalities, features enabling user interface developers to take full advantage of managing the look and feel of out-of-the-box artifacts. In other words, you could customize almost anything on the site which uses the publishing site template.

Let's take a look at the typical publishing site template. If you're using *2010 Information Worker Demonstration and Evaluation Virtual Machine (RTM)*, there is an instance of the publishing site created for you with the URL: www.contoso.com.

Let's take a look at how the branding is structured for publishing sites. Publishing sites still use Masterpages which define the header of the page and main areas on the page. You can change the Masterpage your site is using, and we'll see how in a moment. The concept of themes is still applicable in the publishing site scenario, meaning you can customize themes and extend them to support custom style sheets just as you have done for collaboration site. You can specify the CSS file that your site is going to be using right from the administrative UI or programmatically. This means that you don't have to create a custom theme just to incorporate a custom style sheet for the site. One of the main differences between the collaboration site and publishing is that each page in the publishing site has a choice of a few out-of-the-box **page layouts** that it can inherit from.

Page layouts define zones and areas for the page's main body. Each page which inherits from the particular page layout will have zones and areas defined in the page layout. Those zones and other markup will appear just as defined in page layout on instances of pages inheriting from the layout.

In the collaboration site template, we had one layout defined in the Masterpage; we also had few administrative options allowing us to hide left navigation, for example, or change the order of things. We couldn't, however, add our own custom top navigation menu with slick UI and the behavior we require. By using page layout, we can define the look and feel of anything on the page. Page layouts can use additional style sheets to help them govern the behavior of the page.

You might be thinking, "Why do I need multiple page layouts? One or two should be sufficient." In some cases, yes. In most cases, SharePoint sites and pages on them will have different purposes and different behavior. For example, the home page will have complex structure with multiple zones where different web parts and lists are going to be hosted in. You might also have the news and events page on the site. This page will have the title and body of the news and possibly some additional metadata, such as the date of the news release. For each major type of page, or page with separate behavior, you may require a separate page layout.

You may be thinking, "Why don't I create a universal page layout which has all the zones and areas to satisfy each scenario my user may have?" and this solution might be a good option for your scenario, especially when you have two or three distinct layouts. However, if you have over five layout requirements, it might complicate content authoring experience, and your users might be confused about which zone they should then use for which content. Page layouts can also be used to tie content to a different **content type**. Content type is a SharePoint system feature which combines defined metadata and allows SharePoint to locate instances of content type anywhere on the site by using a content type reference.

For example, you may have a news content type which will define a news piece with a date, title of the news, and the body. This piece of news will also have its layout to structure the data in a specific way. SharePoint 2010 allows users and developers to perform queries on content type and provide pieces of metadata as a result. In practice, we could have a roll-up of the news based on the date for instance, and users would be able to see titles of news releases and the link to the actual news page.

Publishing content types very commonly have an individual page layout attached to them to help content authors identify the piece of content as a separate entity from all the other pages.

Let's take a look at some more of the branding-specific features and SharePoint 2010 out-of-the-box UI to manage them:

1. From http://intranet.contoso.co, click **Site Actions -> Site Settings**.
2. Under **Galleries** click **Masterpages and page layouts**.

In this gallery you will find all of the Masterpages (files with extension **master**) uploaded to the site and page layouts (files with extension **aspx**). In a publishing site scenario it's a standard process to upload new Masterpages and page layouts since those can be selected by site administrators and authorized users to be used throughout the site. Let's see how:

1. From the http://intranet.contoso.com, click **Site Actions ->
   Site Settings**.
2. Under **Look and Feel** click **Masterpage**.

Here you have an option to specify the **Site Masterpage**, which
is the Masterpage which will be used by pages on the site. The
drop-down of options will include more Masterpages as you
upload them, which we'll do later. The **System Masterpage** is the
Masterpage you see right when you're on the settings page or
any other SharePoint system page, for that matter. Since item
forms, such as document upload form or create new list item form,
use a system Masterpage, you may need to customize **System
Masterpage** to ensure your forms on the site look appropriate, if
you're planning to expose those to users. The last option on the
Look and Feel page allows you to set new **Alternate CSS URL**,
which in this case will allow you to inject your own CSS to be used
on the site. By specifying your own CSS file, you will be able to
overwrite the default behavior of the out-of-the-box CSS selectors
for out-of-the-box and custom controls.

Let's take a look at how different the navigation management tool
is for publishing sites:

1. Click **Site Actions -> Site Settings**.
2. Click **Navigation**.

In here, SharePoint power users are able to define not only the
nodes that will appear on the top navigation of the site, but
also the underlying pages or sites. They're also able to add their
own links and nodes and sort them in one of a few options.
By making changes in here, SharePoint saves settings into the
content database and exposes the navigation structure using
a specialized navigation object. The default navigation control
you see rendered on the site connects to that specialized object
and renders HTML based on the data in the object. Further, we'll
take a look at how we can integrate third party controls to render
similar but visually different navigation HTML. The benefit of using
a custom or third party control to render your navigation is that

you have more flexibility of how you can style its elements and manage the behavior.

Going back to **site settings**, you will also see the link to **Site Theme**; there is no difference on how you can manage site themes for the publishing site and collaboration site. The theming engine is the same, and the settings page has the same capabilities. As you can probably see now, one of the reasons why themes are not so crucial to publishing site branding is the fact that you have control over incorporating your own CSS and page structure using Masterpage and alternate CSS.

Let's take a look at how you can change the page layout for the out-of-the-box home page at www.contoso.com:

1. Navigate to the home page of the www.contoso.com.
2. Click **Site Actions** and select **Edit Page**.
3. On the ribbon, select the **Page** tab, and under the **Page Actions** group, click the **Page Layout** button.
4. You will see the list of the out-of-the-box page layouts. Select **Blank Web Part Page** and you will see how the page has transformed to accommodate new zones and layouts.

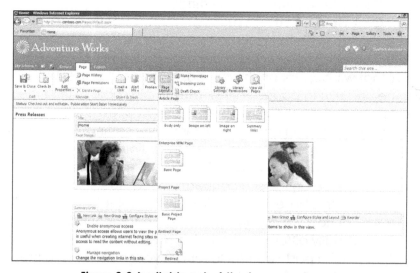

Figure 2-2 Available out-of-the-box page layout

Later, we will see how you can create your own page layouts and incorporate basic and more complex dynamic behavior on pages. In essence, page layout allows you to define the HTML and any other customizations, including .NET controls you want to see on the page. When controls get called on the specific page instance, they will have access to a page context and can render different HTML based on the context.

Just as it is not a good practice to modify out-of-the-box Masterpages in the collaboration site template, the same applies to publishing Masterpages and page layouts. If you like an existing page layout then make a copy of it and extend it; later, we'll see how you can do just that.

SharePoint 2010 specialized sites

Specialized sites is a term we'll use to describe site templates which don't belong to collaboration and publishing site templates. Those are rather specialized site templates, instances of which, in some cases, are only created by SharePoint system. Those templates have limited capabilities in terms of branding, and customizations often require additional steps apart from those in collaboration or publishing scenarios.

One of the examples of specialized sites is a MySite. MySite sites are personal sites providing users with a rich set of social networking features. The MySite site template has a specialized set of features and dependencies on SharePoint 2010 settings, and for this reason you can't modify MySite pages using the typical mechanism you have seen so far.

Let's navigate to your user's personal site on the demo environment:

1. Ensure you are logged in as **contoso\administrator**.
2. Navigate to the following URL: http://intranet.contoso.com/.

3. When the page has loaded, in the top right-hand-side corner, click on the user's name, and from the drop-down, select MySite.

The page you see is a user feed page showing various information and feeds for the currently logged in user.

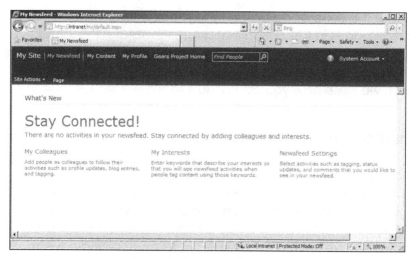

Figure 2-3 Typical user MySite home page

On the home page you get access to modify the page using the **Site Actions** -> **Edit Page** interface. As administrator, you will have the ability to add web parts and not be able to change the page layout of most of the other settings. If you navigate to site settings **Site Actions** -> **Site Settings**, you will see that this site very much resembles functionality available when branding collaboration site.

Changes made here will affect everyones user feed page and related pages.

Navigate to the MySite home page URL by clicking **MySite** in the top left corner of the page. You will also see the option to navigate to the **My Content** and **My Profile** sections of the site.

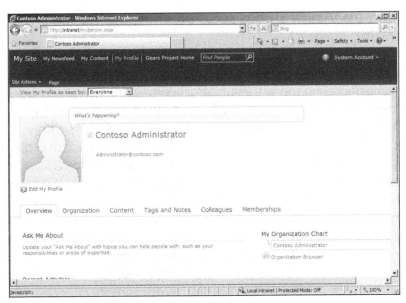

Figure 2-4 Accessing other options available in MySite template

The My Profile option will allow the user to access his or her social profile. In here, administrators also have the ability to customize web parts on the page. Theme changes on My Profile and My Newsfeed pages are going to be shared; those are also going to be shared by all users of the portal. By default, users have no permissions to modify web parts or themes. When changes are made by administrators and a new look and feel is applied, they will apply to all the users.

My Content is an area for users to store their personal and shared documents. If you click on My Content for the first time, the site will be created for that user account. The site created is a new site, also based on the collaboration template, and it looks like a team site. You have the same capabilities to change site themes and basic site settings. This site is personal to individual user, and changes made here are not shared across other users' sites.

Later we'll take a look at how you can make changes to **My Content** site for all users so changes automatically propagate to everyone or selected set of users.

Setting up Visual Studio solution structure for the branding project

As a user experience developer you can apply many of the customizations on the site using SharePoint administrative pages and referencing your custom CSS and other artifact files. This part of the chapter will help you to understand how to apply your customizations using Visual Studio 2010. On a typical project, your solutions will be delivered to the site along with other customizations incorporated by back-end developers. This means that user interface customizations will live in the same package as the rest of the solution artifacts. Usually setting up a solution structure is something your project lead will take care of. However, it's important to understand how a typical SharePoint 2010 project is structured; this will help you with locating existing components when you come back to the solution to implement patches and future versions.

Since the SharePoint solution package will deliver all of the customizations to the site (branding and back-end functionality), it's a good practice to separate your branding project from the other projects you may have in your SharePoint solution. In some cases you will be given the freedom of deploying branding as a separate package, in which case your solution will be independent from others. Here are some of the other types of Visual Studio projects you may see in your solution. They may not have the same name, but will be logically and structurally similar to below.

- Platform project—handles provisioning of core components; all the web parts and list definitions will go here. Typical back-end developers will work in this project.
- Content project—provisions default content to pages when the site is deployed. Usually, the site isn't provisioned with nothing on it. This is a logical way to separate site content pages in a separate project. This is less typical, and sometimes your back-end developers will provision site content in a Platform Visual Studio project.

- Services project—stores all of the constant classes as well as any logic that will interact with non-SharePoint systems. This is handled by back-end developers. In simple solution inplementations, this project may not be included. In more complex solutions, you may have several Visual Studio project of this type.
- Branding project—contains all of the components that will take care of your solution branding—items like themes, along with their CSS files, images, and even any footer and header controls. This is where you will add all of the user interface components and other artifacts.

The naming conventions above (Platform project, Content project) are not set standards. In fact those are the most commonly used names to separate projects in typical SharePoint solutions. The key takeaway is that there will be other projects in your solution and, depending on your solution size, there might be several more granular projects filling a few of the roles above.

Here is a typical solution structure for a Platform project with folder and components in it:

Platform Project Root

- Features
  - ☐ Masterpage provisioning feature
  - ☐ Page layout provisioning feature
  - ☐ Page provisioning feature(s)
  - ☐ General web part provisioning feature
- Pages
  - ☐ Page module
  - ☐ Page-specific web part module
  - ☐ Page-specific list instance
- Page layouts
- Masterpages
- Control templates
  - ☐ Project-specific custom user control
- Template
- Controls
  - ☐ Custom controls

- Layouts
  - ☐ Folder (project name)
  - ☐ Application pages (ASPX)
- List definitions
  - ☐ List definitions
- Lists
  - ☐ List instance
- Web parts
  - ☐ General web part

The rule of the thumb here is that developers keep all of the solution items hierarchical unless they are generic enough for other elements to reuse. For example, you see *Page-specific web part module* right under pages; this is mainly due to those custom web part modules being used on that page only, and nowhere else. If developers anticipate using one or few web part modules throughout your site on multiple pages, the modules for such web parts usually sit under web parts of the root of the SharePoint project (see *General Web Part* in the structure above).

As a user interface developer, you usually would not be expected to go and create artifacts in this solution—you might be expected to incorporate branding in some components (such as web parts, application pages, etc.). We will cover adding a few of the basic components since it's important that you're aware of the structure in your solution.

Content Project Root

- Features
  - ☐ Page provisioning feature(s)
- Pages
  - ☐ Page module

This is a simple enough structure, so here we'll only place content provisioning XML files for your pages. Usually as a user interface developer, you would not add any artifacts to this project since content provisioning is handled by back-end developers. However, we will briefly cover, for your own benefit, what's involved in provisioning basic page and web parts on pages.

Services Project Root

- Constants
  - ☐ List constants
  - ☐ Site constants
  - ☐ Web part constants
- List helpers
  - ☐ Service query helper

This solution project is usually a helper to Platform project, which inherently makes it a responsibility for back-end developer. The main benefit to keeping Service artifacts separate from the Platform is that when it comes to bug fixes or functionality upgrades, it's easier to replace a single or a few libraries that keep all of the supporting functionality than replacing the core **Platform** library. Although, as a user interface developer, you are not generally expected to maintain this project, we'll touch on it further when working with external service integration.

Branding Project Root

- Features
  - ☐ Theme installer
  - ☐ Theme setter
- Controls
  - ☐ Optional header control
  - ☐ Optional footer control
- Template
  - ☐ Layouts
  - ☐ Styles
  - ☐ Project folder (containing images and style artifacts)

As mentioned earlier, the Branding project will hold your theme-related artifacts and elements, style sheets, features setting branding parameters, etc. This way if you need to upgrade a few images or maybe a CSS markup, you can always do it separately without disturbing the rest of the **Platform** solution items.

Now that we know what goes where, let's go through a few small technicalities on how to create all of those projects in Visual Studio 2010.

We will start by firing up an instance of Visual Studio 2010 and creating a new SharePoint 2010 project as shown below.

Figure 2-5 Creating SharePoint 2010 project in Visual Studio 2010

Ensure you use .NET 3.5 since this is the framework that SharePoint 2010 uses.

Next, you will be asked to choose whether your solution is a **Sandbox Solution** or **Farm Solution**. In this book, we will be deploying most of our applications as **Farm Solutions**. You will also be asked about the name of the site you wish to use for debugging. It is handy to specify the site that most closely resembles the site template you are creating solutions for— for example: **Team Site**, or **Publishing Site**. Since we're using a preconfigured virtual machine, for each example I will specify the URL and corresponding template we're going to be using. For now, enter: www.contoso.com.

After you have picked the site and the type of solution, click **Finish** and your SharePoint project will be created. Your Visual Studio Solution Explorer will contain a single solution with a project in it.

NOTE:

One of the advantages of creating a **Sandboxed Solution** is when you're creating a solution to be hosted in the *cloud* on a shared infrastructure. In this case, the shared hosting administrator of the SharePoint farm has a choice to decide what level of access to give to your application as well as define a threshold for when to disable your solution if it reaches the limits defined in the SharePoint 2010 configuration. I will emphasize it when we're creating a Sandbox Solution in our samples; let's keep Farm Solution as our default.

Next, navigate to your **Branding** project properties and give a meaningful name to your assembly and namespace. You can see the convention that I recommend below.

- Assembly Name: **SolutionName. Branding**—for a **Branding** project.
- Default Namespace: **SolutionName. Branding**—assuming it's a **Branding** Visual Studio project.

If you remember our **Branding** project structure, it had number of folders and modules. There is a difference between a regular Visual Studio folder and a special mapped folder. A mapped folder is a folder that is mapped to a specific SharePoint 2010 directory under the SharePoint Root (a.k.a.: *[Drive]:\ Program Files\Common Files\Microsoft Shared\Web Server Extensions\14*).

To create a mapped folder:

1. Right click on the **Branding** project.
2. Select **Add**.
3. Select **SharePoint** mapped folder.
4. Pick the folder you would like to map (**TEMPLATE**, for example).
5. Click **OK**.

Now you will see a new folder in your solution structure. In the **Branding** project structure we outlined above, all of the mapped folders are identified with an asterisk (*). In a Visual Studio 2010, mapped folders are identified with a globe superimposed on a folder icon in the project structure.

After I populate my solution structure with the hierarchy we discussed earlier, my Solution Explorer will look similar to what is shown below.

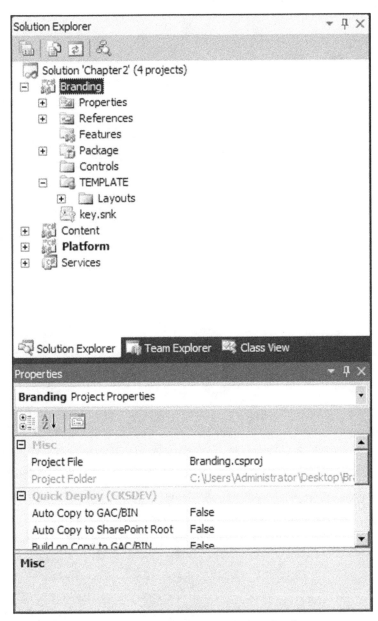

Figure 2-6 Branding project solution structure

Now the remaining pieces left are, at least, **Services** and **Platform** project structure, which follow the same principle. In examples you will see in this book, most of the time we'll skip other types of projects and keep most of our artifacts in our branding project.

CHAPTER 3

Customizing SharePoint 2010
Collaboration Sites

As we looked at previously, SharePoint themes are one of the few main mechanisms to incorporate custom branding on your collaboration site. In this chapter we'll take a look at how you can create basic themes without getting too much into the customization. Of course, with this approach your options are limited, but sometimes it's all you need. Then we'll move on to creating a bit more complex themes; this time we'll use Visual Studio to create the theme and make use of a few advanced features of the branding engine. Some of the capabilities available in the SharePoint 2010 branding engine are truly a huge step ahead.

Although, with themes, there is so much you can do, when it comes to making structural changes on the page, you will have to work with site Masterpage. We will take a look at what one of the default SharePoint collaboration Masterpages is all about. The concept of Masterpage will also be used throughout this book when we work with a variety of other site templates. We'll learn how you can set the alternate Masterpage on the site and a few of the capabilities you can incorporate into your site branding.

Creating basic themes

As we already established, SharePoint themes have a key role in managing the look and feel for SharePoint collaboration sites. Let's take a look at how you can create a simple theme which supports custom color scheme changes and then a more complex theme which supports custom CSS.

From the previous chapter, you have become familiar with how to access out-of-the-box theme settings and change color themes and other basic options. Suppose you need to provide your customer with the new color scheme for your theme. Let's take a look at how you can create a theme and provide it to your customer as a package.

1. From your collaboration site instance at http://intranet. contoso.com, click **Site Actions->Site Settings**.
2. Under **Galleries** click **Themes**. If you're not able to locate this option, it's because the theme gallery is only available on the root of your SharePoint site collection. To navigate to the root, click the **Go to top level site settings** link on the bottom of the page.
3. You see a list of existing themes available on the site. Use the context menu to download one of the themes to your computer.
4. Open the file from the file system. If you have PowerPoint installed on your computer, which is the case for our virtualized demo environment, this will be the default program that will open the file; otherwise, open the file on the computer which has PowerPoint installed.
5. You will see a blank PowerPoint presentation; assuming you are using PowerPoint 2010, access the presentation master slide by clicking on the ribbon **View** tab -> **Slide Master** within PowerPoint.
6. In the **Edit Theme** group of the ribbon, you will be able to define colors, fonts, and other attributes of the theme. Not all of those apply to SharePoint, only colors and fonts do.
7. When ready, save the theme by clicking the **Themes** button on the ribbon and selecting **Save current theme....**

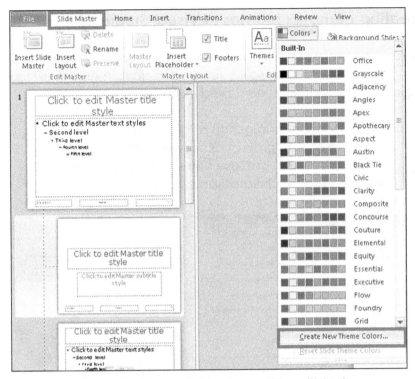

**Figure 3-1 Options available when working with basic
SharePoint themes is PowerPoint 2010**

8. Save the new theme to the file system and upload it back
    to the theme gallery you accessed in step 2.

To check out your new theme you can navigate to:

1. From your collaboration site, click **Site Actions->Site Settings**.
2. Under **Look and Feel** click **Site Theme**.
3. Pick the theme you have just created and click **Preview**
    button below to preview how our site looks with the new
    theme.

Above theme changes are handy but don't provide significant
value in branding terms besides changing few basic color
schemes and fonts. Let's take a look at how you can incorporate
your own CSS into the theme.

Creating complex themes in Visual Studio 2010

As you can see, changes you can make with PowerPoint are not going to get you too far; so if you need to go further, Visual Studio approach is something you should consider.

1. Start up Visual Studio 2010 and create a new Empty SharePoint 2010 project as shown on the figure below; alternatively you can use corresponding Visual Studio downloadable chapter source code:

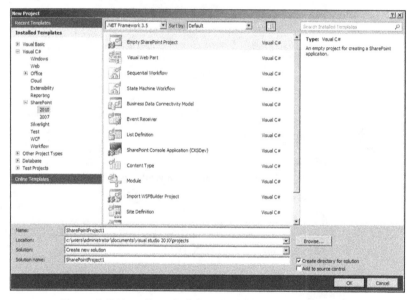

Figure 3-2 New SharePoint project in Visual Studio 2010

2. For debug URL specify the URL of your team site, http://intranet.contoso.com. This is where Visual Studio 2010 will deploy your solution to while you test.
3. Right click on the name of the newly created project and from the context menu select **Add** -> **New Item....**
4. From the list of project items select **Module**, give it the name *ProvisionCS*, and click **Add**.
5. This module will provision our CSS file to the SharePoint database.

6. Right click on the newly added module folder and select **Add-> New Item**.
7. Remove *Sample.txt* file from the module.
8. From the new project item window, select **Web** as a template on the left and **Style Sheet** for the item. The blank style sheet will be added to the module. Ensure the name of the file is *branding.css*
9. Locate *Elements.xml* from the newly added module folder and open it for edit; replace the declarative XML with the one below:

LISTING 3-1

```
<?xml version="1.0" encoding="utf-8"?>
<Elements xmlns="http://schemas.microsoft.com/
sharepoint/">
<Module Name="ProvisionCSS"
    Url="Style Library/Themable">
<File Path="ProvisionCSS\branding.css"
    Type="GhostableInLibrary" Url="branding.css" />
</Module>
</Elements>
```

This XML will ensure that the newly added CSS file we call here *branding.css* has been added to the system document library called **Style Library**. **Style Library**, in turn, contains a folder called *Themable*.

10. You will notice Visual Studio has created a new feature under the **Features** folder in the solution structure called **Feature 1**. Double click on the new feature folder and you will see the user interface similar to what is shown below:

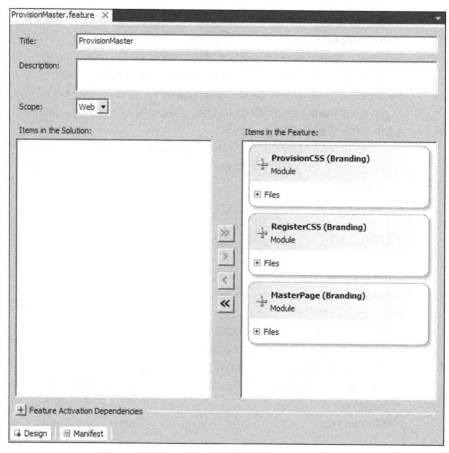

Figure 3-3 New Visual Studio feature edit page

Ensure the **Scope** value of the feature is set to **Web**. As we briefly mentioned earlier, the feature in the Visual Studio project for SharePoint will provision necessary artifacts; in our case, the contents of the module will be provisioned to the SharePoint library. The reason why we set the scope to **Web** is to ensure the feature is activated on the individual site and not on the main site collection. The URL of the deployed solution will be the one you have specified as a debug URL, http://intranet.contoso.com.

Now, just having the CSS file provisioned to the library will not make SharePoint use it by default. We need to ensure that the current Masterpage which is used by the site has the proper reference to our CSS file. To achieve that, we will use a delegate control to inject out style sheet declaration.

Let's take a quick look at how delegates work:

1. From the root of your collaboration site, click **Site Actions->Site Settings**.
2. Under **Galleries** click **Master Pages**.
3. Download *v4.master* to the file system.
4. Open the file from the file system in Visual Studio.
5. You will see markup defining the page. Search for *AdditionalPageHead* and locate the following line of code:
   *<SharePoint:DelegateControl runat="server"
   ControlId="AdditionalPageHead"
   AllowMultipleControls="true"/>*

Now, take a look at the location of this control—it's in page head. This placeholder will allow us to inject our custom markup during execution of the page. In our case we will inject our custom style sheet registration.

Let's add our style sheet registration control to the solution:

1. In Visual Studio right click on the project name and select **Add -> SharePoint Mapped Folder**.
2. From the list of folders open **TEMPLATE** and select **CONTROLTEMPLATES**. This will add new Visual Studio folder to your solution structure, which will map it to the actual physical folder on the SharePoint system at the time of solution deployment.
3. Right click on the newly mapped **CONTROLTEMPLATES** folder and select **Add -> New Item....**
4. From the list of available project items, select **User Control**.
5. Give it the name *CSSRegistration.ascx* and click **Add**.
6. Replace the content s of the newly added user control with the following:

LISTING 3-2

```
<%@ Assembly
Name="$SharePoint.Project.AssemblyFullName$" %>
<%@ Register
Tagprefix="SharePoint" Namespace="Microsoft.SharePoint.
WebControls"
Assembly="Microsoft.SharePoint, Version=14.0.0.0,
Culture=neutral,
PublicKeyToken=71e9bce111e9429c" %>


<SharePoint:CSSRegistration
Name="<% $SPUrl:~sitecollection/Style Library/Themable/
branding.css %>"
After="corev4.css"
runat="server" />
```

Above we reference SharePoint CSSRegistration; **CssLink** control in Masterpage reads this registration to insert a **LINK** element into the resulting page to apply the external CSS defined by the registration.

The URL of our registration is relative to site collection, where we provision **branding.css** plus the document library and folder. The **After** property of the CSSRegistration allows us to specify the order of where the registration will appear. In this case **corev4.css** is an out-of-the-box style sheet which we may want to overwrite with our custom styles; that's why we specify the **After** value to the code style sheet.

Now that we have added the registration control, we need to ensure it's injected into the appropriate placeholder in our Masterpage.

1. Right click on the Visual Studio project name to create a new item.
2. Select **Add** -> **New Item....**

3. From the list of project items, select **Module**, give it the name **RegisterCSS**, and click **Add**.
4. Remove **Sample.txt** file from the module.
5. Locate **Elements.xml** in the newly created module file.
6. Replace the contents of the file with the following:

LISTING 3-3

```
<?xml version="1.0" encoding="utf-8"?>
<Elements xmlns="http://schemas.microsoft.com/
sharepoint/">
<Control Id="AdditionalPageHead"
    Sequence="80"
    ControlSrc="~/_ControlTemplates/Chapter3/
    CSSRegistration.ascx" />
</Elements>
```

The above specifies that the new delegate control should be added to the Masterpage with the delegate ID **AdditionalPageHead**. The sequence in this case is a numeric value specifying in which order multiple such registrations are going to be handled; lower value, in this case, ensures our registration will be the last on the page.

If you glance at the **Feature 1** in our solution structure **Features** folder, you will see that the new module has been added to the list of items this feature will provision.

Let's deploy the solution from within Visual Studio:

1. Right click on the solution name and select **Deploy**.
2. Once the solution is deployed, open the URL of your collaboration site, http://intranet.contoso.com.
3. View the source of the page in the browser. If everything succeeded, you will see the following CSS registration in the HTML of the page:

LISTING 3-4

```
<link rel="stylesheet"
type="text/css"
href="/_catalogs/theme/Themed/9A2213C4/branding-4FA53B74.
css?ctag=27"/>
```

The reason the **HREF** attribute points to a location different than we have specified in our **ProvisionCSS** module is because themes in SharePoint allow you to specify special directives in your CSS. Those directives are then parsed and the new CSS is written. This new CSS is placed into the location you see above and this is what actually gets referenced dynamically.

More on the CSS directives just mentioned, coming up next.

Working with compile time directives in SharePoint style sheets

As I briefly mentioned before, you can incorporate a custom style sheet into the new theme and manage the look and feel of the existing page and site. Since theme artifacts are getting compiled before rendering, SharePoint 2010 supports compile time directives which you can use in your style sheet to achieve certain branding artifact transformations.

As you can see from the figure below, users are able to define colors and fonts on the theme settings page. Those fonts and colors can be referenced in your style sheet as input parameters.

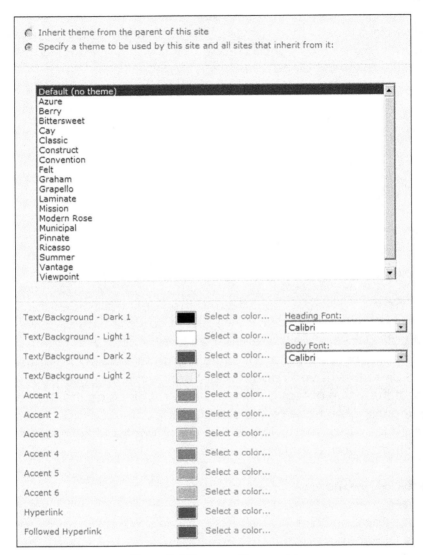

Figure 3-4 Theme settings page

What this allows you to do is define your style sheet and allow it to change later as users adjust their own color schemes on their subsites, if they are allowed to do so. This is very handy because if your users changed the color scheme of the site and your style sheet was hardcoded, some of the elements could become visually incompatible with the new theme.

Let's take a look at the example. Using a solution from the previous example, open **ProvisionCSS** module and edit the **branding.css** file. Add the following piece to the file:

LISTING 3-5

```
.s4-titlelogo
{
border: solid;
/*[ReplaceColor(themeColor:"Dark1")]*/
border-color:#000;
}
```

In this case **.s4-titlelogo** is the class surrounding the site icon on the site. We add a border around it and then define a border color. Right before the border color, we give a compile time directive instructing to replace the referenced border color with the one defined in the **Dark 1** accent of the theme settings page. Compile time directives have to appear right before the property and will affect the value of that particular property. Since on the theme setting page we have only the ability to specify accent colors and fonts, the only property values that are acceptable have to do with the color and font assignment.

Here are few more compile time directives:

- ReplaceColor
- RecolorImage
- ReplaceFont

Let's now take a look at how to work with **RecolorImage**. The **RecolorImage** directive is defined right before you declare your image and uses three methods to recolor the image using the specified color in the theme settings page. The three methods are:

- Tinting
- Blending
- Filling

Let's take a look at the syntax and then see the effect. In the style sheet from our solution, let's define a background image and then apply the recolor directive.

LISTING 3-6

```
body {
/*[RecolorImage(themeColor:"Accent6",method:"Tinting")]*/
background:url("/_layouts/images/siteIcon.png") no-
repeat;
}
```

This instructs the theming engine to recolor the image with **Tinting** and use the tint color that's defined for *Accent 6* in theme settings.

This is really handy when you need to quickly change the overall look and feel and apply it to all of the artifacts without creating copies of images for each scenario.

One other compile directive is **ReplaceFont**, and, as you may have expected, it replaces the font of the style sheet property value with a new font defined in theme settings.

Let's take a look at the syntax:

LISTING 3-7

```
body {
/* [ReplaceFont(themeFont: "MinorFont")] */
font-family:Verdana;
}
```

You may have noticed that the pattern, **MinorFont**, just as in other directive attributes, has to be typed with no space; otherwise you will receive an error when applying your theme.

As you have been modifying the **branding.css** with the directives above, to test the effect, **deploy** the solution using Visual Studio. Once deployed, you can toggle options and accents from the theme settings page, to preview your changes click the **Preview** button.

What collaboration Masterpage is all about

As we established in the last few examples, you can do quite a lot with the collaboration site in terms of customizing user interfaces with themes. If you remember earlier, we talked about the default Masterpage each collaboration site is using. Well, in order for us to make structural changes on the collaboration page, such as: moving things around on the page, adding new web part zones, removing sections on the page and more, we will have to create an instance of our own Masterpage and assign it to be used on the site instead of the default one.

Before we go and start modifying the new instance of the Masterpage, let's spend some time looking at what's in the default Masterpage. Don't get discouraged, poking around the Masterpage is actually the best way to learn it in detail and this is something we'll do in a little bit. Before that, let's look at some of the major components in the Masterpage. This way you'll know what you don't need and where to add new things. Download an instance of the **v4.master** from your collaboration site:

1. From the http://intranet.contoso.com, click **Site Actions->Site Settings**.
2. Under **Galleries** click **Master Pages**.
3. Download **v4.master** to the file system.
4. Open the file from the file system in Visual Studio.

My comments are going to be in bold in the listing below. I will be explaining most of the components on the Masterpage; some items are going to be cut to save space in this book. Plus, in my opinion, if you need more granularities in your work, you can poke around the Masterpage with tools like Firebug, which we'll take a look at in a bit.

LISTING 3-8

```
<%@Master language="C#"%>

<!-- Contains ASP.NET server controls used on
masterpage and in pages of the SharePoitn site -->
<%@ Register Tagprefix="SharePoint"
Namespace="Microsoft.SharePoint.WebControls"
Assembly="Microsoft.SharePoint, Version=14.0.0.0,
Culture=neutral,
PublicKeyToken=71e9bce111e9429c" %>

<!-- Used for utility tasks, things like encoding,
processing of user information etc -->
<%@ Register Tagprefix="Utilities"
Namespace="Microsoft.SharePoint.Utilities"
Assembly="Microsoft.SharePoint, Version=14.0.0.0,
Culture=neutral,
PublicKeyToken=71e9bce111e9429c" %>

<%@ Import Namespace="Microsoft.SharePoint" %>

<! --Supplies classes and functionality allowing work
with ribbon -->
<%@ Assembly Name="Microsoft.Web.CommandUI,
Version=14.0.0.0, Culture=neutral,
PublicKeyToken=71e9bce111e9429c" %>
<%@ Import Namespace="Microsoft.SharePoint.
ApplicationPages" %>

<! --Supplies classes and functionality to work with
web part pages-->
<%@ Register Tagprefix="WebPartPages"
Namespace="Microsoft.SharePoint.WebPartPages"
```

```
Assembly="Microsoft.SharePoint, Version=14.0.0.0,
Culture=neutral,
PublicKeyToken=71e9bce111e9429c" %>

<! -- User control which contain items in the "welcome
menu" on the top right hand side of each page-->
<%@ Register TagPrefix="wssuc" TagName="Welcome"
src="~/_controltemplates/Welcome.ascx" %>

<! -- User control handling multilingual UI selector-->
<%@ Register TagPrefix="wssuc" TagName="MUISelector"
src="~/_controltemplates/MUISelector.ascx" %>

<! -- This control supplies functionality for the edit
bar when the page is in edit mode allowing user to
exit the edit mode etc -->
<%@ Register TagPrefix="wssuc"
TagName="DesignModeConsole"
src="~/_controltemplates/DesignModeConsole.ascx" %>

<! -- This document will conform to strict document
type definition -->
<!DOCTYPE html PUBLIC "-//W3C//DTD XHTML 1.0 Strict//EN"
"http://www.w3.org/TR/xhtml1/DTD/xhtml1-strict.dtd">

<html lang="<%$Resources:wss,language_value%>"
dir="<%$Resources:wss,multipages_direction_dir_value%>"
runat="server" xmlns:o="urn:schemas-microsoft-
com:office:office">

<head runat="server">

<! -- Sets IE browser to render the page compatible
with IE8 -->
<meta http-equiv="X-UA-Compatible" content="IE=8"/>
<meta name="GENERATOR" content="Microsoft SharePoint"/>
<meta name="progid" content="SharePoint.WebPartPage.
Document"/>
```

```
<meta http-equiv="Content-Type" content="text/html;
charset=utf-8"/>


<! -- Intructs not to cache the content of the page -->
<meta http-equiv="Expires" content="0"/>


<! -- Writes HTML instructions for search robots to
index or not index the content based on the settings
for the specific SharePoint web -->
<SharePoint:RobotsMetaTag runat="server"/>


<! -- Placeholder  to populate page title-->
<title id="onetidTitle"><asp:ContentPlaceHolder
id="PlaceHolderPageTitle" runat="server"/></title>


<! -- Adds a LINK element into the HTML adding
external and SharePoint style sheets -->
<SharePoint:CssLink runat="server" Version="4"/>


<! -- Loads CSS associated with selected SharePoint
theme -->
<SharePoint:Theme runat="server"/>
<! -- Enables error reporting from the page -->
<SharePoint:ULSClientConfig runat="server"/>


<! -- For backwards compatible javascript – this
variable says we're working with SharePoint 2010 UI -->
<script type="text/javascript">
var _fV4UI = true;
</script>


<! -- Loads SharePoint  core javascript-->
<SharePoint:ScriptLink language="javascript" name="core.
js" OnDemand="true" runat="server" />


<! -- References any custom JS if any specified to run
-->
<SharePoint:CustomJSUrl runat="server" />
<SharePoint:SoapDiscoveryLink runat="server" />
```

```
<! -- Place holder for additional header information,
ex. custom style sheets -->
<asp:ContentPlaceHolder id="PlaceHolderAdditionalPageHe
ad" runat="server"/>

<! -- Delegate control for injecting references within
header -->
<SharePoint:DelegateControl runat="server"
ControlId="AdditionalPageHead"
AllowMultipleControls="true"/>

<! -- This specifies favicon used on page inheriting
from this masterpage -->
<SharePoint:SPShortcutIcon runat="server" IconUrl="/_
layouts/images/favicon.ico" />

<! -- Place holder for additional body styles, mainly
used for additional style definitions -->
<asp:ContentPlaceHolder id="PlaceHolderBodyAreaClass"
runat="server"/>

<! -- Place holder for the title area class-->
<asp:ContentPlaceHolder id="PlaceHolderTitleAreaClass"
runat="server"/>
<SharePoint:SPPageManager runat="server" />
<SharePoint:SPHelpPageComponent Visible="false"
runat="server" />
</head>
```

Now we have identified most of the elements in the header section of the Masterpage. Those are references to .NET components used later as well as CSS and JavaScript registrations. Next is the body of the Masterpage, which will include the majority of the content. Some of the sections in the body, such as navigation, we will be touching base on in more details in later chapters.

LISTING 3-9

```
<body scroll="no"
onload="if (typeof(_spBodyOnLoadWrapper) != 'undefined')
_spBodyOnLoadWrapper();" class="v4master">

<form runat="server"
onsubmit="if (typeof(_spFormOnSubmitWrapper) !=
'undefined')
{return _spFormOnSubmitWrapper();} else {return true;}">

<!-- Aids with Ajax script libraries and script files,
partial-page rendering etc -->
<asp:ScriptManager id="ScriptManager" runat="server"
EnablePageMethods="false" EnablePartialRendering="true"
EnableScriptGlobalization="false"
EnableScriptLocalization="true" />

<!-- In charge of web parts and events on a webpage -->
<WebPartPages:SPWebPartManager id="m" runat="Server" />

<! -- In case JavaScript is disabled in the client
browser — this control shows a message instructing
users to enable JavaScript and reload the page -->
<SharePoint:SPNoScript runat="server"/>

<! -- Controls related to navigation accessibility -->
<div id="TurnOnAccessibility" style="display:none"
...
</div>

<! -- Delegate control allowing you to inject your own
content into the global navigation area of the page-->
<SharePoint:DelegateControl runat="server"
ControlId="GlobalNavigation" />

<div id="s4-ribbonrow" class="s4-pr s4-
ribbonrowhidetitle">
<div id="s4-ribboncont">
```

```
<! -- Ribbon UI starts here-->
<SharePoint:SPRibbon
runat="server" PlaceholderElementId="RibbonContainer"
CssFile="">


<! -- Left side of the ribbon defined here-->
<SharePoint:SPRibbonPeripheralContent
runat="server"
Location="TabRowLeft"
CssClass="ms-siteactionscontainer s4-notdlg">


<span class="ms-siteactionsmenu" id="siteactiontd">

<! -- Site Actions menu definition and its menu items
defined here-->
<SharePoint:SiteActions runat="server"
accesskey="<%$Resources:wss,tb_SiteActions_AK%>"
id="SiteActionsMenuMain"
PrefixHtml=""
SuffixHtml=""
MenuNotVisibleHtml=" ">
<CustomTemplate>
<SharePoint:FeatureMenuTemplate runat="server"
FeatureScope="Site"
Location="Microsoft.SharePoint.StandardMenu"
GroupId="SiteActions"
UseShortId="true">
<!-- ... Site actions elements were defined here -->
</CustomTemplate>
</SharePoint:SiteActions></span>


<!-- Global navigation menu allowing users to navigate
through the tree to various sites in site collection-->
<asp:ContentPlaceHolder  id="PlaceHolderGlobalNavigati
on" runat="server">
<SharePoint:PopoutMenu
runat="server"
ID="GlobalBreadCrumbNavPopout"
IconUrl="/_layouts/images/fgimg.png"
```

```
IconAlt="<%$Resources:wss,master_breadcrumbIconAlt%>"
IconOffsetX=0
<!-- .... -->


<!-- The "Save and Close" button right beside the site
collection navigation button-->
<SharePoint:PageStateActionButton
id="PageStateActionButton" runat="server"
Visible="false" />


<!-- Right side of the ribbon -->
<SharePoint:SPRibbonPeripheralContent
runat="server"
Location="TabRowRight"
ID="RibbonTabRowRight"
CssClass="s4-trc-container s4-notdlg">


<! --Delegate allowing to inject site links — this
is for backwards compatibility only and not used by
default -->
<SharePoint:DelegateControl runat="server"
ID="GlobalDelegate0" ControlId="GlobalSiteLink0" />


<!-- … -->


<div class="s4-trc-container-menu">
<div>
<! -- Displays "welcome" and login control -->
<wssuc:Welcome id="IdWelcome" runat="server"
EnableViewState="false">
</wssuc:Welcome>


<! — Renders multilingual menu control if applicable on
the site, right beside the "welcome" control -->
<wssuc:MUISelector ID="IdMuiSelector" runat="server"/>
</div>
</div>
```

```
<!-- … -->

<! -- This is a dashboard functionality, when enabled
displaying performance statistics of the page -->
<Sharepoint:DeveloperDashboardLauncher
ID="DeveloperDashboardLauncher"
NavigateUrl="javascript:ToggleDeveloperDashboard()"
runat="server"
ImageUrl="/_layouts/images/fgimg.png"
Text="<%$Resources:wss,multipages_launchdevdashalt_
text%>"
OffsetX=0
OffsetY=222
Height=16
Width=16 />
</span>
</span>
</SharePoint:SPRibbonPeripheralContent>
</SharePoint:SPRibbon>

<! -- Notification area right after the ribbon, that's
where quick notification messages pop up-->
<div id="notificationArea" class="s4-noti">
</div>
<asp:ContentPlaceHolder ID="SPNavigation"
runat="server">
<SharePoint:DelegateControl runat="server"
ControlId="PublishingConsole"
Id="PublishingConsoleDelegate">
</SharePoint:DelegateControl>
</asp:ContentPlaceHolder>
<!-- … -->
<!--This is where ribbon and notification UI ends-->
```

Next is the section which will handle the main area of the
Masterpage. If you notice from SharePoint UI, only the main area
of the page scrolls and ribbon remains in position. The section
we're going to take a look at next is the scrollable area of the
page.

Figure 3-5 Scrollable area of the page

LISTING 3-10

```
<div id="s4-workspace">

<! --Site title area, also area where ribbon tab
content is going to be overlayed on -->
<div id="s4-bodyContainer">
<div id="s4-titlerow" class="s4-pr s4-notdlg s4-
titlerowhidetitle">
<div class="s4-title s4-lp">
<div class="s4-title-inner">
<table class="s4-titletable" cellspacing="0">
<tbody>
<tr>
<td class="s4-titlelogo">

<! -- Link back to the root of the site -->
<SharePoint:SPLinkButton runat="server"
```

```
NavigateUrl="~site/" id="onetidProjectPropertyTitleGrap
hic" >
```

```
<! -- Logo image, can be changed from the
administration UI of the site-->
<SharePoint:SiteLogoImage name="onetidHeadbnnr0"
id="onetidHeadbnnr2" LogoImageUrl="/_layouts/images/
siteIcon.png"
runat="server"/>
</SharePoint:SPLinkButton>
</td>
```

```
<! -- Area right beside the site logo with a breadcrumb
of and link back to the root of the site-->
<td class="s4-titletext">
<h1 name="onetidProjectPropertyTitle">
<asp:ContentPlaceHolder id="PlaceHolderSiteName"
runat="server">
<SharePoint:SPLinkButton runat="server"
NavigateUrl="~site/" id="onetidProjectPropertyTitle">
<SharePoint:ProjectProperty Property="Title"
runat="server" /></SharePoint:SPLinkButton>
</asp:ContentPlaceHolder>
</h1>
<span id="onetidPageTitleSeparator"
class="s4-nothome s4-bcsep s4-titlesep">
<SharePoint:ClusteredDirectionalSeparatorArrow
runat="server" /> </span>
<h2>
<asp:ContentPlaceHolder id="PlaceHolderPageTitleInTitleA
rea" runat="server" />
</h2>
<div class="s4-pagedescription" tabindex="0" >
<asp:ContentPlaceHolder id="PlaceHolderPageDescription"
runat="server"/>
</div>
</td>
<! -- The right hand side area with social data
controls such as "I Like It" and "Tags"-->
```

```
<td class="s4-socialdata-notif">
<SharePoint:DelegateControl ControlId="GlobalSiteLink3"
Scope="Farm" runat="server" />
</td>
</tr>
</tbody>
</table>
</div>
</div>
<! -- "s4-notdlg" will ensure the containing element is
hidden when this page is displayed in modal dialogs -->
<div id="s4-topheader2" class="s4-pr s4-notdlg">
<a name="startNavigation"></a>
<div id="s4-searcharea" class="s4-search s4-rp">

<! -- Search box will be injected here as a delegate
control -->
<asp:ContentPlaceHolder id="PlaceHolderSearchArea"
runat="server">
<SharePoint:DelegateControl runat="server"
ControlId="SmallSearchInputBox" Version="4" />
</asp:ContentPlaceHolder>

<! -- Help icon with supporting code -->
<span class="s4-help">
<span style="height:17px
<! -- … -->
</span>
</span>
</div>

<div class="s4-rp s4-app">
</div>

<! -- Top horizontal navigation menu -->
<div class="s4-lp s4-toplinks">
<asp:ContentPlaceHolder id="PlaceHolderTopNavBar"
runat="server">
```

```
<asp:ContentPlaceHolder id="PlaceHolderHorizontalNav"
runat="server">
<SharePoint:AspMenu
  ID="TopNavigationMenuV4"
  Runat="server"
  EnableViewState="false"
  DataSourceID="topSiteMap"
  AccessKey="<%$Resources:wss,navigation_accesskey%>"
  UseSimpleRendering="true"
  UseSeparateCss="false"
  Orientation="Horizontal"
  StaticDisplayLevels="2"
  MaximumDynamicDisplayLevels="1"
  SkipLinkText=""
  CssClass="s4-tn" />

<! -- … -->

</asp:ContentPlaceHolder>
</asp:ContentPlaceHolder>
</div>
</div>
</div>

<! -- Container displaying page check out information
or other details, right below the top horizontal menu
-->
<div id="s4-statusbarcontainer">
<div id="pageStatusBar" class="s4-status-s1">
</div>
</div>
<SharePoint:VisualUpgradePreviewStatus runat="server" />

<! -- This is the area right below the top navigation
bar -->
<div id="s4-mainarea" class="s4-pr s4-widecontentarea">

<! -- The quick launch area on the left of the page -->
```

```
<div id="s4-leftpanel" class="s4-notdlg">
<div id="s4-leftpanel-content">
<asp:ContentPlaceHolder id="PlaceHolderLeftNavBarDataSo
urce" runat="server" />
<asp:ContentPlaceHolder id="PlaceHolderCalendarNavigator
" runat="server" />
<asp:ContentPlaceHolder id="PlaceHolderLeftActions"
runat="server"></asp:ContentPlaceHolder>
<asp:ContentPlaceHolder id="PlaceHolderLeftNavBarTop"
runat="server"/>
<asp:ContentPlaceHolder id="PlaceHolderLeftNavBar"
runat="server">
<div class="ms-quicklaunchouter">
<div class="ms-quickLaunch">
<asp:ContentPlaceHolder id="PlaceHolderQuickLaunchTop"
runat="server">
<SharePoint:UIVersionedContent UIVersion="3"
runat="server">
<ContentTemplate>
<h3 class="ms-standardheader"><label class="ms-hidden">
<SharePoint:EncodedLiteral runat="server"
text="<%$Resources:wss,quiklnch_pagetitle%>"
EncodeMethod="HtmlEncode"/></label>

<! -- Will automatically decide whether to render the
HTML inside the security trimmer control based on
PermissionsString -->
<Sharepoint:SPSecurityTrimmedControl runat="server" Per
missionsString="ViewFormPages">
<div class="ms-quicklaunchheader">
<! -- … -->
</div>
</SharePoint:SPSecurityTrimmedControl>
</h3>
</ContentTemplate>
</SharePoint:UIVersionedContent>
</asp:ContentPlaceHolder>
<Sharepoint:SPNavigationManager
id="QuickLaunchNavigationManager"
```

```
runat="server"
QuickLaunchControlId="QuickLaunchMenu"
ContainedControl="QuickLaunch"
EnableViewState="false"
CssClass="ms-quicklaunch-navmgr"
>
<! -- … -->
<! -- Backwards compatible rendering of the quick
launch, not required unless you're planning to make
SharePoint 2007 compatible masterpage -->
<SharePoint:UIVersionedContent UIVersion="3"
runat="server">
<! -- … -->
</ContentTemplate>
</SharePoint:UIVersionedContent>

<! -- Rendering the quick launch menu -->
<SharePoint:UIVersionedContent UIVersion="4"
runat="server">
<ContentTemplate>
<SharePoint:AspMenu
  id="V4QuickLaunchMenu"
  runat="server"
  EnableViewState="false"
  <! -- … -->
  CssClass="s4-ql" />
</ContentTemplate>
</SharePoint:UIVersionedContent>
</div>
</Sharepoint:SPNavigationManager>

<! -- Backwards compatible special navigation links -->
<Sharepoint:UIVersionedContent runat="server"
UIVersion="3">
<! -- … -->
</SharePoint:UIVersionedContent>

<! -- Special navigation links displayed on some pages
based on user permissions -->
```

```
<Sharepoint:UIVersionedContent runat="server"
UIVersion="4">
<ContentTemplate>
<Sharepoint:SPNavigationManager
<! -- … -->
</Sharepoint:SPNavigationManager>
</ContentTemplate>
</SharePoint:UIVersionedContent>

<! - Recycle bin link, rendered based on permissions
that user has on the page-->
<asp:ContentPlaceHolder id="PlaceHolderQuickLaunchBotto
m" runat="server">
<SharePoint:UIVersionedContent UIVersion="3"
runat="server" id="PlaceHolderQuickLaunchBottomV3">
<ContentTemplate>
<! -- … -->
</ContentTemplate>
</SharePoint:UIVersionedContent>
<SharePoint:UIVersionedContent UIVersion="4"
runat="server" id="PlaceHolderQuickLaunchBottomV4">
<ContentTemplate>
<! -- … -->
</ContentTemplate>
</SharePoint:UIVersionedContent>
</asp:ContentPlaceHolder>
</div>
</div>
</asp:ContentPlaceHolder>
</div>
</div>

<div class="s4-ca s4-ca-dlgNoRibbon" id="MSO_
ContentTable">
<div class="s4-die">
<! -- … -->
</div>
<SharePoint:VersionedPlaceHolder UIVersion="3"
ID="DesignModeConsoleV3" runat="server">
```

```
<asp:ContentPlaceHolder id="WSSDesignConsole"
runat="server">
<wssuc:DesignModeConsole id="IdDesignModeConsole"
runat="server" />
</asp:ContentPlaceHolder>
</SharePoint:VersionedPlaceHolder>

<! -- Center area of the page, main content -->
<div class='s4-ba'><div class='ms-bodyareacell'>
<div id="MSO_ContentDiv" runat="server">
<a name="mainContent"></a>

<! -- The content for this section is loaded from page
layouts, which define web part zones and web parts.
We'll cover page layouts in further chapters -->
<asp:ContentPlaceHolder id="PlaceHolderMain"
runat="server">
</asp:ContentPlaceHolder>
</div>
</div></div>
<div class="s4-die">
<asp:ContentPlaceHolder id="PlaceHolderBodyRightMargin"
runat="server">
</asp:ContentPlaceHolder>
</div>
</div>
</div>
<! -- Another link to developer dashboard, to monitor
performance of the page -->
<SharePoint:DeveloperDashboard runat="server" />
</div>
</div>
<! -- ... -->
<! -- Displays compatibility message if the browser is
not supported in SharePoint -->
<SharePoint:WarnOnUnsupportedBrowsers runat="server"/>
```

That's it; we've skimmed through the main structure of the typical collaboration masterpage. As promised, right after the next section (*Dynamically discovering granular components of the masterpage and branding a typical site*), we're going to take a look at how to discover more granular parts of the masterpage using various tools like IE Developer Toolbar and Firebug.

Setting alternative Masterpage for collaboration sites

In our extensive Masterpage overview above, we looked at what typical collaboration Masterpage is all about. Next item on the agenda is to see how we can set the existing Masterpage as a default Masterpage for the collaboration site. We'll use Visual Studio solution for this.

1. Open Visual Studio and create a new project using SharePoint 2010 Empty Project template.
2. Specify http://intranet.contoso.com/ as your debug URL.
3. In the soltion folder, locate the **Features** folder and right click on it to add a new feature.
4. Rename the default **Feature1** to **ProvisionMaster** so we can track our items better.
    This feature will be used to upload our custom masterpage to the gallery.
5. In the soltion folder, right click on the project name and select **Add -> New Item....**
6. Select **Module** for an item type and give it the name **Masterpage**.
7. Rename the **Sample.txt** file in the module to **newmaster.master**.
8. Navigate to http://intranet.contoso.com logged in as administrator.
9. Click **Site Actions -> Site Settings** and locate **Masterpages** under **Galleries**.
10. Click on **v4.master** and pick **Download a Copy** on the ribbon. Save the file to disk. The Masterpage you have just downloaded is the default masterpage used on the team site when you it for the first time.

11. Open the newly downloaded Masterpage in Visual Studio and copy its content to the **newmaster.master** we just created. To add a piece of customization to our new Masterpage, locate the following in the code of **newmaster.master**, which is the default logo of the team site:

    siteIcon.gif

    and replace it with:

    PWSCommitments.png

    This piece of custom string replaces the logo of the site with another SharePoint image which will help us easily identify that our custom Masterpage has been applied to the site.

12. Open **Elements.xml** in your Masterpage module and replace its contents with the following:

LISTING 3-11

```xml
<?xml version="1.0" encoding="utf-8"?>
<Elements xmlns="http://schemas.microsoft.com/
sharepoint/">
<Module Name="MasterPage"
List="116"
Url="_catalogs/masterpage">
<File Path="MasterPage\newmaster.master"
Type="GhostableInLibrary"
Url="newmaster.master" />
</Module>
</Elements>
```

In here, the **Module** and **File** element is describing where the Masterpage is going to be uploaded. The **List** attribute specifies the Masterpage gallery URL.

In the **File** element, the URL defines the Masterpage be uploaded. **GhostableinLibrary** tells SharePoint to create a list item to go with your file when it is added to the library.

13. Now that the solution will take care of deploying the Masterpage, let's add the code to set the Masterpage as a new alternative Masterpage on the site. Locate the **Features** folder in your solution and right click on **ProvisionMaster** in it. Select, **Add Event Receiver**.

14. In the **FeatureActivated** section of the code, replace the section with the following:

LISTING 3-12

```
public override void FeatureActivated(SPFeatureReceiver
Properties properties)
{
SPWeb web = properties.Feature.Parent as SPWeb;
web.CustomMasterUrl = "/_catalogs/masterpage/newmaster.
master";
web.Update();
}
```

This functionality of the feature receiver will execute custom. NET code when solution gets deployed and feature gets activated. This will set the custom Masterpage on the site to be our newly uploaded Masterpage.

15. Let's deploy the solution; right click the solution name and click **Deploy**.

Navigate back to the site root http://intranet.contoso.com to see that the logo of the site has changed to another image. I won't spend a lot of time describing to you things that you already know from here.

One example I would like to give here, is incorporating custom JavaScript in your Masterpage to drive its look dynamically.

As you navigate to the http://intranet.contoso.com you see the quick launch and the main area of the site. Suppose I want to give my users ability to hide or show quick launch dynamically to maximize the center area of the page when they require it. The figure below illustrates what I'm trying to achieve.

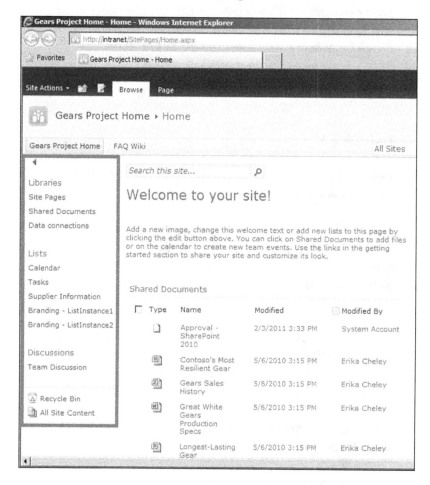

Figure 3-6 Toggling SharePoint quick launch on and off using custom extension in Masterpage

We're going to reuse the same solution structure we have used in this chapter since it already has all of the necessary artifacts such as Masterpage and provisioning code.

1. In Visual Studio, open the **MasterPage** module and containing **newmaster.master**.

2. In your **newmaster.master** locate the following piece of code:
   <div id="s4-leftpanel-content">
   add below code right after it:

LISTING 3-13

```
<a onclick="ExpandCollapseQuickLaunch(); return false;"
href="#">
<img id="LeftPaneCollapseImg" style="padding-left: 8px;
padding-right: 8px;" src="/_layouts/images/mewa_left.
gif" border="0"/>
</a>
```

This is the link to hide the quick launch; for now it calls the JavaScript function which we're going to define in a bit.

3. Now to show the quick launch which was hidden we're going to add another link. Locate the following code in your Masterpage:
   <a name="mainContent"></a>
   and add below right after it:

LISTING 3-14

```
<a onclick="ExpandCollapseQuickLaunch(); return false;"
href="#">
<img id="LeftPaneExpandImg" style="display: none;"
src="/_layouts/images/mewa_right.gif" border="0"/>
</a>
```

4. Now, we're going to add the JavaScript which is going to do all the work. This script relies on JQuery which is already referenced by SharePoint 2010. In your Masterpage, locate the
   </head>
   and add below right before it:

LISTING 3-15

```
<script type="text/javascript">
var quickLaunchVisible=true;
var showECIcon;
var contentTableMargin;
function ExpandCollapseQuickLaunch()
{
ToggleQuickLaunch(quickLaunchVisible, true);
}
function ToggleQuickLaunch(toggleOff, showECIcon)
{
if (toggleOff==null)
{
  toggleOff=true;
}
if (showECIcon==null)
{
  showECIcon=false;
}
var leftPanel = $get("s4-leftpanel");
if (leftPanel !=null)
{
  leftPanel.style.display=toggleOff ? 'none' : '';
  var contentTable = $get("MSO_ContentTable");
if (contentTable !=null)
{
 if (toggleOff)
 {
 contentTableMargin=(window.document.dir !='rtl') ?
contentTable.currentStyle.marginLeft :
 contentTable.currentStyle.marginRight;
 }
 if (window.document.dir !='rtl')
 {
 contentTable.style.marginLeft=toggleOff ?
'0px' : contentTableMargin;
 }
 else
```

```
  {
  contentTable.style.marginRight=toggleOff ?
  '0px' : contentTableMargin;
   }
  }

  var collapsePanelIcon=$get("LeftPaneCollapseImg");
  var expandPanelIcon=$get("LeftPaneExpandImg");
  expandPanelIcon.style.display=showECIcon &&
  toggleOff ? '' : 'none';
  if (collapsePanelIcon !=null)
  {
   collapsePanelIcon.style.display=showECIcon &&
  !toggleOff ? '' : 'none';
  }
  quickLaunchVisible=!toggleOff;
  }
  }
  </script>
```

5. **Deploy** the solution with Visual Studio and navigate to
   http://intranet.contoso.com. You will see the quick launch
   expand and collapse links as shown before.

In essence, this example demonstrates how you can change what
gets rendered on your Masterpage and how to apply it on the site.
Later on, we'll talk about integrating third-party controls on your
pages and making other advanced UI customizations.

Dynamically discovering granular components of the masterpage and branding a typical site

Although this chapter covers work with collaboration sites, this
section is somewhat generic and will apply to variety of site
templates. In here we're going to see how you can use popular
developer tools such as Firebug or IE Developer toolbar to discover
granular elements on the Masterpage and learn how those can

help you apply your custom markup to site Masterpage and other parts rendered to the user.

In the downloadable source code of this book, in *chapter 3* folder, you will find a subfolder called *SampleSite*. This folder will have an HTML page, a style sheet, and few images in a separate folder. If you open an HTML page, you will see it looks like a home page of a typical collaboration site with a header, few menus, and a main content area. In here, we'll go through a typical process you may be involved in when asked to brand a SharePoint site based on the sliced markup similar to what you get with our *SampleSite*.

I'm going to reuse the same solution I have used all along in this chapter. I will keep the Masterpage as **newmaster.master** and for style sheet I will use **branding.css**, which both already exist in my solution.

We'll start by deploying an existing solution from *chapter 3* to our site, http://intranet.contoso.com. This way our **newmaster.master** will be set on the site and we can use tools like Firebug and IE Developer Toolbar to see and edit the markup of the Masterpage in our solution.

Once the solution has been deployed with Visual Studio, open the site and ensure all of the customizations from *chapter 3* are in place; this way you know that our custom Masterpage and style sheet are applied.

From here, I will be using Firebug from Firefox, which requires your site to run in Firefox; you can install Firefox and Firebug in your virtual machine environment. You can also use IE Developer Toolbar by pressing F12 while your site is open in the browser.

1. Open the **style.css** file from your *SampleSite* package.
2. Copy the entire contents of the **style.css** to the **branding.css** file in your Visual Studio solution in the **ProvisionCSS** module.
3. Style classes in this file define the look of the various elements on the page, some of which may need to

be adjusted in order to not collide with out-of-the-box SharePoint markup.

Deploy the **Branding** project in the solution to the site and open the site.

4.   Open the Firebug (F12 key in Firefox). As you can see from the sliced HTML page in *SampleSite*, we need to change the header of the default team site to the custom header. Although the specs in *SampleSite* don't have a ribbon, we'regoing to keep the ribbon on our SharePoint site. You will also notice, that in the markup of out *SampleSite* we have three main *DIVs* within our body: *firstTopNav* (the very top navigation), *header* (image with the site name), and *secondNav* (main horizontal navigation). Everything below is part of the body.

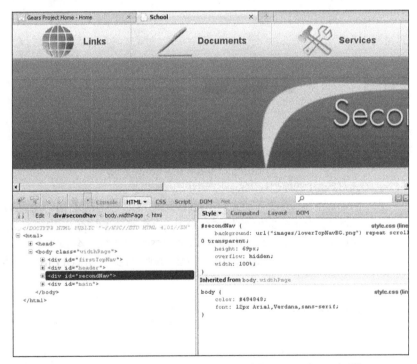

Figure 3-7 The look and associated markup of the spec *SampleSite*

5.   Switch to the http://intranet.contoso.com and open Firebug; here you will see we have the following important *DIVs*: ***s4-title s4-lp*** (the site title and icon area right below the

ribon), and **s4-topheader2** (is the area for the secondary navigation and search tools).

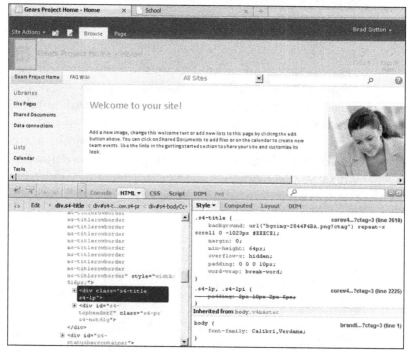

Figure 3-8 The look and associated markup of the SharePoint team site home page

6. Switch to your Visual Studio solution and open **newmaster. master** for editing. Locate the **s4-title s4-lp** within your markup; it'll be within <div class="s4-title s4-lp">
7. Place below listing right above the markup from *step* 6:

LISTING 3-16

```
<div id="firstTopNav">
<ul>
<li><a href="" class="links-Nav"><span>Links</span></
a></li>
<li><a href="" class="doc-Nav"><span>Documents</span></
a></li>
```

```
<li><a href="" class="services-Nav"><span>Services</
span></a></li>
<li><a href="" class="community-Nav"><span>Community</
span></a></li>
<li><a href="" class="contact-Nav"><span>Contact Us</
span></a></li>
</ul>
</div>
<div id="header">
<div class="header-Logo">
</div>
</div>
```

Above code will take care of rendering the very top navigation and a header image. You will notice that we didn't replace the current header; the reason is because we need to transfer some of the mendatory placeholders such as PlaceHolderPageTitleInTitleArea into the area of the page where they're safe to render and at the same time do not disturb our page design.

8. Now is the time to add supporting images. Create a new module in your Visual Studio solution called **ProvisionImages**. Remove **Sample.txt** file from the module and right click on it to add existing images we have in **SampleSite/images** folder.

9. Access the newly created module **Elements.xml** and replace it's contents with the following:

LISTING 3-17

```
<?xml version="1.0" encoding="utf-8"?>
<Elements xmlns="http://schemas.microsoft.com/
sharepoint/">
<Module Name="ProvisionCSS" Url="Style Library/Images">
<File Path="ProvisionImages\comIcon.png"
Type="GhostableInLibrary" Url="comIcon.png" />
<File Path="ProvisionImages\contactIcon.png"
Type="GhostableInLibrary" Url="contactIcon.png" />
```

```
<File Path="ProvisionImages\docIcon.png"
Type="GhostableInLibrary" Url="docIcon.png" />
<File Path="ProvisionImages\headePix.gif"
Type="GhostableInLibrary" Url="headePix.gif" />
<File Path="ProvisionImages\headerBG.png"
Type="GhostableInLibrary" Url="headerBG.png" />
<File Path="ProvisionImages\headerLogo.png"
Type="GhostableInLibrary" Url="headerLogo.png" />
<File Path="ProvisionImages\headeWelcomIcon.png"
Type="GhostableInLibrary" Url="headeWelcomIcon.png" />
<File Path="ProvisionImages\linkIcon.png"
Type="GhostableInLibrary" Url="linkIcon.png" />
<File Path="ProvisionImages\lowerTopNavBG.png"
Type="GhostableInLibrary" Url="lowerTopNavBG.png" />
<File Path="ProvisionImages\lowerTopNavHov.gif"
Type="GhostableInLibrary" Url="lowerTopNavHov.gif" />
<File Path="ProvisionImages\lowerTopNavSection.png"
Type="GhostableInLibrary" Url="lowerTopNavSection.png"
/>
<File Path="ProvisionImages\rightPanelPix.gif"
Type="GhostableInLibrary" Url="rightPanelPix.gif" />
<File Path="ProvisionImages\servicesIcon.png"
Type="GhostableInLibrary" Url="servicesIcon.png" />
<File Path="ProvisionImages\topHovNav.gif"
Type="GhostableInLibrary" Url="topHovNav.gif" />
<File Path="ProvisionImages\topNavBGPix.png"
Type="GhostableInLibrary" Url="topNavBGPix.png" />
<File Path="ProvisionImages\topNavPix.png"
Type="GhostableInLibrary" Url="topNavPix.png" />
<File Path="ProvisionImages\topNavSepPix.gif"
Type="GhostableInLibrary" Url="topNavSepPix.gif" />
<File Path="ProvisionImages\weatherIcon.png"
Type="GhostableInLibrary" Url="weatherIcon.png" />
</Module>
</Elements>
```

This will provision all of the images we added to the module into the **Style Library/Images** folder on the http://intranet.contoso.com site.

10. Now let's ensure we have proper references to images in our **branding.css**. Open **ProvisionCSS** and its update all references in **branding.css** to point to *url(/Style Library/ Images/[image name])*.

11. Now, since at this point we don't know what we're going to do with out-of-the-box header, we'll just hide it in the panel control. We'll wrap our header component within *<div class="s4-title s4-lp">*in the following:

```
<asp:Panel id="HideHeader" runat="server"
visible="false">

...

</asp:Panel>
```

12 Deploy the solution in Visual Studio and navigate to http:// intranet.contoso.com to see results.

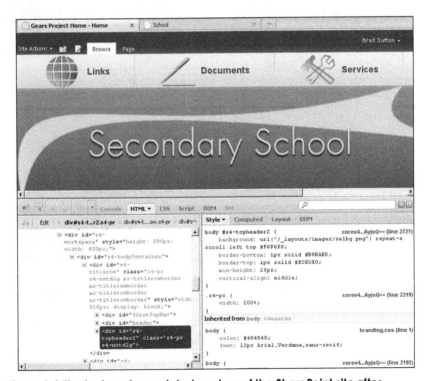

Figure 3-9 The look and associated markup of the SharePoint site after changes applied to the header

Next of the list is the horizontal menu. The only reason we won't just copy and paste the markup as-is is because secondary horizontal menu markup gets rendered dynamically based on the information coming from site map hierarchy. This means we'll just need to transfer only parts of the markup we care about and let SharePoint render the rest of the markup.

Let's take a look at the structure of the menu out-of-the-box in SharePoint.

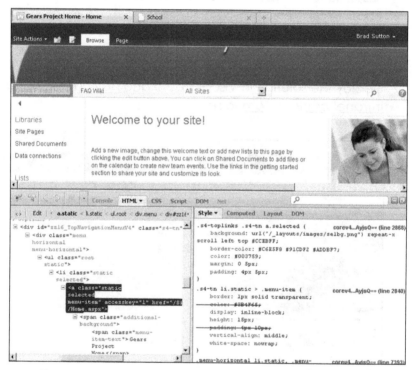

Figure 3-10 SharePoint horizontal navigation structure and look

This structure matches our sliced up *SampleSite* structure:

LISTING 3-18

```
<div id="secondNav">
<ul>
```

```
<li><a href="" class="course-Nav"><span>Course</span></
a></li>
<li><a href="" class="library-Nav"><span>Library</
span></a></li>
<li><a href="" class="honour-Nav"><span>Honour Roll</
span></a></li>
<li><a href="" class="scholarships-
Nav"><span>Scholorships</span></a></li>
<li><a href="" class="support-Nav"><span>Support
Services</span></a></li>
</ul>
</div>
```

The rendering of the secondary menu on our masterpage is done by *SharePoint:AspMenu*. The structure rendered by this control matches the one we have in our *SampleSite* slicing. This is not always the case. In some cases you may be given an HTML for the menu (secondary or primary menu) which looks differently and therefore can not be easily transfered to SharePoint. You will have to convert such menu to match the output rendered by SharePoint. In our case the only thing that's different is that our *secondNav* is a DIV Id and not the class like in SharePoint. This is easy enough to fix. We need to replace the **CssClass** attribute of the *SharePoint:AspMenu* to equal *secondNav*, just like in the listing below:

LISTING 3-19

```
<SharePoint:AspMenu
ID="TopNavigationMenuV4" Runat="server"
EnableViewState="false" DataSourceID="topSiteMap"
AccessKey="<%$Resources:wss,navigation_accesskey%>"
UseSimpleRendering="true" UseSeparateCss="false"
Orientation="Horizontal" StaticDisplayLevels="2"
MaximumDynamicDisplayLevels="1" SkipLinkText=""
CssClass="secondNav"/>
```

Also, in our **ProvisionCSS** module, in **branding.css** we need to replace all references to #secondNav to say .secondNav. That's it, deploy the solution and open http://intranet.contoso.com to see results.

Figure 3-11 The look and associated markup of the secondary navigation on the SharePoint site

Hopefully this gives you an idea of what's involved in branding a typical masterpage. Same techniques will come handy when branding any other part of the collaborations site or publishing site for that matter.

CHAPTER 4

Customizing SharePoint 2010 Publishing Sites

The SharePoint 2010 publishing site is defined by the set of features which make the site distinct from the collaboration site. Publishing site templates are usually used for Internet sites as well as intranets, which require flexibility in site design and the ability to streamline the production of web content. Among other features not available in collaboration sites, SharePoint publishing sites have the ability to pick alternative Masterpages as well as allow for users to choose from multiple layouts of how the information will be structured on the page. In this chapter we'll take a look at the anatomy of the publishing site Masterpage, which will have a few more features than its collaboration counterpart. We're also be making changes to the Masterpage and apply a different style sheet to be used on the site; we'll take a look at how you can automate the setup of those parameters when your site is provisioned. Finally, we'll see how you can modify the look and feel of administrative components and pages on the site.

What publishing Masterpage is all about

Just like in the example with the collaboration site, in order for us to make structural changes to the publishing page, we will have to create an instance of our own Masterpage and assign it to be used on the site.

Let's go ahead and take a look at the typical publishing Masterpage to see which parts are where. Download an instance of the **nightandday.master** from your publishing site, which is the default publishing sample site Masterpage:

1. From the http://www.contoso.com,which is the default publishing site on the virtual machine, click **Site Actions->Site Settings**.
2. Under **Galleries** click **Master pages and page layouts**.
3. Download **nightandday.master** to the file system.
4. Open **nightandday.master** in Visual Studio.

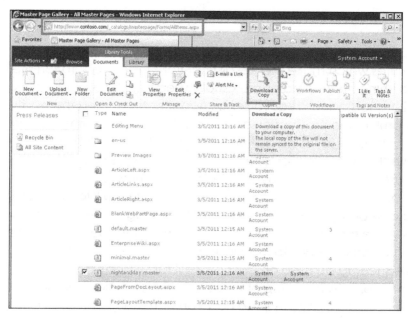

Figure 4-1 Masterpage gallery and typical masterpage file

Just like in the collaboration example from above, my comments are going to be in bold in the listing below. Most of the components will be explained apart from a few not-so-typical instances.

LISTING 4-1

```
<!--Adhering to strict document type definition -->
<!DOCTYPE html PUBLIC "-//W3C//DTD XHTML 1.0 Strict//EN"
"http://www.w3.org/TR/xhtml1/DTD/xhtml1-strict.dtd">
<%@ Master language="C#" %>


<!--Handles majority of site and web operations in
SharePoint -->
<%@ Import Namespace="Microsoft.SharePoint" %>


<!-- References server controls used on site pages -->
<%@ Register Tagprefix="SharePoint"
Namespace="Microsoft.SharePoint.WebControls"
Assembly="Microsoft.SharePoint, Version=14.0.0.0,
Culture=neutral, PublicKeyToken=71e9bce111e9429c" %>


<!-- Provides necessary wiring for creating custom Web
Parts and Web Part pages -->
<%@ Register Tagprefix="WebPartPages"
Namespace="Microsoft.SharePoint.WebPartPages"
Assembly="Microsoft.SharePoint, Version=14.0.0.0,
Culture=neutral, PublicKeyToken=71e9bce111e9429c" %>


<! -- User control which contain items in the "welcome
menu" on the top right hand side -->
<%@ Register TagPrefix="wssuc" TagName="Welcome"
src="~/_controltemplates/Welcome.ascx" %>


<! -- Supplies functionality for the edit bar when the
page is in edit mode of the page-->
<%@ Register TagPrefix="wssuc"
TagName="DesignModeConsole" src="~/_controltemplates/
DesignModeConsole.ascx" %>


<! -- User control handling multilingual UI selector-->
<%@ Register TagPrefix="wssuc" TagName="MUISelector"
src="~/_controltemplates/MUISelector.ascx" %>
```

```
<!-- Contains classes defining the structure,
appearance, and behavior of SharePoint publishing web
controls -->
<%@ Register Tagprefix="PublishingWebControls
" Namespace="Microsoft.SharePoint.Publishing.
WebControls" Assembly="Microsoft.SharePoint.Publishing,
Version=14.0.0.0, Culture=neutral, PublicKeyToken=71e9bce
111e9429c" %>

<!-- Contains classes for nodes, data source, providers
functionality implementing SharePoint navigation-->
<%@ Register Tagprefix="PublishingNavigati
on" Namespace="Microsoft.SharePoint.Publishing.
Navigation" Assembly="Microsoft.SharePoint.Publishing,
Version=14.0.0.0, Culture=neutral, PublicKeyToken=71e9bce
111e9429c" %>

<!-- Contains classes for sites, context and other core
functionality SharePoint portal -->
<%@ Assembly Name="Microsoft.SharePoint.Portal,
Version=14.0.0.0, Culture=neutral, PublicKeyToken=71e9bce
111e9429c" %>

<!-- Contains classes for SharePoint server web
controls and supporting components -->
<%@ Register Tagprefix="MSSWC" Namespace="Microsoft.
SharePoint.Portal.WebControls" Assembly="Microsoft.
Office.Server.Search, Version=14.0.0.0, Culture=neutral,
PublicKeyToken=71e9bce111e9429c" %>

<html xmlns="http://www.w3.org/1999/xhtml"
lang="<%$Resources:wss,language_value %>"
<!-- … -->
<!--Registers SharePoint out-of-the box javascript to
initialize components on the page -->
<SharePoint:ScriptLink name="init.js" runat="server"/>

<!-- Creates a reference to a custom JavaScript file to
run on the page -->
```

```
<SharePoint:CustomJSUrl runat="server" />

<SharePoint:SoapDiscoveryLink runat="server" />
<asp:ContentPlaceHolder id="PlaceHolderAdditionalPageHe
ad" runat="server"/>
<SharePoint:DelegateControl runat="server"
ControlId="AdditionalPageHead"
AllowMultipleControls="true"/>

<! -- Supplies favicon on the page -->
<SharePoint:SPShortcutIcon runat="server" IconUrl="/_
layouts/images/favicon.ico" />
<SharePoint:SPPageManager runat="server" />
<SharePoint:SPHelpPageComponent Visible="false"
runat="server" />

<! -- Registers out-of-the-box style sheets on the
page by emitting LINK tag on the page -->
<SharePoint:CssRegistration name="<%
$SPUrl:~sitecollection/Style Library/~language/Themable/
Core Styles/controls.css %>" runat="server"/>
<SharePoint:CssRegistration name="<%
$SPUrl:~sitecollection/Style Library/~language/Themable/
Core Styles/nightandday.css %>" After="corev4.css"
runat="server"/>
</head>
```

The header area stops above. As you can see, there is some repetition from the collaboration site template. There are quite a few control registrations specific to the publishing template. Below, we continue with the body of the Masterpage.

LISTING 4-2

```
<body scroll="no"
<!--…-->
<!-- Aids with Ajax script libraries and script files,
partial-page rendering etc -->
```

```
<asp:ScriptManager id="ScriptManager" runat="server"
EnablePageMethods="false" EnablePartialRendering="true"
EnableScriptGlobalization="true"
EnableScriptLocalization="true" />


<!-- In charge of web parts and events on a webpage -->
<WebPartPages:SPWebPartManager runat="server"/>


<! -- Controls related to navigation accessibility;
class="s4-notdlg" ensure the container not rendered in
the modal dialog windows-->
<span id="TurnOnAccessibility" style="display:none"
class="s4-notdlg">
<! -- … -->
</span>
<a id="HiddenAnchor" href="javascript:;"
style="display:none;"></a>


<! -- Ribbon area starts here-->
<div class="ribbonbackground">
<div class="s4-notdlg top-row">


<! -- Site logo with link back to the root of the site-
->
<div class="site-image-title">
<h2>
<SharePoint:SPLinkButton id="onetidProjectPropertyTitle
Graphic" runat="server" NavigateUrl="~site/">


<! -- Site logo — in this case Adventure works logo-->
<SharePoint:SiteLogoImage name="onetidHeadbnnr0"
id="onetidHeadbnnr2" LogoImageUrl="<%
$SPUrl:~sitecollection/Style Library/Images/nd_logo.png
%>" runat="server"/>
</SharePoint:SPLinkButton>
</h2>
</div>
```

```
<! -- Area displaying social tags buttons, help button,
and "welcome menu"-->
<div class="s4-trc-container s4-notdlg top-row-
elements">
<SharePoint:DelegateControl runat="server"
ControlId="GlobalSiteLink0" />
<! -- …-->
<div class="s4-trc-container-menu">

<! -- Welcome menu control-->
<wssuc:Welcome id="IdWelcome" runat="server"
EnableViewState="false">
</wssuc:Welcome>

<! -- Multilanguage selector-->
<wssuc:MUISelector runat="server"/>
</div>
<SharePoint:DelegateControl ControlId="GlobalSiteLink2"
Scope="Farm" runat="server" />
<span>
<span style="top:12px;display:inline-
block;position:relative;">

<! -- If enabled by administrator, this will display an
icon to call developer dashboard-->
<Sharepoint:DeveloperDashboardLauncher
ID="DeveloperDashboardLauncher"
NavigateUrl="javascript:ToggleDeveloperDashboard()"
runat="server"
<!-- … -->

<!--Area which will hold ribbon controls and button,
also Site Actions and search controls-->
<div id="s4-ribbonrow" class="s4-pr s4-
ribbonrowhidetitle">
<SharePoint:SPRibbon runat="server"
PlaceholderElementId="RibbonContainer"
CssFile="">
```

```
<!--Left side of the ribbon starts here -->
<SharePoint:SPRibbonPeripheralContent
runat="server"
Location="TabRowLeft"
CssClass="ms-siteactionscontainer s4-notdlg">
    <span class="ms-siteactionsmenu" id="siteactiontd">

<!--Site actions menu -->
<SharePoint:SiteActions runat="server"
accesskey="<%$Resources:wss,tb_SiteActions_AK%>"
id="SiteActionsMenuMain"
PrefixHtml=""
SuffixHtml=""
MenuNotVisibleHtml=" "
>
<CustomTemplate>
<!--… site actions menu items …-->
</CustomTemplate>
  </SharePoint:SiteActions>
</span>

<!--Global navigation menu allowing to navigate to the
parent of the site and other site in the hierarchy-->
<SharePoint:PopoutMenu
runat="server"
ID="GlobalBreadCrumbNavPopout"
IconUrl="/_layouts/images/fgimg.png"
IconAlt="<%$Resources:wss,master_breadcrumbIconAlt%>"
IconOffsetX=0
IconOffsetY=112
IconWidth=16
IconHeight=16

<!-- … -->

NodeImageUrl="/_layouts/images/fgimg.png"
HideInteriorRootNodes="true"
SkipLinkText="" />
```

```
</asp:ContentPlaceHolder>
</SharePoint:PopoutMenu>
```

<!--The "save" button only appearing when the page is in edit mode -->
```
<SharePoint:PageStateActionButto
n id="PageStateActionButton" runat="server"
Visible="false" />
</SharePoint:SPRibbonPeripheralContent>
```

<!--The right side of the ribbon -->
```
<SharePoint:SPRibbonPeripheralContent
runat="server"
Location="TabRowRight"
CssClass="s4-trc-container s4-notdlg">
```

<!--The area holding the search controls -->
```
<div id="s4-searcharea" class="s4-search s4-rp">
<asp:ContentPlaceHolder id="PlaceHolderSearchArea"
runat="server">
```

<!--Search control injected as delegate -->
```
<SharePoint:DelegateControl runat="server"
ControlId="SmallSearchInputBox" Version="4" />
</asp:ContentPlaceHolder>
</div>
</SharePoint:SPRibbonPeripheralContent>
</SharePoint:SPRibbon>
```

<! -- Notification area right after the ribbon, that's where quick notification messages pop up-->
```
<div id="notificationArea" class="s4-noti"></div>
<asp:ContentPlaceHolder ID="SPNavigation"
runat="server">
<SharePoint:DelegateControl runat="server"
ControlId="PublishingConsole"
Id="PublishingConsoleDelegate" />
</asp:ContentPlaceHolder>
<div id="WebPartAdderUpdatePanelContainer">
<!-- … -->
```

```
</div>
</div>
```

This marks the end of the ribbon-related content, which, apart from a few changes, was very similar to the collaboration site template. Next we're moving onto the main body of the publishing site Masterpage.

LISTING 4-3

```
<! --Main content area begind here-->
<div id="s4-workspace">
<div id="s4-bodyContainer">
<div id="s4-titlerow" class="s4-pr s4-notdlg s4-
titlerowhidetitle">
<table class="titlerow-table" border="0" cellspacing="0"
cellpadding="0">
<tr>

<! --Site breadcrumb — right next to the title and the
logo image of the site-->
<td class="breadcrumb">
<asp:SiteMapPath
runat="server"
SiteMapProviders="SPSiteMapProvider,SPXmlContentMapProv
ider"
RenderCurrentNodeAsLink="false"
NodeStyle-CssClass="breadcrumbNode"
CurrentNodeStyle-CssClass="breadcrumbCurrentNode"
RootNodeStyle-CssClass="breadcrumbRootNode"
HideInteriorRootNodes="true"
SkipLinkText="" />
</td>
</tr>
<tr>
<td class="title">
```

```
<! --Used by SharePoint to render title and description
of the site-->
 <h1><asp:ContentPlaceHolder id="PlaceHolderPageTitleInT
itleArea" runat="server" /></h1>
<h3><asp:ContentPlaceHolder
id="PlaceHolderPageDescription" runat="server" /></h3>
</td>
</tr>
</table>
</div>
<div id="s4-statusbarcontainer">

<! --Status bar displaying information such as whether
the page is checked out, when will it be published etc
-->
<div id="pageStatusBar" class="s4-status-s1"></div>
</div>
<!--Begin Nav|Content Area-->
<div class="body-wrapper">
<a name="startNavigation"></a>

<! --Current navigation (left side nav) will be
injected here-->
<asp:ContentPlaceHolder id="PlaceHolderGlobalNavigation"
runat="server" />
<asp:ContentPlaceHolder id="PlaceHolderGlobalNavigationS
iteMap" runat="server" />
<div id="s4-leftpanel" class="left-nav-bar s4-notdlg
res-nav-l">
<asp:ContentPlaceHolder id="PlaceHolderLeftNavBarDataSo
urce" runat="server" />
<asp:ContentPlaceHolder id="PlaceHolderCalendarNavigator
" runat="server" />
<asp:ContentPlaceHolder id="PlaceHolderWikiNavigator"
runat="server" />
<asp:ContentPlaceHolder id="PlaceHolderLeftNavBarTop"
runat="server" />

<! --This defines the datasource for the navigation
control-->
```

```
<PublishingNavigation:PortalSiteMapDataSource
ID="SiteMapDS"
runat="server"
EnableViewState="false"
SiteMapProvider="CurrentNavigation"
StartFromCurrentNode="true"
StartingNodeOffset="0"
ShowStartingNode="false"
TrimNonCurrentTypes="Heading"/>
<asp:ContentPlaceHolder id="PlaceHolderLeftNavBar"
runat="server">

<! --This will render left navigation UI -->
<SharePoint:AspMenu
ID="CurrentNav"
runat="server"
EnableViewState="false"
DataSourceID="SiteMapDS"
UseSeparateCSS="false"
UseSimpleRendering="true"
Orientation="Vertical"
StaticDisplayLevels="2"
MaximumDynamicDisplayLevels="0"
CssClass="nightanday-menu"
SkipLinkText="<%$Resources:cms,masterpages_
skiplinktext%>"/>

<!-- … -->

</asp:ContentPlaceHolder>
<asp:ContentPlaceHolder id="PlaceHolderLeftActions"
runat="server" />
<asp:ContentPlaceHolder id="PlaceHolderNavSpacer"
runat="server" />
</div>
<div class="s4-ca main-container" id="MSO_ContentDiv"
runat="server">
```

```
<!--Main part of the page where all the web parts and
other content is rendered -->
<div class="main-content">
<a name="mainContent"></a>
<asp:ContentPlaceHolder id="PlaceHolderMain"
runat="server" />
</div>
</div>
<!--If enabled, this allows to open a developer
dashboard-->
<div id="DeveloperDashboard" class="ms-
developerdashboard">
<SharePoint:DeveloperDashboard runat="server" />
</div>
```

This concludes the Masterpage body users will see. The rest are several content place holders which are not going to be used on our site but, due to the fact that SharePoint will expect to inject controls in them depending on the page you're on, we have to place those on the page. One of the standard techniques is to hide those place holders using the *asp:panel* set to be hidden.

LISTING 4-4

```
<! --Panel hiding all of the unused content
placeholders — this way if SharePoint inserts any
controls they will be hidden from the user-->
<asp:Panel Visible="false" runat="server">

<!--Site name defined in the Site Settings-->
<asp:ContentPlaceHolder id="PlaceHolderSiteName"
runat="server" />

<!--Site top navigation bar -->
<asp:ContentPlaceHolder id="PlaceHolderTopNavBar"
runat="server" />

<!--Menu within the top nav bar -->
```

```
<asp:ContentPlaceHolder id="PlaceHolderHorizontalNav"
runat="server" />

<!--Site image set in Site Settings-->
<asp:ContentPlaceHolder ID="PlaceHolderPageImage"
runat="server" />

<!--Border for the left page side -->
<asp:ContentPlaceHolder ID="PlaceHolderBodyLeftBorder"
runat="server" />

<!--Border for the left page side in the title area-->
<asp:ContentPlaceHolder ID="PlaceHolderTitleLeftBorder"
runat="server" />

<!-- Border for the left page side in the title area
separator -->
<asp:ContentPlaceHolder ID="PlaceHolderTitleAreaSeparat
or" runat="server" />

<!--Margin of the title area-->
<asp:ContentPlaceHolder ID="PlaceHolderTitleRightMargin"
runat="server" />

<!--Body area class -->
<asp:ContentPlaceHolder id="PlaceHolderBodyAreaClass"
runat ="server" />

<!--Title area class-->
<asp:ContentPlaceHolder id="PlaceHolderTitleAreaClass"
runat ="server" />

<!--Margin of the body area-->
<asp:ContentPlaceHolder id="PlaceHolderBodyRightMargin"
runat="server" />
</asp:Panel>
```

Now that we have taken a look at the structure of a typical
SharePoint publishing Masterpage, let's see what's involved in

making basic modifications and uploading the Masterpage to the server.

Modifying the Masterpage on SharePoint 2010 Publishing site

The Masterpage of the publishing site hosts various components on the page. Page navigation, page header, and references to style sheets are just few elements that reside on the Masterpage. Being able to modify the site Masterpage will allow you to change the positioning of the logo as well as the header of the site.

You may think that it's not often that you will modify the Masterpage of the site because you have access to style sheets and you can apply a new look and feel to the elements on the site using style sheets. However, default styles and attributes which are emitted through SharePoint controls in the Masterpage may be used in more than one place. This means that if you modify the style of a certain CSS class, you will end up modifying all of the instances of such class anywhere on the site where your style sheet is applied. This is sometimes a requirement, but in many cases not. An example might be a menu control which is positioned slightly off on the home page but appears to be fine everywhere else. Another case of when you need to make changes to the Masterpage is to change the default navigation of the site with the custom navigation user control. This is quite a common technique when developers require greater control over the functionality and appearance of the navigation.

Let's see how we can easily access and modify SharePoint 2010 publishing site Masterpages using SharePoint Designer 2010. SharePoint Designer will be installed in your demo environment and if you're using your own environment–you can download the tool online.

1. Open SharePoint Designer 2010 from the start menu, and click **Open Site** from the main menu of the welcome page.

Specify the URL of the site http://www.contoso.com and click **Open**.

2. You may be prompted for credentials, so ensure you provide **contoso\dministrator** as username with a valid password.
3. The site workspace will open, and under **Site Objects** on the left, choose **Masterpages**. SharePoint Designer will open the list of available Masterpages. Click to open **nightandday. master**.
4. The Masterpage file properties will open. Click the **Edit file** option in the workspace area and click OK to confirm that you're OK with the checkout of this file. By checking out this file, you will lock it for your own use, and no one else will see your changes until you're done and check back in the file.

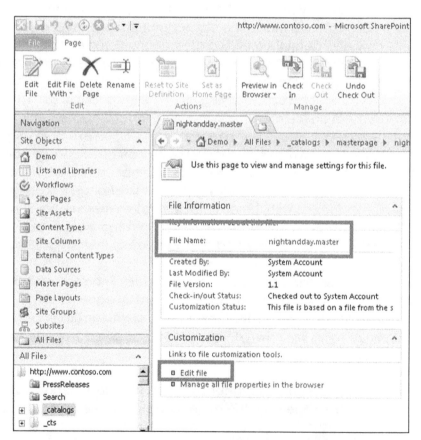

Figure 4-2 Editing Masterpage in SharePoint Designer

The Masterpage will load into the workspace. Now you can make structural changes to the Masterpage to match your particular requirements. This approach is very valid when you have an existing site and you need to make small tweaks. Mainly this is because your changes will be written to the server and no one will ever know how many times you modified the Masterpage over time and what has changed. After a while, when an issue happens related to Masterpage content, neither you nor anyone else will be able to reliably track back and revert problem code.

One of the more sustainable approaches is to make your modifications using Visual Studio and deploy your new Masterpage or existing modified version as a SharePoint solution package. Since SharePoint solution packages reside in the solution gallery, you can always see the version of the solution and when it was deployed, and there is always a way to upgrade or revent back to the previous version. Additionally, if you have to deploy your customizations to several environments (for example, development, QA environment, and production), you just need to run the solution deployment once on all those environments rather than following a list of changes to be applied in SharePoint Designer.

Let's go ahead and create Visual Studio version of the customization we did above.

We're going to create a Visual Studio solution which is going to provision Masterpage to an existing publishing site with our customizations in it. In this example, the customization is going to be very simple. In *chapter 7*, we'll take a look at how you can incorporate custom navigation control in your SharePoint Masterpage:

1. Open Visual Studio and create new project using SharePoint 2010 Empty Project template.
2. Specify http://www.contoso.com/ as your debug URL and choose **Deploy as farm solution** for your deployment method.
3. In the solution folder, locate the **Features** folder and right click on it to add a new feature.

4. Rename the default **Feature1** to **ProvisionMaster** so we can track our items better.
    This feature will be used to upload our custom masterpage to the gallery.
5. In the soltion folder, right click on the project name and select **Add** -> **New Item….**
6. Select **Module** for an item type and give it a name **Masterpage**.
7. Rename the **Sample.txt** file in the module to **newmaster. master**.
8. Navigate to http://www.contoso.com as **contoso\ administrator**.
9. Click **Site Actions** -> **Site Settings** and locate **Masterpages and Page Layouts** under **Galleries**.
10. Click on **nightandday.master** and pick **Download a Copy** on the ribbon. Save the file to disk. The Masterpage you have just downloaded is the default Masterpage used in the **Adventure Works** site when you create the publishing site for the first time.
11. Open the newly downloaded Masterpage in Visual Studio and copy its content to **newmaster.master**, which we created. Now, let's add a piece of customization to our new Masterpage. Locate the following piece of code in **newmaster.master**:

    ```
    <SharePoint:SiteLogoImage name="onetidHeadbnnr0"
    id="onetidHeadbnnr2" LogoImageUrl="<%
    $SPUrl:~sitecollection/Style Library/Images/nd_logo.png %>"
    runat="server"/>
    ```

    Add below right in front of the previous code:

    This Masterpage has been modified

    This piece of custom string will be placed right before global navigation in the Masterpage, which will help us easily identify that our custom Masterpage has been applied to the site.

12. Open **Elements.xml** in your Masterpage module and replace its contents with the following

LISTING 4-5

```xml
<?xml version="1.0" encoding="utf-8"?>
<Elements xmlns="http://schemas.microsoft.com/
sharepoint/">
<Module Name="MasterPage"
List="116"
Url="_catalogs/masterpage">
<File Path="MasterPage\newmaster.master"
Type="GhostableInLibrary"
Url="newmaster.master " />
</Module>
</Elements>
```

In here, the **Module** and **File** element is describing where the Masterpage is going to be uploaded. The **List** attribute specifies the Masterpage gallery URL.

In the **File** element, the URL defines the Masterpage be uploaded. **GhostableinLibrary** tells SharePoint to create a list item to go with your file when it is added to the library.

13. Let's deploy this solution with Visual Studio. Right click the solution name and click **Deploy**.

Now, our Masterpage should be deployed to the site but not automatically set on a site. Let's see how we can set the Masterpage manually first:

1. Navigate to http://www.contoso.com as administrator.
2. Click **Site Actions -> Site Settings** and locate **Masterpage** under **Look and Feel**.
3. You should see the choice to pick *newmaster.master* from the **Site Master Page** drop-down.
4. Once the setting is applied, you will see the new Masterpage available on the site.

Next, let's take a look at how we can automate Masterpage assignment by using the Visual Studio feature; after all, you don't want to instruct your users to set the Masterpage on several sites as manual steps. Essentially, we need to tell SharePoint to assign a new Masterpage on the site programmatically just like we did in the UI using **Site Settings**.

1. Right click on the **Features** solution node and locate **ProvisionMaster**.
2. Replace the code in the **FeatureActivated** method of the feature receiver with the one below:

LISTING 4-6

```
public override void FeatureActivated(SPFeatureReceiver
Properties properties)
{
SPWeb web = (SPWeb)properties.Feature.Parent;
string masterUrl = "newmaster.master";

if (String.IsNullOrEmpty(masterUrl) == false)
{
masterUrl = SPUrlUtility.CombineUrl(web.Site.
ServerRelativeUrl,
"_catalogs/masterpage/" + masterUrl);

foreach (SPWeb site in web.Site.AllWebs)
{
site.CustomMasterUrl = masterUrl;
site.Update();
}
}
}
```

This code will ensure the newly uploaded Masterpage has been set as the site Masterpage. That's all that we require at the moment to apply a new Masterpage to the user site.

3. Replace the code in the **FeatureDeactivated** method of the feature receiver with the one below:

LISTING 4-7

```
public override void FeatureDeactivating(SPFeatureRecei
verProperties properties)
{
SPWeb web = (SPWeb)properties.Feature.Parent;
string masterUrl = SPUrlUtility.CombineUrl(web.Site.
ServerRelativeUrl,
"_catalogs/masterpage/nightandday.master");
foreach (SPWeb site in web.Site.AllWebs)
{
site.CustomMasterUrl = masterUrl;
site.Update();
}
}
```

4. Reset the manually set Masterpage we have set in the previous sequence to **nightandday.master** and deploy our solution from Visual Studio to see how Masterpage gets set on the site.

From example above, you can see how to implement basic and more advanced configurations to the Masterpage. Next, let's take a look at the style sheet modifications and how those are different from the collaboration site scenario.

Setting custom style sheets for the SharePoint 2010 publishing site

In our last example we looked at how we can provision and set up custom Masterpages on the site. You may have also noticed that on the same page in SharePoint UI where you set Masterpage, you can also set custom style sheets. Let's take a look at how we can enhance the same solution we used in the example with provisioning Masterpages to provision a custom style sheet and set it to be used on the site.

Remember earlier we talked about the ability to specify an **Alternate CSS URL** using SharePoint out-of-the-box UI:

1. From www.contoso.com, click **Site Actions** -> **Site Settings**.
2. Under **Look and Feel** click **Masterpage**.

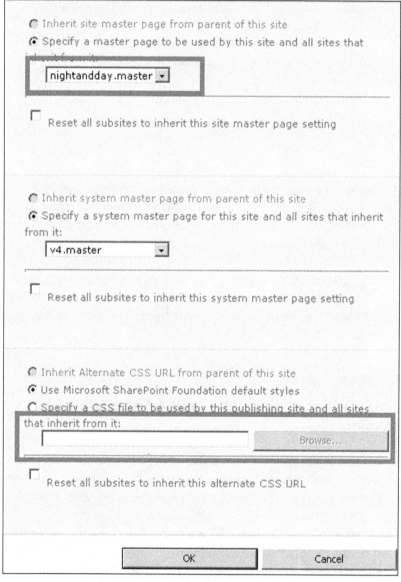

Figure 4-3 Managing Masterpages and Style Sheets using SharePoint 2010 interface

Well, in essence, you can point the value of **Alternate CSS URL** to a document library on the site where you can upload your style sheet. In many cases this is appropriate when you're making small tweaks and pointing the site to a draft version of a Masterpage.

However, for the same reasons we identified earlier for Masterpage, this approach is not the best case scenario. Imagine finding out that someone has deleted the document library where, among other things, you stored your style sheet. Additionally, if your site is a public site visited by at least several users at any given moment, you should avoid tweaking things and instead roll out your changes as versioned solution packages. By placing the style sheet into the appropriate style library using Visual Studio solution, you ensure there is better change control on the site and it will take less time to maintain your solution in the future.

Let's take a look at how we can extend our existing solution we used for provisioning Masterpage to now provision our custom style sheet:

1. In the existing Visual Studio solution, right click on the project name to create a new **Module** called **Styles**.
2. Locate the **ProvisionMaster** feature we created earlier and double click the feature name to ensure the new **Styles** module is in the list of items in the feature. If this is not the case, Visual Studio matched the new module to be provisioned by **SetMaster** feature; this sometimes happens since Visual Studio can't make the correct guess every time. In this case remove the **Styles** module from the list of items in **SetMaster** and add it to **ProvisionMaster**.
3. Open the newly created **Styles** module and rename **Sample.txt** to **Style.css**.
4. Replace the contents of the **Style.css** with the following sample style sheet code:

LISTING 4-8

```
body{
color: red;
}
```

5. Replace the contents of the **Elements.xml** in the **Styles** module with the following provisioning XML:

LISTING 4-9

```xml
<?xml version="1.0" encoding="utf-8"?>
<Elements xmlns="http://schemas.microsoft.com/
sharepoint/">
<Module Name="Styles" Url="Style Library" Path="Styles"
RootWebOnly="FALSE">
<File Url="style.css" Type="GhostableInLibrary"
Path="style.css">
<Property Name="Title" Value="My Custom CSS" />
</File>
</Module>
</Elements>
```

Here we instruct SharePoint to drop the **style.css** file into the **Style Library,** the default document library on the publishing site. This library is automatically created with the publishing site instance and is designed to host styles.

6. So far we have taken care of provisioning the style sheet to the **Style Library**; let's automatically set the style sheet on the site. Locate the **ProvisionMaster** feature, which already takes care of setting the Masterpage, and update the event receiver code of the feature with the following **FeatureActivated** event:

LISTING 4-10

```csharp
public override void FeatureActivated(SPFeatureReceiver
Properties properties)
{
SPWeb web = (SPWeb)properties.Feature.Parent;
string masterUrl = "newmaster.master";
```

```
if (String.IsNullOrEmpty(masterUrl) == false)
{
masterUrl = SPUrlUtility.CombineUrl(web.Site.
ServerRelativeUrl,
"_catalogs/masterpage/" + masterUrl);

foreach (SPWeb site in web.Site.AllWebs)
{
site.CustomMasterUrl = masterUrl;
site.AlternateCssUrl = "Style Library/style.css";
site.Update();
}
}
}
```

7. Here is the **FeatureDeactivated** event code to reverse our changes when solution is uninstalled:

LISTING 4-11

```
public override void FeatureDeactivating(SPFeatureRecei
verProperties properties)
{
SPWeb web = (SPWeb)properties.Feature.Parent;
string masterUrl = SPUrlUtility.CombineUrl(web.Site.
ServerRelativeUrl,
"_catalogs/masterpage/nightandday.master");
foreach (SPWeb site in web.Site.AllWebs)
{
site.CustomMasterUrl = masterUrl;
site.AlternateCssUrl = string.Empty;
site.Update();
}
}
```

8. Now, **deploy** the solution using Visual Studio.
9. Navigate to http://www.contoso.com as administrator.

10. Click **Site Actions** -> **Site Settings** and locate **Masterpage** under **Look and Feel** to verify that the **Custom Style Sheet** setting has been populated with our new style sheet. Depending on what changes you have included in the CSS file, you will also see them applied on the site.

Customizing administrative UI and modal dialogs

As we have discovered in previous chapters, SharePoint Masterpage allows you to customize the base look and feel of the client UI. However, as soon as you switch to administrative UI or open a modal dialog, the look and feel on those is different. The reason behind this is that administrative UI and modal dialog framework use what's known in SharePoint as **System Masterpage**.

To access **System Masterpage**:

1. Navigate to your publishing site URL: www.contoso.com.
2. Click **Site Actions** -> **Site Settings** -> **Masterpage** (under **Look and Feel**).
3. For the **System Masterpage,** you have access to the drop-down box of all the Masterpage choices.

When designing a custom system Masterpage, it's important to remember that Site Masterpage and System Masterpage have different purposes. This means you can't or rather shouldn't reuse an already existing Site Masterpage as a system one.

Consider a scenario such as www.contoso.com. Here we're dealing with a public site. Public sites usually have heavily customized UI; you would probably replace quick launch with custom right side navigation or have no quick launch at all. You would also probably use customized or custom top navigation, and you might have a highly interactive header section of the site. When such a Masterpage gets applied as a system Masterpage, it may add unnecessary controls and confuse your content contributors. Some other areas and controls which are normally displayed on administrative pages may be missing. Quick launch, for example, is used for a number of out-of-the-box management functions, such as accessing SharePoint security groups. If your Site Masterpage does not have a quick launch area, your site administrators will not be able to assign permissions to site users in a normal way.

This is one of the reasons you should consider creating a separate Masterpage and try to keep default UI elements which you're not sure about. The base for System Masterpage is **v4.master**, the same masterpage which is used for collaboration site templates as a default for all pages.

Since we've already taken a look at how to provision custom masterpages, I would like to add a part of the feature receiver code which will demonstrate how to set your custom Masterpage to be used as a System Masterpage.

The **FeatureActivated** event of the **ProvisionMaster** feature will look like this:

LISTING 4-12

```
public override void FeatureActivated(SPFeatureReceiver
Properties properties)
{
SPWeb web = (SPWeb)properties.Feature.Parent;
string masterUrl = "newmaster.master";

if (String.IsNullOrEmpty(masterUrl) == false)
{
masterUrl = SPUrlUtility.CombineUrl(web.Site.
ServerRelativeUrl,
"_catalogs/masterpage/" + masterUrl);

foreach (SPWeb site in web.Site.AllWebs)
{
site.MasterUrl = masterUrl;
site.CustomMasterUrl = masterUrl;
```

```
site.AlternateCssUrl = "Style Library/style.css";
site.Update();
}
}
}
```

The *FeatureDeactivated* event will look like this:

LISTING 4-13

```
public override void FeatureDeactivating(SPFeatureRecei
verProperties properties)
{
SPWeb web = (SPWeb)properties.Feature.Parent;
string masterUrl = SPUrlUtility.CombineUrl(web.Site.
ServerRelativeUrl,
"_catalogs/masterpage/nightandday.master");
string systemMasterUrl = SPUrlUtility.CombineUrl(web.
Site.ServerRelativeUrl,
"_catalogs/masterpage/v4.master");

foreach (SPWeb site in web.Site.AllWebs)
{
site.MasterUrl = systemMasterUrl;
site.CustomMasterUrl = masterUrl;
site.AlternateCssUrl = string.Empty;
site.Update();
}
}
```

Let's now **deploy** the solution using Visual Studio and test our functionality.

1. Navigate to http://www.contoso.com as administrator.
2. Click **Site Actions** -> **Site Settings**. Since the settings page uses System Masterpage, already you will see administrative UI has changed to conform to what has been defined in a System Masterpage.

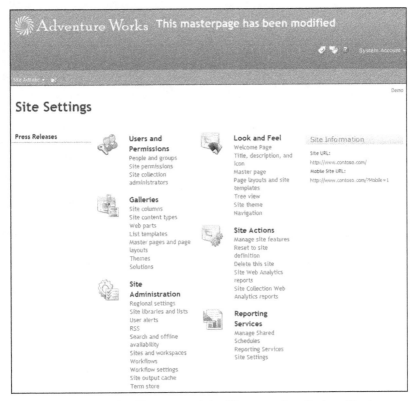

Figure 4-4 The look of settings page inheriting a custom System Masterpage

In your actual customer scenario, you may see a need to use custom System Masterpage to display consistent look across list item forms such as calendar event forms etc.

In this chapter you've become more familiar with the structure and branding customizations you can apply to a publishing site. Publishing site templates and pages are used in many different places in SharePoint. Later, we'll be dealing with publishing site template again, particularly in chapter 8, where we look at working with publishing pages.

Before we jump further, let's take a look at customizing SharePoint 2010 specialized site templates. This topic will cover some of the things you already know from the collaboration site template, plus we'll see what makes specialized site templates so different from others.

CHAPTER 5

Customizing SharePoint 2010 Specialized Sites

In general overview in **chapter 2**, we talked about what specialized sites are all about. Particularly, we looked at My Site and its components. So how exactly do you go about modifying users' **MySites** -> **My Content** sites and applying custom branding? The process is a bit more different than typical collaboration or publishing sites.

In the case of modifying users' private site, we will be using **feature site template associations**, also known as the **feature stapling** technique. As does every site in SharePoint, MySite derives from a template, and this template is what SharePoint is using every time a new instance of the site is created.

Unfortunately, we can't modify and add new features to a MySite template. By using the feature stapling approach, we're going to **staple** our new customizations to the existing site template. Here are two Visual Studio features which will be involved in this process:

1. **Staplee** feature—containing the functionality you want to add to a MySite template.

2. **Stapler** feature—contanining the association XML allowing binding the staplee feature to a particular site template, in our case the MySite user site.
3. Masterpage, which will be just an ASP.NET page that has the file name extension .master. Masterpage will allow us to create a consistent appearance and layout for our MySite pages.
4. ASP.NET web control, in our case ASP.NET server control, which consists of a .NET assembly and will be added to a page to instantiate an instance of our control.

Usually, when customizing MySites across an enterprise, the most typical requirement is to:

1. Use a custom Masterpage with a custom style sheet to add the desired look and feel to the site
2. Add, remove, or move web parts on the page.

Those are the main items we're going to look at here. However, the approach here is flexible enough to perform any other customizations.

Let's go ahead and create a Visual Studio solution which is going to modify our MySite user site template:

1. Open Visual Studio and create a new project using SharePoint 2010 Empty Project template.
2. Specify http://intranet.contoso.com/ as your debug URL and choose **Deploy as farm solution** for your deployment method.
3. In the soltion folder, locate the **Features** folder and right click on it to add a new feature.
4. Rename the default **Feature1** to **MySiteStaplee** so we can track our items better.
   This feature will be used to upload our custom masterpage to the gallery.
5. In the solution folder, right click on the project name and select **Add** -> **New Item....**

6. Select **Module** for an item type and give it the name **Masterpage**.
7. Rename the **Sample.txt** file in the module to **newmaster. master**.
8. Navigate to the MySite at http://intranet.contoso.com as administrator.
9. Click **Site Actions** -> **Site Settings** and locate **Masterpages** under **Galleries**.
10. Click on **v4.master** and pick **Download a Copy** on the ribbon. Save the file to disk.
11. Open the newly downloaded out-of-the-box Masterpage in Visual Studio and copy its content to the **newmaster. master** we created. Now, let's add a piece of customization to our new Masterpage. Locate the following piece of code in **newmaster.master**:
    <SharePoint:DelegateControl runat="server" ControlId="GlobalNavigation" />
    Add below right in front of the previous code:
    Custom Masterpage test
    This piece of custom string will be placed right before global navigation in the Masterpage, which will help us easily identify that our custom Masterpage has been applied to the site.
12. Open **Elements.xml** in your Masterpage module and replace its contents with the following:

LISTING 5-1

```xml
<?xml version="1.0" encoding="utf-8"?>
<Elements xmlns="http://schemas.microsoft.com/
sharepoint/">
<Module Name="MasterPage"
    List="116"
    Url="_catalogs/masterpage">
<File Path="MasterPage\newmaster.master"
    Type="GhostableInLibrary"
    Url="newmaster.master " />
</Module>
</Elements>
```

In here, the **Module** and **File** element is describing where the Masterpage is going to be uploaded. The **List** attribute specifies the Masterpage gallery URL.

In the **File** element, the URL defines the Masterpage to be uploaded. **GhostableinLibrary** tells SharePoint to create a list item to go with your file when it is added to the library.

13. Next, we need to tell SharePoint to assign the new Masterpage on the site programmatically just like we did in the UI using Site Settings. For that, right click on the **MySiteStaplee** feature we created earlier and select **Add Event Receiver**.

14. In a newly created feature receiver class file, locate **FeatureActivated** method and uncomment its code (select the code and hit CTRL+K+U).

15. Add the code below to the **FeatureActivated** method of the receiver:

LISTING 5-2

```
public override void FeatureActivated(SPFeatureReceiver
Properties properties)
{
SPWeb web = (SPWeb)properties.Feature.Parent;
string masterUrl = "newmaster.master";

if (String.IsNullOrEmpty(masterUrl) == false)
{
masterUrl = SPUrlUtility.CombineUrl(web.Site.
ServerRelativeUrl,
"_catalogs/masterpage/" + masterUrl);

foreach (SPWeb site in web.Site.AllWebs)
{
site.MasterUrl = masterUrl;
site.Update();
}
}
}
```

This code will ensure the newly uploaded Masterpage has been set as the site Masterpage. That's all that we require at the moment to apply the new Masterpage to the user site. As I mentioned earlier, we will see how we can rearrange web parts on the page as a separate sample.

The *MySiteStaplee* feature has all of the required functionality; now the feature stapler comes into play. The stapler will establish an association between a site template (**MySite**) and a feature, meaning that whenever a new site is created based on a specific template, our staplee feature will get activated. When it does, our Masterpage is going to be provisioned to the site and set as a new site Masterpage.

16. In the soltion folder, locate the **Features** folder and right click on it to add a new feature.
17. Rename the default name from **Feature1** to **MySiteStapler**. This feature will be used to establish an association between a site template (**MySite**) and a feature.
18. In the soltion folder, right click on the project name and select **Add** -> **New Item....**
19. Select **Module** for an item type and give it the name **StaplerHelper.**
20. In a newly created module folder, remove **Sample.txt** file. Also, double click on **MySiteStaplee** to see its properties. Remove **StaplerHelper** from the list of items in the feature; by default Visual Studio assigns modules to features scoped to a **web**, which in our case won't work.
21. Double click on the **MySiteStapler** feature name and add the **StaplerHelper** to the list of items in the feature. Then, set the **Scope** attribute of the feature to **Farm**.
22. Switch to the feature properties page of **MySiteStaplee** and click the **Manifest** option at the bottom of the properties page; you will be switched to the XML with various properties we have assigned using a UI.

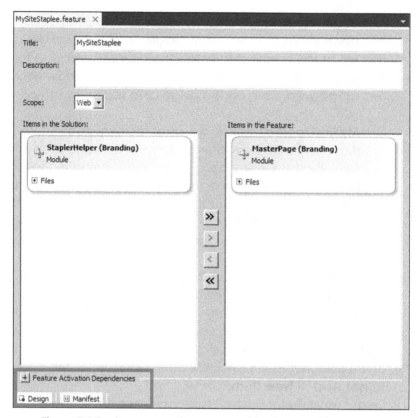

Figure 5-1 Feature properties page and Feature Manifest option

Locate the attribute called **Id** of the **Feature** element and copy the value of it, which is going to look something like this: **2ea7bfd3-01a6-4fde-8b2e-87d57e598315**. We will be referencing this Id further in our **StaplerHelper**.

Figure 5-2 Attribute to copy from the Feature Manifest

23. Now, we will ensure our newly created module
(**StaplerHelper**) can be referenced in our **MySiteStapler**
feature by extending the scope of the module to **Farm**.
In the Solution Explorer window, click the button to **Show
All Files**.

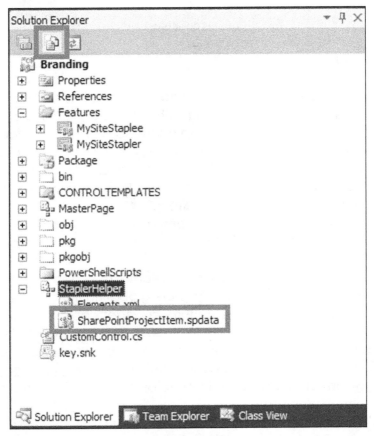

Figure 5-3 Show All Files option in Visual Studio Solution Explorer

24. Inside the **StaplerHelper** folder, locate the file called
SharePointProjectItem.spdata and open it. Locate the
attribute called **SupportedDeploymentScopes** and change
its value to **Farm**. Save the file.
25. Open **Elements.xml** of the **StaplerHelper** module and
replace its contents with the following:

LISTING 5-3

```xml
<?xml version="1.0" encoding="utf-8"?>
<Elements xmlns="http://schemas.microsoft.com/
sharepoint/" >
    <FeatureSiteTemplateAssociation
    Id="2ea7bfd3-01a6-4fde-8b2e-87d57e598315"
TemplateName="SPSPERS#0"/>
</Elements>
```

Here we link our staple feature with the **Id** we copied earlier (ensure you replace the **Id** with the value you have copied from the **FeatureStaplee**) to a template responsible for **MySite** personal user sites. Templates in SharePoint have IDs allowing one template to have different sets of features depending on the circumstances. The MySite personal site template and Id in here is **SPSPERS#0**.

26. Right click on the project name and select **deploy**; allow Visual Studio to complete the deployment to the farm.

In this scenario we have applied a custom Masterpage to the site with a simple headline right before the global navigation on the site. You can see how other structural changes can be added to the Masterpage just as you would do to a collaboration site. If you'd like to use a custom style sheet or graphics on the site, those can be placed on the parent site, in our case http://intranet. contoso.com, and have permission to be readable from user sites.

In this case the situation is pretty simple—you make a reference in your custom Masterpage to a style sheet, which resides on the main site, in this case.

Alternatively, you can place such artifacts into individual user sites when those are created. This is a less common scenario because you will have to maintain a copy of the artifacts on each site. In some cases, however, you need to customize web parts which appear on the pages of the users' personal site. Such customizations may fall into the branding scenario. For example, you may need to ensure the department logo appears as a web part on the page; in this case you would need to place a web part into the zone of the Masterpage once the site is created.

When a new site is created, such as users' **MySites**, not all of the libraries or artifacts are right away available during provisioning of the custom feature. This means if we have a custom feature which provisions a file to a document library, the provisioning may fail if your feature has been activated before the document library provisioning feature has. This is a common scenario, and one of the approaches is to use a server control to perform the provisioning role.

In this case the server control will be referenced on the site's Masterpage, and when the page is hit for the first time, the control will execute all of the provisioning actions which are required to complete setup.

Let's take a look at the scenario like this in action. We will reuse the same Visual Studio solution from above and build on the top of it.

1. Open the **MasterPage** module we created earlier and the **newmaster.master** file.
2. We will register a new .NET control on the Masterpage so the contents of it run when the Masterpage is called. Locate the existing below code in the Masterpage:
   <%@ Register TagPrefix="wssuc" TagName="DesignModeConsole" src="~/_controltemplates/DesignModeConsole.ascx" %>

   And right below it, add the following

   <%@ Register Tagprefix="Custom" Namespace="SharePointProject1" Assembly="Chapter5. Branding, Version=1.0.0.0, Culture=neutral, PublicKeyToken= dc8455ec5d98810e" %>

   Ensure the assembly name, which in our case is **Chapter5. Branding**, is the name you gave to your project assembly. Also, the value of **PublicKeyToken** can be determined by accessing the properties of the assembly. Locate your assembly by opening *C:\Windows\assembly* in Windows Explorer and accessing the properties of the assembly name matching the one you gave for the Visual Studio project (**Chapter5.Branding** unless you have changed it).

3. Now that the control is declared, we referenced it in the body of the Masterpage. Locate the test text we placed in **step 11** of the previous sequence (hint: *Custom masterpage test*) and replace it with the following code:

   <Custom:CustomControl runat="server">Add new Content Editor webpart</Custom:CustomControl>

4. Let's create the .NET control we have just declared. Right click on the project name and select **Add**-> **Class....**
5. Give the class the name **CustomControl** and add it to the solution.
6. Right click on references in your project structure to add the reference to:
   Microsoft.SharePoint.DLL (in .NET list).
7. Replace the code in your newly created user control with the following:

LISTING 5-4

```
using System;
using System.Collections.Generic;
using System.Linq;
using System.Text;
using System.Web.UI;
using Microsoft.SharePoint;
using Microsoft.SharePoint.WebPartPages;
using System.Web.UI.WebControls;

namespace Chapter5.Branding
{
public class CustomControl : LinkButton
{
```

```
protected override void OnClick(EventArgs e)
{
base.OnClick(e);

SPWeb thisWeb = SPContext.Current.Web;

if (!thisWeb.Properties.ContainsKey("CustomActionExecut
ed1"))
{
thisWeb.AllowUnsafeUpdates = true;

SPFile defaultPage = thisWeb.GetFile("default.aspx");
if (defaultPage.CheckedOutByUser == null)
{
defaultPage.CheckOut();
}

SPLimitedWebPartManager webpartManager =
defaultPage.GetLimitedWebPartManager
(System.Web.UI.WebControls.WebParts.
PersonalizationScope.Shared);

ContentEditorWebPart contentEditorWP = new
ContentEditorWebPart();
contentEditorWP.Title = "My WebPart Title";
contentEditorWP.ChromeType =
System.Web.UI.WebControls.WebParts.PartChromeType.
TitleOnly;

webpartManager.AddWebPart(contentEditorWP, "Left", 0);
webpartManager.SaveChanges(contentEditorWP);

defaultPage.CheckIn("Added Content Editor");
thisWeb.Properties.Add("CustomActionExecuted1", "true");
thisWeb.AllowUnsafeUpdates = false;
}
}

protected override void OnLoad(EventArgs e)
```

```
{
base.OnLoad(e);
}
}
}
```

Here, we run our custom code as soon as the control loads. Since we want to execute the code only once, when the user first accesses the site, we record a value inside the site's **Properties** called *CustomActionExecuted* which will ensure we run the code only if this property value is blank.

Then we simply access the current site and the default page on it and add a new web part to the page with some of the basic properties assigned.

8. Deploy the solution using Visual Studio and navigate to the administrator's **MySite** from http://infranet.contoso.com/.

9. Once on the users feed bage, click **My Content** located in the top link area.

10. You will see the link to *Add new Content Editor web part* on the top of the page. Click this link to add the web part, in our case Content Editor web part.

Once the administrator's MySite site has loaded, you will see the additional web part added to the page. This demonstrates how you can incorporate additional UI elements using web parts for specialized sites which haven't been created yet. When the site is created we inject additional feature into the list of template features. What if you need to make changes to existing instance of the site? Next example focuses on demonstrating just that.

Applying common design artifacts and settings on existing specialized sites

If you noticed, the logic we have implemented works only for sites that have not been created yet. When we staple our custom branding provisioning feature to the personal site template, the feature actions will only execute upon the new site being created and not on existing sites.

So what do you do when you need to apply branding to quite a few existing sites? Well, one of the most common ways is to go through all of the sites, specialized or not, and set your customizations as planned. You would automate such a procedure so it takes very little down time and implementation time. Just like we implemented a custom code to add web parts in the example with specialized sites, you can access SharePoint site properties and assign new value to them and provision artifacts in the same way.

This example involves steps which are likely to be performed by a back-end developer on your team; however, if your role involves those responsibilities or if you like to see what's involved, this example is for you.

As I mentioned, you could use the approach of deploying custom code in the Visual Studio solution, but this approach comes at the price of leaving artifacts which are not going to be used again. Each time you deploy a new Visual Studio solution, the solution package will end up residing in the solution store even after you have accomplished your goal. One of the better options can be using PowerShell script, which will run your customizations. PowerShell script will execute in a shell environment and will have access to the same SharePoint objects you would have when accessing them in Visual Studio code.

PowerShell script can be created as a text file and referenced in the shell. Let's see how we can create a script which will update the properties of the web part with the new set of values.

1. Ensure you're logged in to your development machine as administrator.
2. Create a new text file on your desktop with the name **addnewwebpart.ps1**. PS1 will specify the PowerShell script.
3. Open the file and replace its content with the following:

LISTING 5-5

```
function UpdateWebpart([Microsoft.SharePoint.Publishing.
PublishingPage]$page)
{
if($page.CheckOutBy -eq $null)
{
    $page.CheckOut()
}
$webpartmanager=$web.GetLimitedWebPartManager($page.
Url,
[System.Web.UI.WebControls.WebParts.
PersonalizationScope]::Shared)
for($i=0; $i -lt $webpartmanager.WebParts.Count; $i++)
{
    if($webpartmanager.WebParts[$i].GetType()
    -eq [Microsoft.SharePoint.WebPartPages.
    ContentEditorWebPart])
    {
    $wp = $webpartmanager.WebParts[$i];
    $wp.ChromeType=
      [System.Web.UI.WebControls.WebParts.
      PartChromeType]::TitleOnly;
      $wp.Title="New Webpart"
      $webpartmanager.SaveChanges($wp);
    }
}
}

function PublishPage ([Microsoft.SharePoint.Publishing.
PublishingPage]$page)
{
    " Page: " + $page.Name
    $listitem = $page.ListItem.File
    UpdateWebpart($page)
    if ($listitem.Level -eq [Microsoft.SharePoint.
    SPFileLevel]::Checkout)
{
    $listitem.CheckIn("Checked in by Administrator",
```

```
         [Microsoft.SharePoint.SPCheckInType]::MajorCheckin)
}
if ($page.ListItem.ParentList.EnableModeration)
{
     if($page.ListItem.ModerationInformation.Status -eq
     Microsoft.SharePoint.SPModerationStatusType]::Pending)
     {
     $listitem.Approve("Approved by Administrator")
     }
     if($page.ListItem.ModerationInformation.Status -eq
     [Microsoft.SharePoint.SPModerationStatusType]::Draft)
     {
       $listitem.Publish("Published by Administrator")
     }
   }
}

function PublishPages([Microsoft.SharePoint.SPWeb]$web)
{
$pubweb =
[Microsoft.SharePoint.Publishing.PublishingWeb]::GetPubl
ishingWeb($web);
if ($pubweb.DefaultPage -ne $null)
{
$pubpages=$pubweb.GetPublishingPages()
for($i=0; $i -lt $pubpages.count; $i++)
{
PublishPage $pubpages[$i]
}
}
}

$site = spsite "http://www.contoso.com"
$site.allwebs | foreach-object {PublishPages $_ }
```

In the script above we have the following parts:

UpdateWebpart—the method accesses the page (which was passed as a parameter) and gets a hold on the web part manager. The web part manager contains the web part which we would like to modify. We access the web part and modify its properties. When done, we save the web part manager with changes to the web part.

PublishPage—this method is responsible for publishing the page which was edited to make changes on the web part. Pages which are not published will remain in the draft state, and changes on them will not be visible to anyone except the author of the draft.

At the very bottom of our script we have two lines which specify the URL of the site and in turn parse site pages and set new web part properties to web parts of type **Content Editor**:

LISTING 5-6

```
$site = spsite "http://www.constoso.com"
$site.allwebs | foreach-object {PublishPages $_ }
```

4. Save the script.
5. Assuming you have access to the administrator's desktop, click **Start** -> **All Programs** -> **Microsoft SharePoint 2010 Products** -> **SharePoint 2010 Management Shell**.
6. In the shell window, switch to the desktop by typing: cd .\Desktop
7. Execute our script from the desktop by typing: & '.\New Text Document1.ps1'

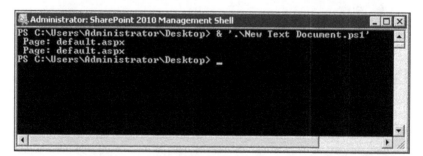

Figure 5-4 PowerShell script execution results

The script will run and display each page which has been modified. After the script has completed setting the web part title and chrome, check a few of the pages on www. contoso.com to see the results. Ensure you're checking the pages that actually have the **Content Editor** web part.

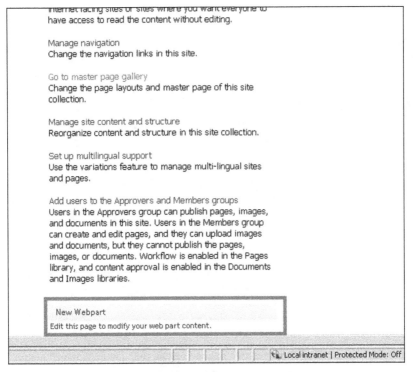

Figure 5-5 Content editor web part added to the page

CHAPTER 6

Extending Search Look and Feel

SharePoint search is a whole set of functionalities which includes a set of features and user interfaces related to searching on the site and rendering results. There are two types of search output features available in SharePoint. When you create a team site, you automatically get a search box on the top of your site, which lets you search for a term on a site and redirects you to a results page once you're done. This results page has some out-of-the-box capabilities, such as RSS feeds, alerts, and so on. Don't try to edit this page, you won't be able to; it's a simplest result page that comes with SharePoint.

If you like to choose what will be displayed on your search page, just as you do on any other SharePoint pages, you're going to have to create a separate subsite for an Enterprise Search Center. In this chapter, we'll focus on the Enterprise Search Center template, which in essence is a SharePoint template just like a team site. This template contains features allowing users to search for people and information on the site and renders rich set of results.

Customizing search center look and feel

Since the search center is part of the overall site structure, there are scenarios where you will be asked to customize the look and feel of the search site.

Let's go ahead and create an instance of your new search center and see what it's all about.

1. Navigate to http://intranet.contoso.com, which is your team site. You will notice that this site already has a **Search** link on the top navigation—this takes you to the FAST search center in our demo virtual machine. The FAST search center is an extended version of a search center but similar in its branding structure to an enterprise search center. For consistency we'll create an enterprise search center here.
2. From the http://intranet.contoso.com, click **Site Actions -> New Site ->**. From the category on the left pick **Search ->** and for the template pick **Enterprise Search Center**.
3. Set the name and URL of the site to *esearch* so it doesn't conflict with the FAST search center, and click **Create**.
4. When the site is created, you will see its basic structure. Click **Site Actions -> Site Settings**. As you will see from the settings user interface, this site is very similar to the publishing site. Under Look and Feel, you see the ability to modify Masterpages and style sheets applied on the site as well as themes. Click on **Masterpage** under **Look and Feel**.

You will notice the search center is using *minimal.master* as its default Masterpage. This Masterpage is a simplified version of *v4.master*, and this is the reason why you don't see some of the elements you used to see on the site using **v4.master**, such as site breadcrumbs beside the **Site Actions** menu allowing you to navigate up. Let's take a look at what **minimal.master** is all about and then see how we can customize it and add some additional controls to enhance it.

1. Open SharePoint Designer 2010 and click the **Open Site** button.
2. In the URL, specify http://intranet.contoso.com/esearch, which is our search center, and click **Open**.
3. When your site loads into SharePoint Designer, under **Site Objects** select **All Files**.
4. Open the **Pages** library. This is the library where Enterprise Search Center holds pages with web parts which facilitate searching and returning results to the user. We have:

   ■ **Advanced.aspx**—a page which facilitates advanced search.
   ■ **Default.aspx**—this is the default page which opens when you open the search center and allows users to enter their one-line keyword.
   ■ **People.aspx**—allows the user to launch the people search query.
   ■ **Peopleresults.aspx**—page which returns results of people search.
   ■ **Results.aspx**—page which returns results of a regular search term query (not people).

All of those are web part pages, and if you open a page in the edit mode, you can see associated web parts in various zones on the page.

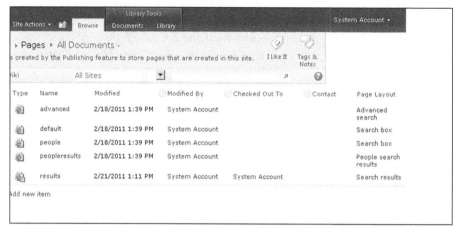

Figure 6-1 Types of pages on the default instance of Enterprise Search Center

You can edit the page right from SharePoint Designer or as we saw before in Visual Studio. By default, all pages are using **minimal. master**.

5. Click **Masterpages** under **Site Objects** on the left, and click **minimal.master**. Under the Customization section on the workspace, click **Edit file**.

   Let's take a look at the body of the **minimal.master**. Here I will only call out elements which are relevant or different from the publishing Masterpage, since we already looked at the publishing Masterpage earlier and you probably have a good idea what it's all about.

LISTING 6-1

```
<head runat="server">
<!-- ... -->
<!--In here I would like to call out two references to
style sheets which are specific to minimal.master-->
<SharePoint:CssRegistration Name="minimalv4.css"
runat="server"/>
```

```
<SharePoint:CssRegistration Name="layouts.css"
runat="server"/>
<!-- ... --->
</head>
<body
<!-- ... -->

<!-- This is where Site Actions and ribbon is going to
be injected. As you can see this is a bit more different
method comparing to publishing Masterpage -->
<asp:ContentPlaceHolder ID="SPNavigation"
runat="server">
</asp:ContentPlaceHolder>

<div id="s4-mini-header" class="s4-pr s4-notdlg">
<div class="s4-rp">

<!-- Ribbon notifications area where flyout messages are
displayed-->
<div id="notificationArea" class="s4-mini-noti"></div>
<SharePoint:DelegateControl ControlId="GlobalSiteLink3-
mini" Scope="Farm" runat="server"/>

<!-- Help button area-->
<asp:ContentPlaceHolder id="PlaceHolderHelpButton"
runat="server">
<div class="ms-mini-trcHelp">
<!-- ... -->
</asp:ContentPlaceHolder>

<!-- Welcome and login menu placeholder -->
<asp:ContentPlaceHolder id="PlaceHolderWelcomeMenu"
runat="server">
<div class="lb ms-mini-trcMenu">
```

```
<!-- Welcome menu control -->
<wssuc:Welcome id="IdWelcome" runat="server"
EnableViewState="false">
</wssuc:Welcome>


<!-- Multilingual selector control -->
<wssuc:MUISelector runat="server"/>
</div>
</asp:ContentPlaceHolder>
<!-- ... -->
</div>


<!-- Area of the site title, right under site actions
-->
<div id="s4-mini-titlearea" class="s4-lp">


<!-- Site logo injected here, this is set from site
actions -->
<SharePoint:DelegateControl ControlId="MinimalMasterSit
eLogo" Scope="Web" runat="server">
<Template_Controls>
<SharePoint:SPLinkButton runat="server"
NavigateUrl="~site/" id="onetidProjectPropertyTitleGraph
ic" CssClass="s4-mini-sitelogo-a">
<SharePoint:SiteLogoImage id="onetidHeadbnnr0"
LogoImageUrl="/_layouts/images/siteIcon.png"
runat="server" CssClass="s4-mini-sitelogo" />
</SharePoint:SPLinkButton>
</Template_Controls>
</SharePoint:DelegateControl>
<h1 class="s4-mini-header">


<!-- Site name goes here with the link to the top of
the search site -->
<asp:ContentPlaceHolder id="PlaceHolderSiteName"
runat="server">
<SharePoint:SPLinkButton runat="server"
NavigateUrl="~site/" id="onetidProjectPropertyTitle"
CssClass="s4-mini-h1-a">
```

```
<!-- Title of the default.aspx page, this is set through
page properties -->
<SharePoint:ProjectProperty Property="Title"
runat="server" />
</SharePoint:SPLinkButton>
</asp:ContentPlaceHolder>
</h1>
<!-- ... -->
</div>
</form>
</body>
</html>
```

That's all that **minimal.master** has. Let's now take a look at how we can enhance this page with something useful and particular to the search page. One of the quite common requests from users is the ability to get the **Navigate Up** breadcrumb control on the search page; as you can see, it's available in the team site and publishing site but not in the **minimal.master** and consequently the search page.

Let's take a look at how we can incorporate this element into the search site. In here, we'll use steps tailored for SharePoint Designer, but the downloadable source code for this chapter has the same implementation approach as Visual Studio solution.

1. We'll start by copying the existing **minimal.master** from within SharePoint Designer. From **Site Objects**, click **Masterpages** and right click on the **minimal.master**. Select **Copy**, then right click on the workspace to **Paste** the copy. Highlight the copy and give it a new name, such as **newminimal.master**.
2. Click on the newly renamed file, and in the workspace **Configuration** section, click **Edit file**.
3. In the Masterpage code, right after the below:
    <h3 class="s4-mini-header">
    <asp:ContentPlaceHolder id="PlaceHolderPageSubTitle"
    runat="server" />
    </h3>

Add the following code:

LISTING 6-2

```
<!--Placeholder for the dynamic menu -->
<asp:ContentPlaceHolder id="PlaceHolderGlobalNavigation"
runat="server">

<!--Calling dynamic menu -->
<SharePoint:PopoutMenu
runat="server"
ID="GlobalBreadCrumbNavPopout"
IconUrl="/_layouts/images/fgimg.png"
IconAlt="<%$Resources:wss,master_breadcrumbIconAlt%>"
IconOffsetX=0
IconOffsetY=112
IconWidth=16
IconHeight=16
AnchorCss="s4-breadcrumb-anchor"
AnchorOpenCss="s4-breadcrumb-anchor-open"
MenuCss="s4-breadcrumb-menu">
<div class="s4-breadcrumb-top">
<asp:Label runat="server" CssClass="s4-
breadcrumb-header" Text="<%$Resources:wss,master_
breadcrumbHeader%>" />
</div>

<!-- Calling actuall breadcrumb; this control will also
take care of formatting of breadcrumb nodes -->
<SharePoint:ListSiteMapPath
runat="server"
SiteMapProviders="SPSiteMapProvider,SPContentMapProvid
er"
RenderCurrentNodeAsLink="false"
PathSeparator=""
CssClass="s4-breadcrumb"
NodeStyle-CssClass="s4-breadcrumbNode"
CurrentNodeStyle-CssClass="s4-breadcrumbCurrentNode"
```

```
RootNodeStyle-CssClass="s4-breadcrumbRootNode"
NodeImageOffsetX=0
NodeImageOffsetY=353
NodeImageWidth=16
NodeImageHeight=16
NodeImageUrl="/_layouts/images/fgimg.png"
RTLNodeImageOffsetX=0
RTLNodeImageOffsetY=376
RTLNodeImageWidth=16
RTLNodeImageHeight=16
RTLNodeImageUrl="/_layouts/images/fgimg.png"
HideInteriorRootNodes="true"
SkipLinkText="" />
</SharePoint:PopoutMenu>
<div class="s4-die">
<asp:ContentPlaceHolder id="PlaceHolderGlobalNavigation
SiteMap"
 runat="server" Visible="false">
</asp:ContentPlaceHolder>
</div>
</asp:ContentPlaceHolder>
```

There are actually two items involved in the code above: the dynamic menu and the breadcrumb control. Both of those were copied from **v4.master** and placed in the appropriate place where breadcrumb control will not look awkward. You can certainly change where it's rendered as well.

4. We're almost there; a few more adjustments to make, since, as of right now, the dynamic menu will appear a bit off. Navigate to the top of your Masterpage right to the <head> section and add the following style declaration inline:

LISTING 6-3

```
<style type="text/css">
#s4-mini-titlearea
```

```
{
color:#676767 !important;
font-size:1.4em;
white-space:nowrap;
}

.ms-popoutMenu{
top:85px !important;
}
</style>
```

Both of those elements, as you can see from Firebug, will reposition the dynamic menu and change the color of the border a bit.

5. Now let's save the Masterpage from SharePoint Designer and navigate back to http://intranet.contoso.com/esearch in the browser. Click **Site Actions** -> **Site Settings** -> **Masterpage** and specify *newminimal.master* as **Site Masterpage**.

6. Navigate back the search site and you will see our new control added to the page.

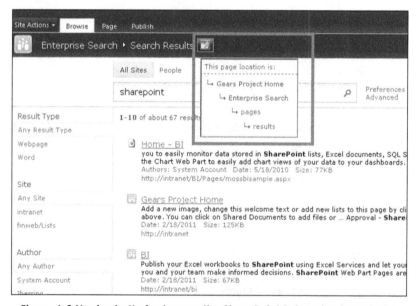

Figure 6-2 Navigate Up feature on the SharePoint Enterprise Search site

This demonstrates some of the functionality available to extend **minimal.master** and the sites which use it. Just to mention again that all pages involved in user interaction on the search site are web part pages, and you can apply the same branding techniques to them as we did before in the section dedicated to the publishing site template.

Next, we'll take a look at how you can make customizations to some of the web parts which facilitate in the rendering of search results, and how you can change the way search results look and behave by using a few simple techniques.

Adding new metadata to your search results view

The central focus of any search page is a results section. After all, that's the whole reason your users will navigate to the search page. Depending on your scenario, some of your users may find more value if the search results look a certain way; maybe they are more used to a document management system which your solution is trying to replace.

In this example, we'll take a look how you can remove some metadata from the search results and add a new metadata property which exists in SharePoint.

Take a look at the default search result returned by SharePoint.

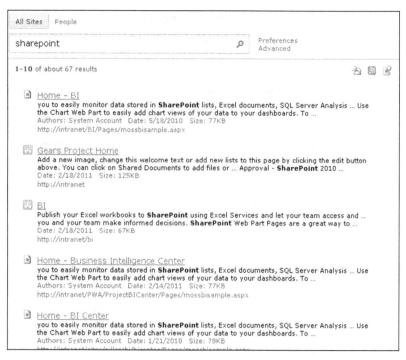

Figure 6-3 Default search result

As you can see, there are a few key properties that are present, and some of them are more unusual than they may appear at first. We have a link to our item, a date, a text with what seems like item content, and the URL of the item. On the other hand, take a look at the following item:

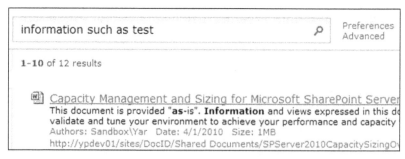

Figure 6-4 Search result of an item with a large body text

First, a few basic rules in terms of a SharePoint search. SharePoint search uses a special calculated field to define what is going to show in an area where the item body is displayed. The property is called **HitHighlightedSummary**, and it will change depending on your search keyword. The **HitHighlightedSummary** will display the area surrounding your search keyword in the body of an item. SharePoint already knows that the item has to be displayed because it contains the text or metadata you searched for. Now, SharePoint will try to prove it to you that this search result is worth looking at because it contains a body that may be something that will help you identifying it. If you searched for a text that is contained in the metadata of the item, that metadata will show up. If your keyword is showing more in the body of the document, then this part of the body will be displayed in the **HitHighlightedSummary**. This is an important piece of functionality to understand, since you may want to customize your search results to hide certain pieces of metadata that will still show up in search results as a part of the **HitHighlightedSummary** field.

Let's take a look at the default markup of the search results web part.

1. While on the search results page, click **Site Actions -> Edit Page**.
2. The page will switch into the edit mode. Locate the **Search Core Results** web part and choose to view web part properties by clicking **Edit Web Part**.
3. From the web part editing panel, expand the **Core Results** category and then expand the **Default Properties** category.
4. Locate and uncheck the **Use Location Visualization** option and you will see **Fetched Properties** and **XSL editor** options become available.
5. Copy the contents of **Fetched Properties** to your clipboard.
6. Switch to the Visual Studio solution we're using for testing and add a new item of type **XML**, under the **Data** category of the **Add New Item** dialog.
7. Replace the contents with the XML from the clipboard. Your XML markup will look similar to what is below.

LISTING 6-4

```xml
<Columns>
    <Column Name="WorkId"/>
    <Column Name="Rank"/>
    <Column Name="Title"/>
    <Column Name="Author"/>
    <Column Name="Size"/>
    <Column Name="Path"/>
    <Column Name="Description"/>
    <Column Name="Write"/>
    <Column Name="SiteName"/>
    <Column Name="CollapsingStatus"/>
    <Column Name="HitHighlightedSummary"/>
    <Column Name="HitHighlightedProperties"/>
    <Column Name="ContentClass"/>
    <Column Name="IsDocument"/>
    <Column Name="PictureThumbnailURL"/>
    <Column Name="PopularSocialTags"/>
    <Column Name="PictureWidth"/>
    <Column Name="PictureHeight"/>
    <Column Name="DatePictureTaken"/>
    <Column Name="ServerRedirectedURL"/>
</Columns>
```

Those are all of the properties that SharePoint requests from each search result. If search results don't have any of the property items, nothing really happens; the field just gets ignored and it's not rendered on a page.

Let's take a look at how the look and feel of the search results is built.

1. Assuming your search results page is still in edit mode and the **Search Core Results** web part properties are opened, click on the **XSL Editor** button located in the **Display Properties** category we looked at before.
2. Copy the contents of the editor dialog to the clipboard.

3. Switch to your Visual Studio and paste the contents of your clipboard to a new XML file similar to where we pasted search properties.

4. Collapse all markup outlining (**CTRL+M+L**) and expand the first node.

You will notice that most of the nodes are templates that define the rendering of various components displayed on the search page. The main part of the XSL sheet is located at the very bottom of the sheet and calls rendering of sub elements. Here is how this part looks:

LISTING 6-5

```
<!-- XSL transformation starts here -->
<xsl:template match="/">
<xsl:if test="$AlertMeLink">
<input type="hidden" name="P_Query" />
<input type="hidden" name="P_LastNotificationTime" />
</xsl:if>
<xsl:choose>
<xsl:when test="$IsNoKeyword = 'True'" >
<xsl:call-template name="dvt_1.noKeyword" />
</xsl:when>
<xsl:when test="$ShowMessage = 'True'">
<xsl:call-template name="dvt_1.empty" />
</xsl:when>
<xsl:otherwise>
<xsl:call-template name="dvt_1.body"/>
</xsl:otherwise>
</xsl:choose>
</xsl:template>
```

In here, we verify that there is a search keyword entered in the body and start rendering content using the **dvt_1.body** template defined above in the XSL.

If you navigate the XSL structure, you will eventually find the template of your interest.

Let's remove the **HitHighlightedSummary** from the search result and add the value of our new search property instead.

1. Assuming you're still in Visual Studio and you have the XSL of the search style sheet open, search for the following string *<div class="srch-Description2">*.
2. You will find the section similar to what is below.

LISTING 6-6

```
<div class="srch-Description2">
<xsl:choose>
<xsl:when test="hithighlightedsummary[. != '']">
<xsl:call-template name="HitHighlighting">
<xsl:with-param name="hh"
select="hithighlightedsummary" />
</xsl:call-template>
</xsl:when>
<xsl:when test="description[. != '']">
<xsl:value-of select="description"/>
</xsl:when>
<xsl:otherwise>
<img alt="" src="/_layouts/images/blank.gif" height="0"
width="0"/>
</xsl:otherwise>
</xsl:choose>
</div >
```

This section is responsible for showing the summary abstract of your search result, if applicable.

3. Let's now add additional metadata to the file markup.

LISTING 6-7

```
<div class="srch-Description2">
<xsl:choose>
<xsl:when test="hithighlightedsummary[. != '']">
```

```
<xsl:call-template name="HitHighlighting">
<xsl:with-param name="hh"
select="hithighlightedsummary" />
</xsl:call-template>
</xsl:when>
<xsl:when test="description[. != '']">
<xsl:value-of select="description"/>
</xsl:when>
<xsl:otherwise>
<img alt="" src="/_layouts/images/blank.gif" height="0"
width="0"/>
</xsl:otherwise>
</xsl:choose>
<xsl:if test="string-length(Authors) &gt; 0">
The value of the Authors is:
<xsl:value-of select="Authors"/>
</xsl:if>
</div >
```

Above, we added a comparison to see whether our new property has a value, and, if so, we will output its value.

4. Copy a modified version of your XSL to the clipboard and replace the contents of the **Search Core Results** XSL with it.
5. In your **Search Core Results Fetched Properties**, ensure you have added a new property to your XML right before the closing tag of columns definition **</Columns>**, the value of the column is <Column Name="Authors"/>.
6. Save web part properties and stop page editing mode.

Launch another search query and you will see all of your other search results returning item descriptions as usual. Your custom description will show up for the items you have created for your test list. If you can't find those items, ensure you searched for a keyword that you might have used in one of the item properties.

This example is meant to demonstrate how you can use XSL to leverage the way your search results are going to appear. Here we replaced the actual values which are going to show in the results.

You can also edit the rendering template to add additional HTML markup or JavaScript interaction to your results to change the way they are structured. Just as with any other SharePoint out-of-the-box web part, the **Search Core Results** web part has many existing CSS selectors which you can overwrite with your desired look and feel.

If you open the search results page in Firefox and launch Firebug or IE Developer Toolbar, you can explore the markup and see how you can change the existing look on the fly. Since Enterprise Search Center uses the publishing site paradigm in terms of branding, you can create an alternate style sheet with your styles defined and apply it to the site just like we did in the publishing site example before.

Adding graphic representation of item ratings to your search results

In the last sample, we looked at how to add a simple column to the search results and style it to match your requirements. This time we'll add more functionality to our search results—a graphic rating coming from the rated content on the site.

If you haven't tried rating SharePoint functionality already, you can easily enable the rating feature on items in lists and libraries by following the steps below: Since all of the back-end infrastructure has been already set up in SharePoint demo environment we use, here is what's involved in enabling the feature on a particular list or document library.

1. Navigate to http://intranet.contoso.com.
2. Click **Shared Documents** from the quick launch of the site.
3. On the ribbon, click the **Library** tab and the select **Library Settings.**
4. From the **General Settings** section, click **Rating settings**.
5. Choose **Yes** to **Allow items in this list to be rated** and click **OK.**

When you navigate back to the library, you will see *rating stars* beside each item. Similar steps apply to other SharePoint lists.

In this sample we'll take a look at how we can display similar rating functionality on the search result, since it's not available by default. After all, it'd be nice if your users could see the rating of the item. At the end, our users won't be able to vote on the item, but they will see the rating for items.

Since rating is enabled on one of our document libraries, cast at least one rating in the library item so that average rating is calculated for that item. The reason for that is because we're going to consume the average in our search and display it to the user. Since metadata displayed for search results is managed by managed properties in the SharePoint search service application, we will create a new managed property that will pick up our rating column. This rating column will only be recognized in our service application if there is at least one value in the rating column.

If you've rated at least one item in our library, perform the following so that your rating is picked up by the search service application:

1. Navigate your browser to http://demo2010a:2010/ which is SharePoint Central Administration site.
2. From under **Application Management**, click **Manage Service Applications**.
3. From the list of available applications, click on **Search Service Application** link.
4. On the quick launch from the **Crawling** section, click **Content Sources**.
5. From the list of available sources you will see **Local SharePoint sites**. Access the context menu of this item and select **Start Full Crawl**.

Give it a few minutes for the crawl to complete and pick up our newly created rating column. This set of tasks is normally going to be performed by a member of your infrastructure support team; however, it's handy when you understand the underlying principles and are able to quickly get through the routine tasks like this one when you need to try this out in your development environment.

Assuming you're still in Central Administration in **Search Service Application**, click **Metadata Properties** on the left-hand side of your search service application window. We'll create a new property which is going to carry our rating information which we can use in our site.

1. Click **New Managed Property**.
2. For the name of the property, chose **Rating** of type **Decimal**, then click **Add Mapping**.
3. In the new modal box, search for **rating** and pick column named ***ows_AverageRating(Decimal)***.
4. Click **OK** to add new managed property.

Now that we have the property created, it's time to use it on the search site to tweak our result set, just like we did in the last example.

1. Navigate to the search results page of your site, http://intranet.contoso.com/esearch and access the **Search Core Results** web part properties, as you did in the last sample.
2. Open the **Display Properties** category, and for **Fetched Properties**, add **Rating** as follows:
   <Column Name="Rating"/>.
3. Choose to edit your XSL and, using Visual Studio, locate the same section you've been working with before by searching *<div class="srch-Description2">*.
4. Replace the section with the code below.

LISTING 6-8

```
<div class="srch-Description2">
<xsl:choose>
<xsl:when test="hithighlightedsummary[. != '']">
   <xsl:call-template name="HitHighlighting">
```

```
    <xsl:with-param name="hh"
    select="hithighlightedsummary" />
</xsl:call-template>
</xsl:when>
    <xsl:when test="description[. != '']">
<xsl:value-of select="description"/>
</xsl:when>
<xsl:otherwise>
    <img alt="" src="/_layouts/images/blank.gif"
    height="0" width="0"/>
</xsl:otherwise>
</xsl:choose>
<xsl:choose>
<xsl:when test="rating > 0">
    <span>
    <xsl:attribute name="title">
    <xsl:value-of select="rating"/>
    </xsl:attribute>
    <xsl:call-template name="stars">
    <xsl:with-param name="starCount" select="rating"/>
    </xsl:call-template>
    <xsl:if test="round(rating) > rating">
    <img src="/_Layouts/Images/Ratings/RatingsNew.png"/>
    </xsl:if>
    </span>
    <br/>
</xsl:when>
<xsl:otherwise>
    <b>Not Rated</b>
    <br/>
</xsl:otherwise>
</xsl:choose>
</div >
```

Just as we did last time, this time we add logic to verify whether there is a rating for an item, and, if so, we call a template to render the output.

5. Now, add the template that we call from the previous steps; search for <!-- *XSL transformation starts here* --> and add code below right before this item.

LISTING 6-9

```
<xsl:template name="stars">
<xsl:param name="starCount"/>
<xsl:param name="value" select="1"/>
<xsl:if test="$value &lt;= $starCount">
    <img src="/_Layouts/Images/Ratings/RatingsNew.png"/>
    <xsl:call-template name="stars">
    <xsl:with-param name="starCount"
    select="$starCount"/>
    <xsl:with-param name="value" select="$value + 1"/>
    </xsl:call-template>
</xsl:if>
</xsl:template>
```

Above, we define a template that will receive an average rating and display the appropriate value for the graphical representation of that rating using *rating stars*.

6. Copy the contents of the file from Visual Studio and paste it into the **Edit XSL** of your **Search Core Results** web part.
7. Click **OK** to save the properties of the web part and exit the edit mode.

When you execute a search again, you will see that whatever items are not rated have received a *Not Rated* label, and the ones that are rated will have *rating stars* beside the summary of the search result.

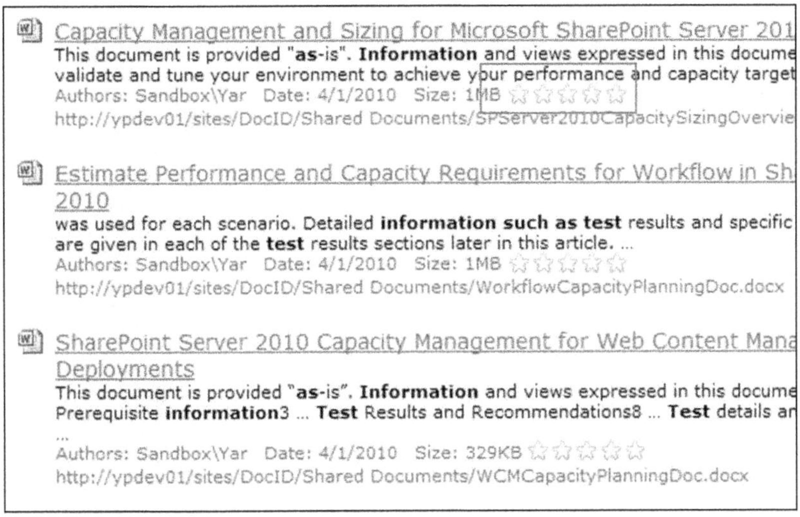

Capacity Management and Sizing for Microsoft SharePoint Server 201
This document is provided "as-is". Information and views expressed in this docume
validate and tune your environment to achieve your performance and capacity target
Authors: Sandbox\Yar Date: 4/1/2010 Size: 1MB
http://ypdev01/sites/DocID/Shared Documents/SPServer2010CapacitySizingOvervie

Estimate Performance and Capacity Requirements for Workflow in Sh
2010
was used for each scenario. Detailed information such as test results and specific
are given in each of the test results sections later in this article. ...
Authors: Sandbox\Yar Date: 4/1/2010 Size: 1MB
http://ypdev01/sites/DocID/Shared Documents/WorkflowCapacityPlanningDoc.docx

SharePoint Server 2010 Capacity Management for Web Content Mana
Deployments
This document is provided "as-is". Information and views expressed in this docume
Prerequisite information3 ... Test Results and Recommendations8 ... Test details ar
...
Authors: Sandbox\Yar Date: 4/1/2010 Size: 329KB
http://ypdev01/sites/DocID/Shared Documents/WCMCapacityPlanningDoc.docx

Figure 6-5 Rating showing for the search results

CHAPTER 7

Integrating Third-Party UI Components into SharePoint

While working on branding projects, you might have developed a collection of reusable components and approaches, and now you might want to port them over to SharePoint. You also might be aware of existing components and would like to integrate them with SharePoint. In this chapter we're going to look at how you can integrate independently developed UI components with SharePoint and replace default SharePoint user controls with those components. As an example, we will use a few Telerik controls due to their popularity on the market—the process, however, is the same even with in-house-developed components.

Examples described in this chapter will have a lot of overlap in responsibilities which would typically be performed by a back-end developer rather than a UI developer. If you're involved with configuring and provisioning third-party UI assemblies you're using in your SharePoint solution, this chapter is for you.

Getting started with third-party UI components integration

One of the most common enchancements UI developers implement is related to SharePoint navigation. Top level navigation and quick launch links are among the most commonly enhanced navigation elements, and SharePoint provides a navigation model which makes it very easy to separate the navigation hierarchy, the data portion providing the data known as **site-map data source**, from the rendering and presentation portion, or navigation controls.

The purpose of the site-map data source is to separate the navigation hierarchy data from the navigation control responsible for the presentation of the data. This simplifies the integrating of custom UI controls into a SharePoint site by simply configuring them to receive the navigation hierarchy from the SharePoint site-map data sources.

In the next section, let's take a look at what's involved in referencing third-party UI components in your Visual Studio solution.

You may think that just by providing a project reference in your solution, SharePoint project will take care of your extra third party DLLs and use them in the solution package it generates; however, there are few extra steps you need to take to make that happen.

Let's see what the steps are to incorporate Telerik controls in our solution:

1. In your Solution Explorer, in SharePoint project, locate **Package** and expand it.
2. Double click on expanded child element of **Package**.
3. Click **Advanced** from the newly opened window and click **Add**.

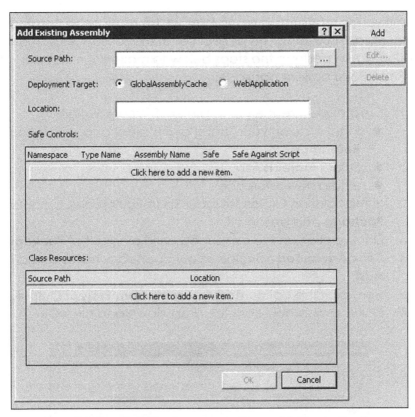

Figure 7-1 SharePoint Package properties and Advanced option

4. Here pick the option **Add Existing Assembly**.
5. Locate an assembly from the disk (usually Telerik assemblies are located here: *C:\Program Files (x86)\Telerik\ RadControls for ASP.NET AJAX Q3 2010\Bin35*); you would be looking for *Telerik.Web.UI.dll*. Click **OK**.

NOTE:

The assembly you have received from the third-party vendor must be signed with a strong name key, which usually is the case for commercial components. The reason we need to sign it is so it has a unique identity when it's deployed along with all the other assemblies on your server's Global Assembly Cache.

Now, if you're referencing assemblies which have been created by your team in a separate project but in the same Visual Studio solution, you'd perform the steps below to make your DLLs part of the SharePoint project package.

1. Create a reference to the project in your solution.
   - Right click on your SharePoint project and select **Add a Reference**.
   - Select **Projects** tab.
   - Add a new reference.
2. In the Solution Explorer of your SharePoint project, locate **Package** and expand it.
3. Double click on the expanded child element of **Package**.
4. Click **Advanced** from the newly opened window and click **Add**.
5. Here pick the option **Add Assembly from Project Output**.
6. Pick the assembly from the drop-down and click **OK**.

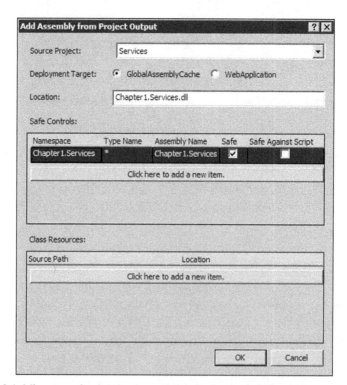

Figure 7-2 Adding a project output assembly to the package of SharePoint project

Visual Studio will compile the assemblies in the package and will reference them as safe assemblies in the configuration files of your site by provisioning all of the necessary **Safe Control** attributes into your IIS site **web.config** file to make sure your assembly is loaded properly.

Replacing SharePoint out-of-the-box menu control with third-party components

If you have successfully referenced Telerik controls from the previous walkthrough, we can now proceed with using Telerik menu control (and other controls available in the referenced library) on your SharePoint sites.

In this example we will be using the SharePoint 2010 publishing site.

If you haven't already, navigate to www.contoso.com and ensure an instance of the publishing site is created on this URL.

Let's first take a look at how we can use SharePoint Designer 2010 to replace default navigation with a Telerik control. If you completed some of the tasks in previous examples, you will already have SharePoint Designer 2010 installed.

1. Open SharePoint Designer 2010 from the start menu and click **Open Site** from the main menu of the welcome page.
2. Specify the URL of the site http://www.contoso.com and click **Open**.
3. You may be prompted for credentials, so ensure you provide administrators' credentials, since it's one user on the site that we know has access to modifying the site Masterpage.
4. The site workspace will open, and under **Site Objects** on the left, choose **Masterpages**. SharePoint Designer will open the list of available Masterpages. Click to open *nightandday. master*.

5. The Masterpage file properties will open. Click the **Edit file** option in the workspace area and click OK to confirm that you're OK with the check out of this file. By checking out this file, you will lock it for your own use, and no one else will see your changes until you're done and checked back in the file.

6. The Masterpage will load into the workspace. At the bottom of the workspace area, click **Code** to switch into the code view of the page; this will help us locating the right element on the page.

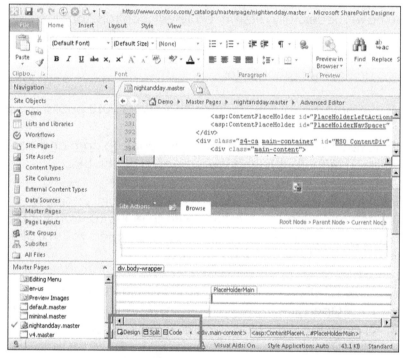

Figure 7-3 SharePoint Designer workspace and toggle between code and design view

7. Alternatively you can click on the **Split** to see both the code and designer parts of the workspace.

8. Locate the following piece of code:

LISTING 7-1

```
<SharePoint:AspMenu
ID="CurrentNav"
runat="server"
EnableViewState="false"
DataSourceID="SiteMapDS"
UseSeparateCSS="false"
UseSimpleRendering="true"
Orientation="Vertical"
StaticDisplayLevels="2"
<!-- … -->
```

This is our current navigation menu. To visualize where it's located, select the code block and view it in **Design** or **Split** view. The default instance of the newly created **Publishing** site will have current navigation on the left side of the page.

9. To replace the current navigation with a custom navigation, we will replace the *SharePoint:AspMenu* control with our own control. In essence all that *SharePoint:AspMenu* control does is it binds to a data source with its property *DataSourceID="SiteMapDS"* and accepts a couple of other properties to govern its look. Let's place the following line of code right above *SharePoint:AspMenu*:

LISTING 7-2

```
<asp:GridView runat="server" id="GridView1"
DataSourceID="SiteMapDS">
</asp:GridView>
```

In here, we're using ASP.NET GridView control, which is usually used to display grids to render the contents of the menu.

10. Save the Masterpage from within SharePoint Designer. You will be prompted to agree to the fact that this Masterpage will be modified and no longer be in its original version.

When saved, navigate back to the home page of www. contoso.com and see how GridView is displayed right before our menu. Since GridView is set to automatically render all of the properties, you will see some of them available in the data source which is displayed.

The same concept applies to using third-party controls; let's see how Telerik's RadMenu will handle the situation. In this case we will be using Visual Studio to demonstrate the example, purely because we want to make sure Telerik assemblies are installed on your server before the Telerik **RadMenu** is referenced on the page. If those assemblies are not installed—Visual Studio will provision them providing they have been referenced in the solution using the steps from our last example about referencing third party components. In the downloadable source code for this chapter you can see the entire solution except references to Telerik assemblies. Due to licencing considerations you will need to download full or trial Telerik assemblies and reference them in the project. In step sequence below I assume this is already done.

1. Let's open the Visual Studio solution you created in the previous section titled *Getting started with third-party UI components integration*. This solution already referenced **Telerik.Web.UI** assembly, and it's just a matter of adding the control to the Masterpage.
2. In the solution folder, locate the **Features** folder and right click on it to add a new feature.
3. Rename the default **Feature1** to **ProvisionMaster**.
    Just like in the example when we started with the publishing site templates, this feature will be used to upload our custom Masterpage to the gallery.
4. In the solution folder, right click on the project name and select **Add -> New Item....**
5. Select **Module** for an item type and give it the name **Masterpage**.
6. Rename the **Sample.txt** file in the module to **newmaster. master**.
7. Navigate to http://www.contoso.com as administrator.
8. Click **Site Actions -> Site Settings** and locate **Masterpages and Page Layouts** under **Galleries**.

9. **Download a Copy** of *nightandday.master* using the ribbon. Save the file to disk.

10. Open the newly downloaded Masterpage in Visual Studio and copy its content to *newmaster.master* we created. Now, let's replace the current navigation of the default Masterpage to our custom navigation control from Telerik. Locate the *html* tag in *newmaster.master* and add the following piece of registration code right before it:

    <%@ Register TagPrefix="telerik" Namespace="Telerik.Web.UI" Assembly="Telerik.Web.UI, Version=2010.3.1317.35, Culture=neutral, PublicKeyToken=121fae78165ba3d4" %>

    This piece will go along with all of the other registrations and will reference our **Telerik.Web.UI** assembly.

11. Now, search for

    <SharePoint:AspMenu ID="CurrentNav"runat="server"

    and replace it with

LISTING 7-3

```
<telerik:RadMenu ID="RadMenu1" runat="server"
DataSourceID="SiteMapDS" />
```

which is the Telerik menu referencing our site map data source **SiteMapDS**.

12. Open **Elements.xml** in your Masterpage module and replace its contents with the following

---

LISTING 7-4

```
<?xml version="1.0" encoding="utf-8"?>
<Elements xmlns="http://schemas.microsoft.com/
sharepoint/">
<Module Name="MasterPage"
    List="116"
```

```
    Url="_catalogs/masterpage">
<File Path="MasterPage\newmaster.master"
    Type="GhostableInLibrary"
    Url="newmaster.master " />
</Module>
</Elements>
```

The piece above will add the Masterpage to the library.

13. Let's deploy this solution with Visual Studio. Right click the solution name and select **Deploy**.
14. Now that the Masterpage is deployed, we'll set it to be used on the site. Navigate to http://www.contoso.com as administrator.
15. Click **Site Actions -> Site Settings** and locate **Masterpage** under **Look and Feel**.
16. Ensure the *newmaster.master* from the **Site Masterpage** drop down is set.
17. Once the setting is applied, you will see the new menu replacing the default out-of-the-box navigation on the site once you navigate to it.

If you haven't added any new subsites to the www.contoso.com site, you will only see one button as a menu item for your navigation. Let's create a hierarchy of two or three sites to see the difference.

1. Click **Site Actions -> New Site**.
2. Pick **Publishing Site** as a template and give the site any name and URL.
3. On the newly created site, repeat step 2 again.
4. Navigate back to home and see how the new structure drives navigation. You can also try switching **RadMenu** with **RadTreeView** in your Masterpage like this:

LISTING 7-5

```
<telerik:RadTreeView ID="RadMenu1" runat="server"
DataSourceID="SiteMapDS" />
```

or this:

LISTING 7-6

```
<telerik:RadPanelBar ID="RadMenu1"
    runat="server" DataSourceID="SiteMapDS"
    Skin="Windows7" />
```

This is going to give yet another version of the menu control.

It's also worth mentioning that once our third-party library has been deployed to the server farm, in our case **Telerik.Web.UI**, you can create instances of controls from this library by using SharePoint Designer 2010. The steps to modifying the Masterpage in that case are exactly the same as modifying it with Visual Studio.

As you can see, this technique allows you to enhance your solutions with a different look and feel and functionality. One of the ways you can enhance the behavior of the control is to create a class in your solution which inherits from it. The class would then override the logic of the control according to your needs. Since this technique is a bit out of the scope of traditional branding and more back-end development task, I will leave it out of this chapter, but you're welcome to contact me for a sample.

CHAPTER 8

Getting Started with and Branding SharePoint Publishing and Custom Pages

Most of the SharePoint solutions are built around managing content and structure. Sites and their subsites, along with pages, make up a hierarchy that business users navigate through to access their data stored in lists, libraries, and other containers. One of the main features leveraged when building SharePoint solutions is pages. Pages are stored in page libraries just like documents are stored in document libraries. Just like list items, pages can have a generic or specific content type, and you can treat them as list items. Pages can contain metadata properties that represent various values on a page, including a page's content.

As we saw earlier, SharePoint Masterpages allow you to customize where various page elements are going to be placed and which ones you need to hide. If you come from the traditional ASP.NET development environment, you probably expect that your page instances, which users will see, directly inherit from Masterpages. This is not the case for SharePoint; there is additional construct involved—**page layouts**.

A page layout defines what web part zones your page will have and any additional markup shared across all page instances using it. In some cases, you may want additional metadata to be captured from a user to represent a page. This additional metadata will have to be captured with appropriate controls (drop-down lists, text boxes) right on a page in page editing mode. The controls and their look and type will also be defined in page layout. In more complex solutions, chances are you will have at least a few page layouts that will represent a specific or generic look for many of your page instances.

When few page layouts are available on the site, SharePoint allows site users with sufficient permissions to edit an instance of the page and change its page layout. By doing so, the page will change what web part zones and other controls are available; any existing web part instances will be placed into zones according SharePoint's best guess. Not to worry, changing page layout for a particular page is not the most common activity your users will do; just as you do, your users understand that page layouts will change the look of the page instance, and they will adhere to guidelines you established in your SharePoint solution.

What publishing page layout is all about

Before we dive into scenarios, just as we did with Masterpages earlier, I would like to show you one of the out-of-the-box page layouts and what it's all about.

On the publishing site, in our case www.contoso.com, page layouts are located in the same folder with Masterpages. Let's download one of the most common page layouts:

1. From the www.contoso.com, click **Site Actions->Site Settings**.
2. Under **Galleries** click **Masterpages and page layouts**.
3. Locate and download *BlankWebPartPage.aspx* to the file system.
4. Open the file from the file system in Visual Studio.

Let's take a look at what is involved in a typical page layout structure. Just as before, I will skip the most obvious or irrelevant pieces. I will comment on areas that you are most likely to work with. Also, to discover more granular pieces of the page layout it's easier and way more efficient to use Firebug or IE Developer Toolbar.

LISTING 8-1

```
<!--Defines the page layout and inherits functionality
from the base class-->
<%@ Page language="C#"  Inherits="Microsoft.SharePoint.
Publishing.PublishingLayoutPage,Microsoft.SharePoint.Pub
lishing,Version=14.0.0.0,Culture=neutral,PublicKeyToken=71
e9bce111e9429c" %>


<!-- Contains ASP.NET server controls used on
masterpage and in pages of the SharePoitn site -->
<%@ Register Tagprefix="SharePointWebControls
" Namespace="Microsoft.SharePoint.WebControls"
Assembly="Microsoft.SharePoint, Version=14.0.0.0,
Culture=neutral, PublicKeyToken=71e9bce111e9429c" %>


<! --Supplies classes and functionality to work with
web part pages-->
<%@ Register Tagprefix="WebPartPages"
Namespace="Microsoft.SharePoint.WebPartPages"
Assembly="Microsoft.SharePoint, Version=14.0.0.0,
Culture=neutral, PublicKeyToken=71e9bce111e9429c" %>


<!-- Contains classes defining the structure,
appearance, and behavior of SharePoint publishing web
controls -->
<%@ Register Tagprefix="PublishingWebControls
" Namespace="Microsoft.SharePoint.Publishing.
WebControls" Assembly="Microsoft.SharePoint.Publishing,
Version=14.0.0.0, Culture=neutral, PublicKeyToken=71e9bce
111e9429c" %>
```

```
<!-- Contains classes for nodes, data source, providers
functionality implementing SharePoint navigation-->
<%@ Register Tagprefix="PublishingNavigati
on" Namespace="Microsoft.SharePoint.Publishing.
Navigation" Assembly="Microsoft.SharePoint.Publishing,
Version=14.0.0.0, Culture=neutral, PublicKeyToken=71e9bce
111e9429c" %>

<!--Below will be inserted into the
PlaceHolderAdditionalPageHead of the masterpage -->
<asp:Content ContentPlaceholderID="PlaceHolderAdditional
PageHead" runat="server">

<!--Specific adjustments to CSS on SharePoint 2007
version-->
<SharePointWebControls:UIVersionedContent UIVersion="3"
runat="server">
<ContentTemplate>
<!-- … -->
</ContentTemplate>
</SharePointWebControls:UIVersionedContent>

<!--Out-of-the-box style sheet references for SharePoint
2010-->
<SharePointWebControls:UIVersionedContent UIVersion="4"
runat="server">
<ContentTemplate>

<!--Since this is 2 column page layout, the style sheet
below facilitates UI features for 2 column page-->
<SharePointWebControls:CssRegistration
name="<% $SPUrl:~sitecollection/Style Library/~language/
Core Styles/page-layouts-21.css %>" runat="server"/>

<!--Contents of this control will render only when
the page is in edit mode; this usually contains style
sheets which facilitate rendering of the page in edit
mode -->
<PublishingWebControls:EditModePanel runat="server">
```

```
<!-- Styles for edit mode only-->
<SharePointWebControls:CssRegistration
name="<% $SPUrl:~sitecollection/Style Library/~language/
Core Styles/edit-mode-21.css %>"
After="<% $SPUrl:~sitecollection/Style Library/~language/
Core Styles/page-layouts-21.css %>" runat="server"/>
</PublishingWebControls:EditModePanel>
</ContentTemplate>
</SharePointWebControls:UIVersionedContent>
</asp:Content>


<!--Below will be inserted into PlaceHolderPageTitle
part of the masterpage -->
<asp:Content ContentPlaceHolderId="PlaceHolderPageTitle"
runat="server">

<!--References for backwards compatible version of
SharePoint UI; you don't need to include those unless
there is a chance your page layout to be used on
2007versions of SharePoint UI-->
<SharePointWebControls:UIVersionedContent UIVersion="3"
runat="server">
<ContentTemplate>
<!-- … -->
</ContentTemplate>
</SharePointWebControls:UIVersionedContent>
<SharePointWebControls:UIVersionedContent UIVersion="4"
runat="server">
<ContentTemplate>

<!--This will render page title to the title are in the
browser-->
<SharePointWebControls:ListProperty Property="Title"
runat="server"/> - <SharePointWebControls:FieldValue
FieldName="Title" runat="server"/>
</ContentTemplate>
</SharePointWebControls:UIVersionedContent>
</asp:Content>
```

```
<!--This be inserted into the
PlaceHolderPageTitleInTitleArea placeholder on your
masterpage, which is right under the ribbon and before
the rest of the page content goes-->
<asp:Content ContentPlaceHolderId="PlaceHolderPageTitleI
nTitleArea" runat="server">
<!--SharePoint 2007 version of the content inserted in
the placeholder-->
<SharePointWebControls:VersionedPlaceHolder
UIVersion="3" runat="server">
<ContentTemplate>
<!-- … -->
</ContentTemplate>
</SharePointWebControls:VersionedPlaceHolder>

<!—This will display the title of the page in the
placeholder above-->
<SharePointWebControls:UIVersionedContent UIVersion="4"
runat="server">
<ContentTemplate>
<SharePointWebControls:FieldValue FieldName="Title"
runat="server" />
</ContentTemplate>
</SharePointWebControls:UIVersionedContent>
</asp:Content>

<!--Below is placed inside PlaceHolderTitleBreadcrumb
on the masterpage, this is located in the dynamic menu
when you press "Navigate Up" button beside the Site
Actions menu-->
<asp:Content ContentPlaceHolderId="PlaceHolderTitleBread
crumb" runat="server">

<!--This is SharePoint 2007 version of the content,
which s essentially a breadcrumb -->
<SharePointWebControls:VersionedPlaceHolder
UIVersion="3" runat="server"> <ContentTemplate>
<!-- … -->
</ContentTemplate>
</SharePointWebControls:VersionedPlaceHolder>
```

```
<SharePointWebControls:UIVersionedContent UIVersion="4"
runat="server">
<ContentTemplate>

<!--Displays the breadcrumb of the site in form of the
dynamic menu; control uses CurrentNavigation datasource
to grab data for the breadcrumb -->
<SharePointWebControls:ListSiteMapPath runat="server"
SiteMapProviders="CurrentNavigation"
RenderCurrentNodeAsLink="false"
PathSeparator="" CssClass="s4-breadcrumb"
<!-- … -->
NodeImageUrl="/_layouts/images/fgimg.png"
HideInteriorRootNodes="true" SkipLinkText="" />
</ContentTemplate>
</SharePointWebControls:UIVersionedContent>
</asp:Content>

<!--Places description information entered in page
properties into PlaceHolderPageDescription area on the
masterpage which is right after the title of the page
in this layout -->
<asp:Content ContentPlaceHolderId="PlaceHolderPageDescri
ption" runat="server">
<SharePointWebControls:ProjectProperty
Property="Description" runat="server"/>
</asp:Content>
<asp:Content ContentPlaceHolderId="PlaceHolderBodyRightM
argin" runat="server">
<div height=100% class="ms-pagemargin">
<IMG SRC="/_layouts/images/blank.gif" width=10 height=1
alt=""></div>
</asp:Content>
```

Now, we're past the header of the page layout as well as some of the control registrations. We've also taken a look at some of the items in the body of the page, such as values from fields on the page being extracted and rendered. Above, when we extract title and description information, that is an example of how you can extract other pieces of available metadata on the page. Later we'll take a look at how to add and render that additional metadata. Let's now take a look at the main part of the page where all the content and web part zones are rendered. The main part of the page is something you will be tweaking pretty often to match your scenario.

LISTING 8-2

```
<!--Contents of this area will be placed in the
PlaceHolderMain  place holder of the masterpage
designed to render main content of the page-->
<asp:Content ContentPlaceHolderId="PlaceHolderMain"
runat="server">

<!--This part is rendered only for version 4 of the
SharePoint UI - 2010-->
<SharePointWebControls:UIVersionedContent UIVersion="4"
runat="server">
<ContentTemplate>
<div class="welcome blank-wp">

<!--EditModePanel ensures the contents of it will be
rendered only when the page is in edit mode, usually
used so that content contributors assign values for
page metadata such as title etc. You can add more
custom fields that will capture page metadata-->
<PublishingWebControls:EditModePanel runat="server"
CssClass="edit-mode-panel">

<!--This will display field to edit title of the page-->
<SharePointWebControls:TextField runat="server"
FieldName="Title"/>
</PublishingWebControls:EditModePanel>

<!--You can create your own structure of DIVs here,
this is just an example how this page is structured-->
<div class="welcome-content">
```

```
<!--This controls will render the contents of the
PublishingPageContent metadata field on the page which
in this case contains the body of the page-->
<PublishingWebControls:RichHtmlField
FieldName="PublishingPageContent"
HasInitialFocus="True"
MinimumEditHeight="400px" runat="server"/>
</div>
</ContentTemplate>
</SharePointWebControls:UIVersionedContent>
<table cellpadding="4" cellspacing="0" border="0"
width="100%">

<!--This section is to render the same content as above
but for version 3 of SharePoint UI – SharePoint 2007.
Main difference here is that the content is structured
with tables. You don't need to supply version 3 UI
rendering if you're not planning to support your UI in
SharePoint 2007>
<SharePointWebControls:UIVersionedContent UIVersion="3"
runat="server">
<ContentTemplate>
<!-- … -->
</ContentTemplate>
</SharePointWebControls:UIVersionedContent>

<!--At this point this page layout will render web part
zones as a table. You can render your web part zones
using your own structure. Remember the reason why
this out-of-the-box layout uses tables so much is to
make it as much compatible with version 3 of the UI as
possible-->
<tr>
<td valign="top" style="padding:0">
<table cellpadding="4" cellspacing="0"
border="0" width="100%" height="100%">
<tr>
```

```
<!--In here the id of the element "_invisibleIfEmpty"
gets styled in CSS as collapsible element if there
is no web part placed in it. This is quite useful
technique if you want to hide the web part zone if
user didn't add any webpart to it, in some other cases
this is not desirable behavior-->
<td id="_invisibleIfEmpty" name="_invisibleIfEmpty"
colspan="3" valign="top">

<!--This is how we define web part zones. The value
of "title" attribute will be displayed to the user,
this way you can assign some helpful and short text
for users to know what this zone is all about. The
"ID" attribute is used when developers automatically
provision web parts to specific zones. -->
<WebPartPages:WebPartZone runat="server" Title="<%$Reso
urces:cms,WebPartZoneTitle_Header%>" ID="Header"/>
</td>
</tr>
<tr>
<td width="100%" colspan="3" valign="top"
style="padding:0">
<table cellpadding="4" cellspacing="0" width="100%"
height="100%">

<!--Next two web part zones will be defined in this
section. They will appear right below the Header zone
defined earlier and will each share 50% of the width of
the header-->
<tr>
<td id="_invisibleIfEmpty" name="_invisibleIfEmpty"
valign="top">
<WebPartPages:WebPartZone runat="server" Title="<%$Res
ources:cms,WebPartZoneTitle_TopLeft%>" ID="TopLeftRow"
/>
</td>
<td id="_invisibleIfEmpty" name="_invisibleIfEmpty"
valign="top">
<WebPartPages:WebPartZone runat="server" Title="<%$Resour
ces:cms,WebPartZoneTitle_TopRight%>" ID="TopRightRow" />
```

```
</td>
</tr>
</table>
</td>
</tr>

<!--Right after above two web part zones we define three
columns each containing a web part zone. All of the
are collapsible, meaning if users or developers don't
add any webpart — the zones will not appear -->
<tr>
<td id="_invisibleIfEmpty" name="_invisibleIfEmpty"
valign="top" height="100%"> <WebPartPages:WebPartZone
runat="server" Title="<%$Resources:cms,WebPartZoneTit
le_CenterLeft%>"
ID="CenterLeftColumn" />
  </td>
<td id="_invisibleIfEmpty" name="_invisibleIfEmpty"
valign="top" height="100%"> <WebPartPages:WebPartZone
runat="server" Title="<%$Resources:cms,WebPartZoneTit
le_Center%>"
ID="CenterColumn"   />
  </td>
<td id="_invisibleIfEmpty" name="_invisibleIfEmpty"
valign="top" height="100%"> <WebPartPages:WebPartZone
runat="server" Title="<%$Resources:cms,WebPartZoneTit
le_CenterRight%>"
ID="CenterRightColumn" />
</td>
</tr>

<!--Footer web part zone defined below all the web parts
-->
<tr>
<td id="_invisibleIfEmpty" name="_invisibleIfEmpty"
colspan="3" valign="top"> <WebPartPages:WebPartZone
runat="server" Title="<%$Resources:cms,WebPartZoneTit
le_Footer%>" ID="Footer"/>
</td>
```

```
</tr>
</table>
</td>
```

```
<!--Finally right hand side zone is defined here. It
will share vertical the real estate with all of the
rest zones and if nothing is placed in it — it will
collapse and allow allow web parts on the right zone to
take over its space-->
<td id="_invisibleIfEmpty" name="_invisibleIfEmpty"
valign="top" height="100%"> <WebPartPages:WebPartZone
runat="server" Title="<%$Resources:cms,WebPartZoneTit
le_Right%>"
ID="RightColumn" Orientation="Vertical"/>
</td>
</tr>
```

```
<!--Script which will take care of hiding elements if
they are set to be invisible if empty -->
<script language="javascript">
if(typeof(MSOLayout_MakeInvisibleIfEmpty) == "function")
{MSOLayout_MakeInvisibleIfEmpty();}
</script>
</table>
<SharePointWebControls:UIVersionedContent UIVersion="4"
runat="server">
<ContentTemplate>
</div>
</ContentTemplate>
</SharePointWebControls:UIVersionedContent>
</asp:Content>
```

That's all there is to the page layout. In essence, as you can see, the main part of the content is the structural container for web part zones. The zones which in the end are going to contain web parts are placed appropriately on the page surrounded with respective markup to match your desired look and feel. The sample we looked at above is quite a complex page layout, which is trying to facilitate various scenarios and make zones invisible if there was no web parts placed in them. This allows the layout to be repurposed. If your requirements call for functionality similar to above, you can borrow ideas from the page layout above. Otherwise, you can make the page layout more simplified, which may be easier to maintain in a long term.

Getting started with creating custom SharePoint pages

In the last few chapters we talked a lot about page layouts and Masterpages. Now is the time to take a look at the real-life scenario of how this all fits together.

Let's assume you want to have a unique section on your site dedicated to company news. You also want to be able to display the most recent news on a home page of your site. One way to approach this is to create a site that will host your news as a publishing site. Each page on the site will be of a custom type denoting a news item. The type of page, in our case the *news* page type, is known in SharePoint as a content type. Your content type will define any out-of-the-box and additional metadata your page may include. Out-of-the-box metadata are things such as created date, author, etc. The custom metadata for our news page can be a department this particular piece of news belongs to, etc. Having a content type defined, we will define a page layout that drives markup of your news page.

Having those two, we can create a news page automatically or a content author on the site can create the instance of a page. This page will use a content type and a page layout to drive its structure and presentation. Once an instance of a news page is created, along with its custom content type, site users can use out-of-the-box web parts to query our news items and filter them out based on the metadata you care about to display them on a home page. In this chapter, we'll take a look at how you go about provisioning your pages and building your site structure with pages.

Let's assume you have a section on your site just like in the example from above that will host company news. We want your users to be able to create news pages in a **Pages** library. We also want to make sure your users will have an area to enter the piece of news they would like to post and choose a department from which the news is coming.

Let's start with creating our custom page layout tied to a custom content type for our pages:

1. In your Visual Studio, create a new Empty SharePoint 2010 project and set the debug URL to www.contoso.com, which is our publishing site.
2. Right click the project name in your Visual Studio solution to **Add -> New Item...** of type **Content Type**. Give it the name *MyCustomPage*, and set it to inherit from **Page**. Click **Finish**.
3. The *Elements.xml* file of the newly created content type will open and you will get a chance to edit its title and other details. Take a note of the **ID** attribute of the content type, as you'll need it in later steps.
4. Right click the project name in your Visual Studio solution to **Add -> New Item...** of type **Module**. Give it the name *LandingPage* and click **Add**.
5. Delete the *Sample.txt* file from the module we just created.
6. Our newly created module will provision a page layout to the Masterpage and **Page Layouts Gallery**, which you're already familiar with from before. The best starting point to creating a new page layout based of the existing page layout is to make a copy of existing page layout and modify it. Let's copy an existing page layout. In the publishing site you use for a test, click **Site Actions -> Site Settings**.
7. Under the **Galleries** category, click **Masterpages and page layouts**.
8. From the list of available files, select and download to disk *BlankWebPartPage.aspx*. If you want to learn more about different types of page layouts available out of the box, create a new page on your publishing site by using the **Site Actions -> New Page** menu option. Once the page is created under the **Page** ribbon tab, click **Page Layout** to

explore various layouts and how you could use one over another as a starting point.

9. Switch back to your Visual Studio and locate your **Landing Page** module that we created earlier. Add an existing item to your module, which is the **BlankWebPartPage.aspx** you saved to disk.

10. Rename the file to **LandingPage.aspx** just for consistency.

11. Open the **Elements.xml** file in your **LandingPage** module and replace its content with the following:

LISTING 8-3

```xml
<?xml version="1.0" encoding="utf-8"?>
<Elements xmlns="http://schemas.microsoft.com/
sharepoint/">
<!-- page layouts -->
<Module Name="PageLayouts"
    Url="_catalogs/masterpage"
    RootWebOnly="TRUE">
<File Url="LandingPage.aspx"
    Type="GhostableInLibrary"
    Path="LandingPage\LandingPage.aspx">
<Property Name="Title" Value="LandingPage Page Layout" />
<Property Name="MasterPageDescription"
Value="LandingPage Page Layout" />
<Property Name="ContentType" Value="MyCustomPage" />
<Property Name="PublishingAssociatedContentType"
Value=";#MyCustomPage;#0x010100C568DB52D9D0A14D9B2FDCC96
666E9F2007948130EC3DB064584E219954237AF3900bc25837a141242
eabc35dc6a382e3fd6;#" />
</File>
</Module>
</Elements>
```

Above, we provisioned the **ASPX** file representing your page layout to the gallery. The page layout is identical to one of the out-of-the-box layouts, but we will change that later. Another important property value in XML above is the **PublishingAssociatedContentType** representing the name and the **ID** attributes of the content type we created in step 3 from above. Make sure you copy those from your content type definition, called **MyCustomPage**.

The first part is done. Now we have a page layout that, although it looks the same as out-of-the-box layout, will have its separate identity since it inherits our custom page content type. Next let's create a page instance that will use our custom page layout:

1. Right click the project name in your Visual Studio solution to **Add** -> **New Item...** of type **Module**, called **HomePage**.
2. Similar to the module we used in the page layout above, this module will provision pages to the **Pages** library on the site, which is a default library on each publishing site.
3. Rename the **Sample.txt** file to **Default.aspx** and open the file to replace its content with the following:

LISTING 8-4

```
<%@ Page Inherits="Microsoft.SharePoint.Publishing.
TemplateRedirectionPage
    ,Microsoft.SharePoint.Publishing,Version=14.0.0.0
    ,Culture=neutral,PublicKeyToken=71e9bce111e9429c" %>
<%@ Reference VirtualPath="~TemplatePageUrl" %>
<%@ Reference VirtualPath="~masterurl/custom.master" %>
```

The above code will mark the page as a publishing page. In fact, all of the publishing pages that you create will have exactly the same content.

4. What appears on the page will be defined in the accompanying module XML file. Let's rename it to **Landing.xml** so we know that this XML definition will provision the landing page. Open the **Landing.xml** and replace its content with the following code:

LISTING 8-5

```
<%@ Page Inherits="Microsoft.SharePoint.Publishing.
TemplateRedirectionPage
    ,Microsoft.SharePoint.Publishing,Version=14.0.0.0
    ,Culture=neutral,PublicKeyToken=71e9bce111e9429c" %>
<%@ Reference VirtualPath="~TemplatePageUrl" %>
<%@ Reference VirtualPath="~masterurl/custom.master" %>
```

In the above, we defined a module and a file within that module that will be copied over to the **Pages** folder of the site this module will be delivered to. Among other properties, two important ones are:

- **PublishingPageLayout**—defining the page layout used for this page.
- **ContentType**—the content type of the page if you use a custom one, which we do.

At this point, we did all that SharePoint requires to provision a page to the site, but there are a few things that happened behind the scenes.

The page module we created is a generic page that doesn't have any content on it. We'll add the content to the page manually once it's provisioned to the site. The mechanism by which SharePoint delivers content to the site is by using **Features** which you're familiar with from previous chapters. The same approach applies when provisioning pages. If you open the **Features** folder in your Visual Studio site structure, you will see that there have been a few features automatically created as we added our modules; those all have generic names. SharePoint created those features so that they can be activated when your solution is deployed, and all of the modules that belong to a feature will get provisioned to their respective places. Since you selected www.contoso.com as a **debug** site, all features will be activated on that site, and all the pages with their relative parameters will be deployed to the pages library on your main site specified as **debug** URL. To keep things simple and not overlap with some of the developer tasks, we're going to provision our new page layout automatically and page instance based on the layout - manually. We will also get another instance of the page created automatically for us based on the page module we defined in the solution.

1. From your Visual Studio solution, right click on the project name and select **Deploy.** This will copy over the content type and page layout to our site, www.contoso.com. As you remember from one of the modules we have defined, we specified the page called ***AutoProvisioned.aspx*** to be provisioned to the site. This page will also have our custom page layout assigned to it.

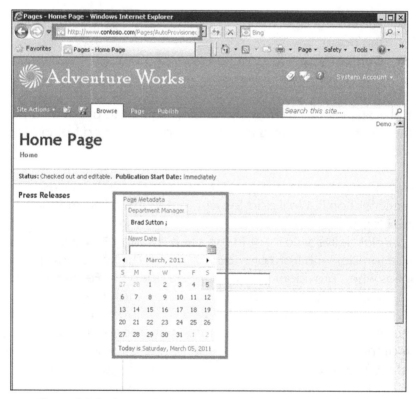

Figure 8-1 Custom metadata when editing AutoProvisione page

2. Open www.contoso.com in the browser, and click **Site Actions** -> **New Page ->** and provide a title to the page, such as **newpage**; it will automatically get assigned an ASPX extension.

3. From the ribbon select the **Page** tab and click **Page Layout** on the flyout menu.

4. From the list of available page layouts, pick our newly created **LandingPage Page Layout**.

The page will receive our new layout, which happens to be the copy of **BlankWebPartPage.aspx**. In the next sample, we'll take a look at how we can add additional metadata-related fields to the page layout so content authors can assign value to them while the page is in edit mode. Also, this will be a good example for you to see how changes on the page layout will affect the instances of pages which use them.

Provisioning several pages with one module

In last few samples, we created a landing page in one of our modules—and you might be thinking about the scenario when we have more than one page on the site. Do we need to create modules for each of them? If all of the pages will end up being deployed to the same page library, it's safe to define their XML in the same module.

Assuming we already have our module that deploys our landing page, here is how we go about adding a few other page definitions:

1. In your Visual Studio, locate the module that deploys your landing page on the site.

2. Right click on the **Landing.xml** file and select **Copy**.

3. Right click on the module name and select **Paste**. Your **Landing.xml** page will be copied to the same module.

4. Rename the page with another name; in our case let's call it **Contact.xml**.

5. By default, Visual Studio assumes that the file you just pasted is just a content file and, therefore, when compiling, it will ignore the entire markup and not provision your page, even if you define correct parameters in it. Since Visual Studio assumes you have just added the file and not the XML definition, it's trying to provision a file as content using one of the default modules it created. Select the newly added file and in the file properties window, locate the **Deployment Type** property and ensure its value is set to **Element Manifest**.

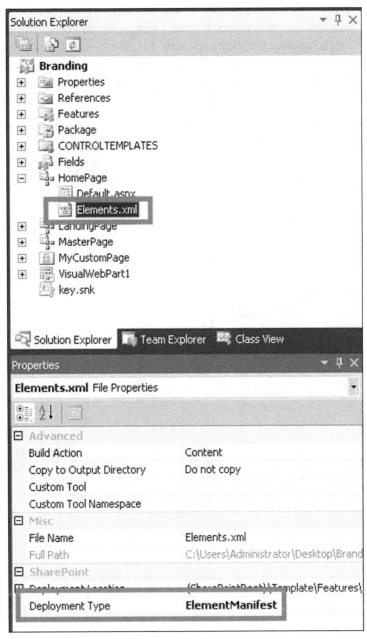

Figure 8-2 Visual Studio item properties for the SharePoint manifest file

6. While you have your **HomePage** module structure expanded in the Solution Explorer on the very top of the panel, click the **Show All Files** button.

7. You will see the Visual Studio hidden file show up called **SharePointProjectItem.spdata**. This file keeps track of all the items and their role in the solution. This is where Visual Studio has taken a note that our newly added **Contact.xml** is now an element manifest file.

Figure 8-3 Visual Studio solution structure including the module provisioning multiple pages

8. Now open the **Contact.xml** and replace its content with the following:

LISTING 8-6

```
<?xml version="1.0" encoding="utf-8"?>
<Elements xmlns="http://schemas.microsoft.com/
sharepoint/">
<Module Name="HomePage" Url="Pages" Path="">
<File Url="Contact.aspx" Type="GhostableInLibrary"
```

```
    Path="HomePage\default.aspx">
<Property Name="Title" Value="Contact Page" />
<Property Name="PublishingPageLayout"
    Value="~SiteCollection/_catalogs/masterpage/
LandingPage.aspx
    , MyCustomPage;" />
<Property Name="ContentType" Value="MyCustomPage" />
</File>
</Module>
</Elements>
```

Notice how at the beginning of the definition we defined the **URL** attribute of the file to be **Contact.aspx**; this defines the resulting page name. On the other hand, the **Path** attribute is still pointing to **Default.aspx**; this is source location of where the page is copied from: *<File Url="Contact.aspx" Type="GhostableInLibrary" Path="HomePage\default.aspx">*.

9. Now that we're done with provisioning, we can build the solution and deploy it using Visual Studio.

After the script is complete, navigate to the page library of the site which you used for **debug** deployment in Visual Studio. Whne you access the **Pages** library on the site by clicking **Site Actions -> View All Site Content**, you will notice that two pages are inside the page library and one of them without any web parts is **Contact.aspx**. You can provision web parts or other components just like you would to a home page.

Rendering additional page-specific metadata during page edit

Custom metadata rendered on a form for content authors to fill out is one of the most common requests which you will hear from business users.Although in this sample we'll try to keep things general and add only out-of-the-box user controls, you can take the idea to the next level and render any other third party of custom controls on the page instance just by provisioning appropriate controls to the page layout. If you think about your page as a list item, users also may want to define some metadata as they create a page. In our example, we're creating an instance of a news page and want to type out our news text and define the news release date. Those additional controls would be very helpful when rendered right there when you're in the middle of typing up your news details.

Let's take a look at how we can define custom fields on the instance of a page when users create it:

1. Assuming we're using the same Visual Studio solution we have used in the previous example, you already have defined a content type and set the page layout to be inherited from the content type.
2. Locate the content type definition within your Visual Studio structure: **MyCustomPage.**
3. Right click the folder of a custom content type to add a new item to it of type: **Empty Element.** This container will take care of provisioning our custom fields to SharePoint.
4. Give your empty elements definition the name **Fields**, and, once finished, open the **Elements.xml** created.
5. Replace the contents of the file with the following:

LISTING 8-7

```
<?xml version="1.0" encoding="utf-8"?>
<Elements xmlns="http://schemas.microsoft.com/
sharepoint/">
<Field ID="{B4EC7C97-EB21-4171-9B64-B56CDC7D9EBA}"
    Name="DepartmentManager" DisplayName="Department
    Manager"
    Type="User" List="UserInfo"
    SourceID="http://schemas.microsoft.com/sharepoint/v3"
```

```
      StaticName="DepartmentManager"
      Group="MyCustomFields">
</Field>
<Field ID="{B9CC7A6F-3753-4d47-A7CD-B6B88F82B683}"
      Name="NewsDate" DisplayName="News Date"
      Type="DateTime" Format="DateOnly"
      SourceID="http://schemas.microsoft.com/sharepoint/v3"
      Hidden="FALSE" ReadOnly="FALSE"
      Required="TRUE"
      xmlns="http://schemas.microsoft.com/sharepoint/"
      Group="MyCustomFields" >
<Default>[Today]</Default>
</Field>
</Elements>
```

Here we have **Department Manager** and **News Date**
defined. Take a look at how both fields were defined and
some of the attributes they use for your future reference.

6. Next, we'll reference defined fields in our content type.
    Open the **Elements.xml** file from your content type and
    locate the **<FieldRefs>** section in the file; replace the section
    with the following reference to our custom fields:

LISTING 8-8

```
<FieldRefs>
<FieldRef ID="{B4EC7C97-EB21-4171-9B64-B56CDC7D9EBA}"
      Name="DepartmentManager" />
<FieldRef ID="{B9CC7A6F-3753-4d47-A7CD-B6B88F82B683}"
      Name="NewsDate" />
</FieldRefs>
```

At this point, if we were to deploy our solution with the
custom deployment script, the newly provisioned page
would show two new fields we have added if you were to
switch to the item property view from the **Pages** document
library.

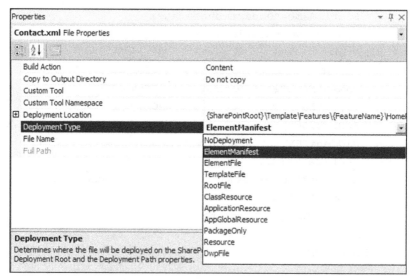

Figure 8-4 Additional fields available to set using an item property page

However, it takes a few steps to get to the item in order to modify its properties in the **Pages** document library. Therefore, the next change will take care of asking users to enter the metadata right into the page while users interact with it in the edit mode.

7. Locate the **MyCustomPage** page layout module and open the **MyCustomPage.aspx** file that defines the markup of your page, including web part zones. Locate the following section in the file:

LISTING 8-9

```
<PublishingWebControls:EditModePanel runat="server"
CssClass="edit-mode-panel">
<SharePointWebControls:TextField runat="server"
FieldName="Title"/>
</PublishingWebControls:EditModePanel>
```

The above section defines any controls that will be rendered to the user once the page enters edit mode. You can see that we already have one control that is rendered and one references item title. The item in this case is page, meaning that this control will let you enter the title of the page and save it to the appropriate field in the page library.

8. Replace the content of the section from above with the following code:

LISTING 8-10

```
<PublishingWebControls:EditModePanel runat="server"
    CssClass="edit-mode-panel">
<legend>Page Metadata</legend>
<SharePointWebControls:UserField
id="DepartmentManagerEdit"
    FieldName="DepartmentManager" runat="server" />
<SharePointWebControls:DateTimeField id="NewsDateEdit"
    FieldName="NewsDate" runat="server" />
<SharePointWebControls:TextField runat="server"
FieldName="Title"/>
</PublishingWebControls:EditModePanel>
```

Above, we have added two more controls that bind to the respective field names we have provisioned to the content type. At this point, the page will allow us to enter the content in the respective fields, but those fields will not be rendered on the page once it's published because there is no control to render them. If you would like the metadata pieces below to be rendered, you will need to place those fields into the markup of the page layout where you want them to appear. We'll place them right below the edit mode panel. Also, because you don't want those fields to appear again when the page is in the edit mode, you can specify that controls will be rendered only in the display mode, as below:

LISTING 8-11

```
<SharePointWebControls:UserField
id="DepartmentManagerDisplay"
    FieldName="DepartmentManager" runat="server"
    ControlMode="Display" />
<SharePointWebControls:DateTimeField
id="NewsDateDisplay"
    FieldName="NewsDate" ControlMode="Display"
    runat="server" />
```

9. The last step required for our custom fields to appear on a page is to make sure the content type that defines our custom page with fields will be permitted in a pages library on a given site. By default having a content type specified in your page XML definition file does not mean this content type will be allowed in the **Pages** library. In order to bind the content type to a library, we need to make a binding definition. Open the **HomePage** module and its containing **Landing.xml** file to define a binding.

10. Add the following definition right after Elements node in your XML:
    <ContentTypeBinding ContentTypeId="{ID}" ListUrl="Pages" />
    In here, replace the **{ID}** with the **ID** of our custom content type (**MyCustomPage**); the **ID** is located in **Elements.xml** file of the content type definition.

11. Let's build and deploy the solution using Visual Studio.

Navigate to the page we have provisioned in the previous example by using a **HomePage** module.

The page on the site will look as before at first. Switch the page to edit mode and you will see two new fields available to edit.

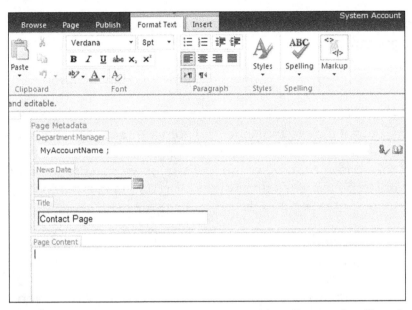

Figure 8-5 Additional properties available to set from the page's edit mode

If you enter valid values into the fields, check in the page, and navigate to the pages library, you will see that entered metadata was preserved in the properties of your pages. Notice how each of our controls has a proper type (**DateTimeField, UserField**, etc.).

While working with pages, you will see a lot of overlap in responsibilities between a back-end developer and yourself. In some cases you will have to add user controls to the page and style them. In other cases a back-end developer will do all of the provisioning for you. Whatever the case might be, one thing I would like you to take away from this sample is that you can provision not just SharePoint out-of-the-box controls bound to SharePoint library fields but any other third party or custom controls which will interact with your users during page view or edit.

For the list of other SharePoint out-of-the-box data bound controls, search **Microsoft.SharePoint.WebControls** on MSDN.

Provisioning page content to your pages programmatically

From the last example, you've seen how you can provision pages to your sites and create a hierarchy of sites on the site collection. However, all of the sites and pages on them have no content on them, except the site that inherited from the **Team Site** template.

Let's take a look at some of the techniques we can use to add new content to pages. We'll start with adding simple text content by using the content editor web part:

1. Navigate to the root of your SharePoint publishing site, www.contoso.com, and switch to the edit mode of the main page.
2. Locate any of the web part zones and click **Add a Web Part**.
3. Click on the **Media and Content** category and select **Content Editor** from the available options.

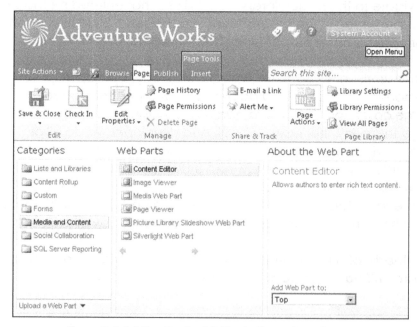

Figure 8-6 Adding Content Editor to the web part zone

4. Once the web part has been added, type any text into the web part editing zone.

5. Click on the **Content Editor** web part maintenance arrow located in the top left-hand side of the web part chrome, and click **Export**.

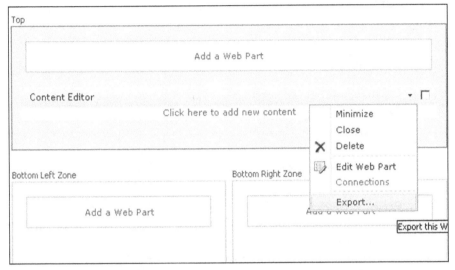

Figure 8-7 Exporting Content Editor definition as XML

6. Save the file you're offered to disk. The file is an XML definition of the web part along with its state and content you've just typed in.

7. Open the file and copy its entire contents to the clipboard.

8. Switch to Visual Studio and locate the **HomePage** module in your Visual Studio structure from last few samples.

9. Open the configuration XML file **Landing.xml**, and locate the section of the file that looks like this:

LISTING 8-12

```
</File>
</Module>
</Elements>
```

The section before the **</File>** is used to define web parts and any other components that will go on the pages appropriate sections.

10. Insert the code below right before the **</File>** closing tag from the previous step:

LISTING 8-13

```
<AllUsersWebPart WebPartZoneID="CenterLeftColumn"
WebPartOrder="0">
<![CDATA[
<?xml version="1.0" encoding="utf-8"?>
<WebPart xmlns:xsi="http://www.w3.org/2001/XMLSchema-
instance" xmlns:xsd="http://www.w3.org/2001/XMLSchema"
xmlns="http://schemas.microsoft.com/WebPart/v2">
<Title>Content Editor</Title>
<FrameType>Default</FrameType>
<Description>Allows authors to enter rich text
content.</Description>
<IsIncluded>true</IsIncluded>
<ZoneID>TopZone</ZoneID>
<PartOrder>0</PartOrder>
<FrameState>Normal</FrameState>
<Height />
<Width />
<AllowRemove>true</AllowRemove>
<AllowZoneChange>true</AllowZoneChange>
<AllowMinimize>true</AllowMinimize>
<AllowConnect>true</AllowConnect>
<AllowEdit>true</AllowEdit>
<AllowHide>true</AllowHide>
<IsVisible>true</IsVisible>
<DetailLink />
<HelpLink />
<HelpMode>Modeless</HelpMode>
```

```
<Dir>Default</Dir>
<PartImageSmall />
<MissingAssembly>Cannot import this Web Part.</
MissingAssembly>
<PartImageLarge>/_layouts/images/mscontl.gif</
PartImageLarge>
<IsIncludedFilter />
<Assembly>Microsoft.SharePoint, Version=14.0.0.0,
Culture=neutral
    ,PublicKeyToken=71e9bce111e9429c</Assembly>
<TypeName>Microsoft.SharePoint.WebPartPages.
ContentEditorWebPart</TypeName>
<ContentLink xmlns="http://schemas.microsoft.com/
WebPart/v2/ContentEditor" />
<Content xmlns="http://schemas.microsoft.com/WebPart/v2/
ContentEditor">
Sample Content
</Content>
<PartStorage xmlns="http://schemas.microsoft.com/
WebPart/v2/ContentEditor" />
</WebPart>
]]>
</AllUsersWebPart>
```

It seems like a lot of text, but all we have is an XML copied from the exported web part on the site surrounded by the following markup:

LISTING 8-14

```
<AllUsersWebPart WebPartZoneID="CenterLeftColumn"
WebPartOrder="0">
<![CDATA[
]]>
</AllUsersWebPart>
```

The markup defines that the containing XML will be a web part placed into the **CenterLeftColumn** eb part zone. If we had more than one web part in that zone, the **WebPartOrder** attribute would set the order of them rendered on the page.

11. Let's build the solution and **deploy** it with Visual Studio. Navigate to the same page we have provisioned earlier using the **HomePage** module. You will see that pages that use our custom template will have a web part with our sample content provisioned to it.

One of the things you probably noticed is our knowing the exact name of the web part zone where our web part will go. To find out the available web part zones, you would refer to the **PageLayouts** folder and the module we have defined for the page layout. If you open the **ASPX** file defining the actual page layout, you will see the web part zone definitions coming up among the other markup, just like we saw before when looking at the structure of the page layout:

LISTING 8-15

```
<WebPartPages:WebPartZone
    runat="server"
    Title="<%$Resources:cms,WebPartZoneTitle_Center%>"
    ID="CenterColumn"   />
```

The above definition tells us the **ID** of the web part zone. Since we copied the existing page layout from the out-of-the-box SharePoint layout definition, we know what web part zones our definition has. If we add more web part zones, those will be named differently and those are the zones we could use to place web parts into.

Custom web parts and their role in SharePoint branding

We've looked at what out-of-the-box web parts are and how we can provision them to a page. As you may suspect, back-end developers create their own custom web parts to facilitate the custom functionality they would like to bring to the site. The whole reason to create a custom web part is to not just execute functionality, but also to provide user interface, and this is where you as a user interface developer come in to play. So what are custom web parts? They are .NET components which render controls on the page. As you already know, web parts get provisioned into the web part zones, so, in essence, your web part will inject HTML into the web part zone. In SharePoint 2010 version, the most common web part back-end developers are creating is a **Visual Web Part**. This type of web part uses ASP.NET User Control, which is rendered on the page. Even if you're not familiar with user controls, SharePoint will take care of the back end for you. Having said that, I would like for you to be comfortable with creating a basic web part so you can practice with functionality on your own. We will only cover those necessary basics.

Let's take a look at how you would add your custom web part to the project and add some custom logic and branding to it.

1. Open Visual Studio and create a new Empty SharePoint 2010 project.
2. Assign http://www.contoso.com as a debug URL and select **Farm solution** as a deployment method.
3. Right click on the project name to **Add -> New Item...** and pick **Visual Web Part** from the list of templates.

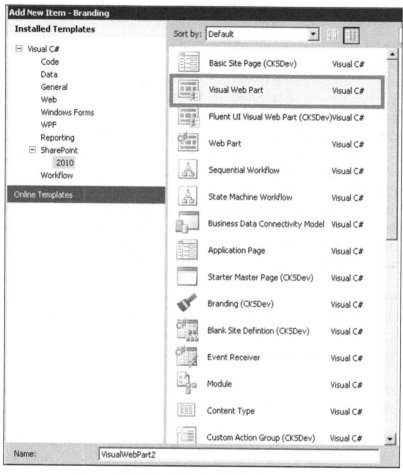

Figure 8-8 Adding Visual Web Part component

You will see Visual Studio adding all of the necessary artifacts for the project. Locate the newly created **VisualWebPart1** folder in the solution structure. Locate the file called **VisualWebPart1UserControl. ascx**. This is the user control which will render the required web part markup and any other markup you decide to render on the page. This user control will also be opened for you in the Visual Studio main workspace area. This is where you can type in your markup, JavaScript, style sheet references, ASP.NET, and third-party controls. We're going to try to keep things very basic here, and later we'll take a look at how you can host external services from your web part and return results back to the user.

4. Add the following piece of code right after this control declaration:
   <%@ Control Language="C#" AutoEventWireup="true" CodeBehind="VisualWebPart1UserControl.ascx. cs" Inherits="SharePointProject1.VisualWebPart1. VisualWebPart1UserControl" %>

LISTING 8-16

```
<h1>
<asp:Label ID="Label1" runat="server" Text="Label">
</asp:Label>
</h1>
<br/>
<asp:LinkButton ID="LinkButton1" runat="server">
Click Me
</asp:LinkButton>
```

In here we just have a label and a button on the page. Let's add a piece of code which will change the value of the label on button clicked.

5. In the Visual Studio View menu, select Designer. Visual Studio will switch to designer mode of the workspace. Double click the **Click Me** button and you will be taken to the code behind of the solution to the file located under **VisualWebPart1** folder and the corresponding **VisualWebPart1UserControl.ascx** within it. Add the following code to the *LinkButton1_Click* method:

LISTING 8-17

```
protected void LinkButton1_Click(object sender,
EventArgs e)
{
Label1.Text = DateTime.Now.ToShortTimeString();
}
```

6. That's's it; now let's deploy the web part to the site. Right click Visual Studio and select **Deploy**.
7. Once deployment is complete, open the http://intranet.contoso.com in your browser.
8. Edit the page: **Site Actions -> Edit Page**. Scroll to the bottom until you see the **Top** web part zone, click **Add a Web Part** for this zone. From the ribbon, click on **Insert** tab, then select **Web Part**, from the area below the ribbon select **Custom** as a Category and *VisualWebPart1* as a web part and click **Add**.
9. Save the page and you will see the **Click Me** button, when clicked the current date and time will be displayed on the page.

As you can see, provisioning your own Visual Web Part did not involve a whole lot of effort. This task will be taken care of by your back-end developer on the project mainly because they would like to place web parts in the related SharePoint *Platform* project and potentially separate web parts by folder if there are many of those in the project. However, don't discount the power of building web parts; as a user interface developer you can take a huge advantage of building interactive client side functionality and making it available as a component on the site.

Branding specific instances of out-of-the-box web parts

By now, you have seen how we brand the content inside the web part as well as the page around it. But what if you have an existing out-of-the-box web part or view and you need to change how it's rendered? Out-of-the-box web parts and controls usually have many CSS classes, IDs which you can use to overwrite and adjust the look and feel of those according to your requirements.

Figure 8-9 Hierarchy of markup surrounding a typical web part in a web part zone

However, if you put those changes in your general style sheet which gets called in the Masterpage, your changes will be applied across the entire site and on all new instances of sites and web parts. You can also choose to apply the style within a content editor web part, as we did in one of the examples. The only thing is that in that example, the page was highly unlikely to be edited; but in your case, if someone goes into the edit mode as part of their normal content editing and accidently deletes your web part, all of your changes will go with it.

One of the better approaches in this case is to create a customized page layout for this particular page and add your style sheet changes right around the web part zone which you want to target. If you're concerned about the fact that we're duplicating the page layout just for the small purpose of adjusting the look and feel of one or few instance of the web part—don't be...usually such requests target a very small number of pages, such as a home page or a landing page of a major section on the site, so you might need to create one or two such page layouts. If business users request too many exceptions, it might be a good idea to generalize those exceptions and explore the idea of applying customization globaly on the site.

Let's take a look at the scenario of customizing the look of the calendar which is going to be placed in one of the web part zones:

1. We'll use the same page layout we looked at the example earlier: **BlankWebPartPage.aspx**. From the www.contoso.com, click **Site Actions->Site Settings**
2. Under **Galleries** click **Masterpages and page layouts**.
3. Locate and download **BlankWebPartPage.aspx** to the file system.
4. Open the file from the file system in Visual Studio.
5. Assuming our calendar web part is going to be in the **Header** web part zone, locate the following code: *<WebPartPages:WebPartZone runat="server" Title="<%$Resources:cms,WebPartZoneTitle_Header%>" ID="Header"/>* This defines the **Header** zone in the page layouts; let's add a border around this zone.
6. Wrap the web part zone code with the following code so it looks like below:

LISTING 8-18

```
<div id="calborder" style="border: solid">
    <WebPartPages:WebPartZone runat="server" Title="<%$R
esources:cms,WebPartZoneTitle_Header%>"
    ID="Header"/>
</div>
```

7. Before proceeding to the next customization, let's preview our changes. Save the page layout you're editing and upload it to the **Masterpages and page layouts** under **Galleries** of your www.contoso.com site. Ensure the page layout is **Published** and **Approved.**
8. Now, let's add a calendar to the site. Since www.contoso.com is a publishing site, collaboration features like a calendar are not enabled on it by default. To enabled collaboration features, click **Site Actions -> Site Settings -> Manage site features**.
9. Locate the **Team Collaboration Lists** feature and click **Activate**. Now let's create an instance of a calendar on our site. Click **Site Actions -> More options....** Under categories

on the right, click **Lists** and select Calendar. Set the calendar **Title** to **Calendar.**

10. Navigate back to www.contoso.com home and slick **Site Actions –> Edit Page**. Locate the **Header** web part zone and click **Add a Web Part** under it.Pick the **Calendar** web part from the **Lists** category.

As you save the page you will notice how the border was applied to the web part zone. Let's see how we can make a style change within the calendar web part so that some cells of a calendar are colored differently.

1. Go back to the **BlankWebPartPage.aspx** page layout and locate the following section within code: *<script language="javascript">...</script>.*

2. We'll add the following code right below it. The code will parse through the elements of the calendar classifying **Sunday** and change the background of those cells to blue:

LISTING 8-19

```
<script language="javascript">
var calendarElements = new Array();
calendarElements.length = 0;
getElementsByClassName('ms-acal-day0', document.body);

for ( var i = 0; i < calendarElements.length; i++ )
{
calendarElements[i].style.background="blue";
}
function getElementsByClassName(calendarClass, node)
{
if (node.className == calendarClass)
{
calendarElements[calendarElements.length] = node;
}
for ( var i = 0; i < node.childNodes.length; i++ )
```

```
getElementsByClassName( calendarClass, node.
childNodes[i] );
}
</script>
```

3. Just like before, save the page layout you've edited and upload it to the **Masterpages and page layouts** under **Galleries** of your www.contoso.com site. Ensure the page layout is **Published** and **Approved.**

As a result, when you navigate to the home page of www.contoso.com, you will be able to see color-coded days of the calendar. The customization you can perform here virtually limitless, I've seen some creative idea of placing a weather icon in each day on the calendar. In this case the JavaScript hits the third party web service and injects a resulting markup into each calendar cell.

Hopefully this illustrates capabilities you have in terms of ad-hoc customizations of various web part elements by using page layouts. As you can imagine, this operation can be done using SharePoint designer or Visual Studio. You want to use Visual Studio in case you're making updates to your production site so that there is a consistent versioning of changes applied to the system. For small tests you can safely use the method from above.

Provisioning web parts directly to page layouts

So far we have looked at how to add your custom web parts directly to pages. Although this approach works most of the time, there are scenarios where you would want to have web parts provisioned to the page layout that your page instance will end up inheriting. For example, your users want to create pages for a particular type of content, and, besides just look and feel, they want the page to initially have a few web parts on it which they can fill in with required information. You can provision web parts during the automated page provisioning using a feature, but when a user creates a page manually, no web parts will be provisioned on a page unless placed into a page layout definition.

Let's see how that can be achieved:

1. In your Visual Studio solution structure we have used so far in samples in this chapter, locate the custom page layout module called **LandingPage**. Open the **Elements.xml** file.
2. Locate the following node in the XML file:

LISTING 8-20

```
<Property
Name="PublishingAssociatedContentType" Value=";#MyCust
omPage;#0x010100C568DB52D9D0A14D9B2FDCC96666E9F2007948130
EC3DB064584E219954237AF3900bc25837a141242eabc35dc6a382e3
fd6;#" />
```

3. Right after the property definition above, insert the XML of the web part you're planning to provision on the page layout. In our case, we provision the **Content Editor** web part, and our page layout looks like this:

LISTING 8-21

```
<?xml version="1.0" encoding="utf-8"?>
<Elements xmlns="http://schemas.microsoft.com/
sharepoint/">
<!-- page layouts -->
<Module Name="PageLayouts" Url="_catalogs/masterpage"
RootWebOnly="TRUE">
<File Url="LandingPage.aspx" Type="GhostableInLibrary"
    Path="LandingPage\LandingPage.aspx">
<Property Name="Title" Value="LandingPage Page Layout" />
<Property Name="MasterPageDescription"
Value="LandingPage Page Layout" />
<Property Name="ContentType" Value="MyCustomPage" />
```

```
<Property Name="PublishingAssociatedContentType" Value=
";#MyCustomPage;#0x010100C568DB52D9D0A14D9B2FDCC96666E9F2
007948130EC3DB064584E219954237AF3900bc25837a141242eabc35dc
6a382e3fd6;#" />


<AllUsersWebPart WebPartOrder="0" WebPartZoneID="Center
RightColumn" >
<![CDATA[
<?xml version="1.0" encoding="utf-8"?>
<WebPart xmlns:xsi=http://www.w3.org/2001/XMLSchema-
instance
    xmlns:xsd=http://www.w3.org/2001/XMLSchema
    xmlns="http://schemas.microsoft.com/WebPart/v2">
<Title>Content Editor</Title>
<FrameType>Default</FrameType>
<Description>Allows authors to enter rich text
content.</Description>
<IsIncluded>true</IsIncluded>
<ZoneID>wpz</ZoneID>
<PartOrder>0</PartOrder>
<FrameState>Normal</FrameState>
<Height />
<Width />
<AllowRemove>true</AllowRemove>
<AllowZoneChange>true</AllowZoneChange>
<AllowMinimize>true</AllowMinimize>
<AllowConnect>true</AllowConnect>
<AllowEdit>true</AllowEdit>
<AllowHide>true</AllowHide>
<IsVisible>true</IsVisible>
<DetailLink />
<HelpLink />
<HelpMode>Modeless</HelpMode>
<Dir>Default</Dir>
<PartImageSmall />
<MissingAssembly>Cannot import this Web Part.</
MissingAssembly>
<PartImageLarge>_layouts/images/mscontl.gif</
PartImageLarge>
```

```
<IsIncludedFilter />
<Assembly>Microsoft.SharePoint, Version=14.0.0.0,
Culture=neutral,
    PublicKeyToken=71e9bce111e9429c</Assembly>
<TypeName>Microsoft.SharePoint.WebPartPages.
ContentEditorWebPart</TypeName>
<ContentLink xmlns="http://schemas.microsoft.com/
WebPart/v2/ContentEditor" />
<Content xmlns="http://schemas.microsoft.com/WebPart/v2/
ContentEditor">
    Sample content</Content>
<PartStorage xmlns="http://schemas.microsoft.com/
WebPart/v2/ContentEditor" />
</WebPart>
]]>
</AllUsersWebPart>
</File>
</Module>
</Elements>
```

4. Build the solution in Visual Studio and deploy it

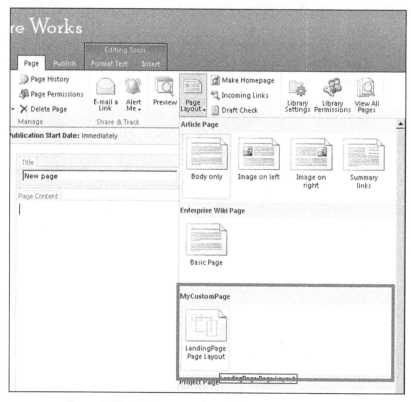

Figure 8-10 Custom page layout deployed to the site

5. Open your site www.contoso.com.

As you can see, although we haven't provisioned anything to the right web part zone of the page, it still has content because it was provisioned through a page layout.

CHAPTER 9

Changing the Look of SharePoint Forms

SharePoint functionality and features are built upon lists and libraries of various types. When you create a calendar event, you're working with a list; when you create a blog post, you're looking at the list item form. All lists and libraries have basic interface for users to create, edit, and view items. If you compare a calendar event entry form and a blog post entry form, you will see a significant difference. In this chapter we'll take a look at why there is a difference between various types of list item entry forms. We'll also take a look at how to modify list item forms for out-of-the-box and custom lists; we'll see how you can add new content to your forms and third-party controls that changes the look and feel of the form.

Applying branding to SharePoint list views

Working with lists is one of the most common tasks SharePoint users face every day. After all, lists are nearly everything in SharePoint. Blog articles, discussions, calendars, document libraries are all lists. Due to the fact that SharePoint allows users to create many instances of lists, applying visual customizations on your style sheet with purpose to affect that one instance will actually affect all of the future instances of the component on the site where your custom style sheet applies.

In short, lists are sets of data which are transformed by XSL to look more like UI applicable to the scenario. For example, if we take a look at the calendar event and the blog post, although those look completely different, they represent the same data rendered in a different way.

The way SharePoint achieves this is by using a web part called **XslListView**.

Let's take a look at how we can do basic management of the look of items using XSL.

1. Navigate to http://intranet.contoso.com.
2. Click **Site Actions -> New Site**.
3. Under **Content** category, pick **Blog** and give the site a title and URL value of *blog*.
4. Open Microsoft SharePoint Designer 2010 and click **Open Site**.
5. Specify URL http://intranet.contoso.com/blog.
6. Once the site has opened in SharePoint Designer, click **All Files** under **Site Objects** on the left pane.
7. In the list of all of the files, pick *default.aspx*, which is our default blog page.
8. Once the page has loaded, select the **Split** view (on the View tab of the ribbon) to give you the code and the design view of the page.
9. In the design view, in the center of the page, locate the **XslListViewWebPart** as shown in the figure and click on its chrome.

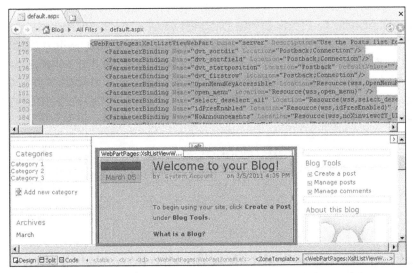

Figure 9-1 Editing XslListViewWebPart using SharePoint Designer

10. The following web part XML will be highlighted in the code view:

LISTING 9-1

```
<WebPartPages:XsltListViewWebPart
runat="server"
Description="Use the Posts list for posts in this
blog."
....
GhostedXslLink="blog.xsl"
MissingAssembly="Cannot import this Web Part."
HelpMode="Modeless"
ListUrl=""
.....
```

11. Change the value of **GhostedXslLink** from *blog.xsl*, the file responsible for rendering the blog look and feel of the list, to *main.xsl*, which is the default XSL for each list.

12. Save the page in SharePoint Designer and you will see the design view refresh with the new look.

You will notice the look of the blog list view has changed to a view that a typical SharePoint list would have. If you switch back to SharePoint Designer and search for **blog.xsl** on the page, you will find a few instances of files being referenced. In fact, the main page of the blog site template, http://intranet.contoso.com/blog, uses **blog.xsl** to render blog categories, blog posts, and links.

In next sample, we'll take a look at how we can make more changes to the look and feel of templates using XSL for their rendering.

Making changes to list view and list item detail view using XSL

As mentioned earlier, SharePoint uses the notion of views and templates on many other components—for example, a list view. List view look and feel is driven by an XSL template. Every time you access the list view or create your own view in the list with any parameters you wish, the data from the list is loaded and its look transformed with XSL. You can actually remove the XSL reference from the list rendering and all you will see is a plain table with rows of data in it.

To better understand how far you can go with extending the list view, let's take a look at the out-of-the-box **Blog** template.

1. Navigate to the root of your collaboration site: http:// intranet.contoso.com.
2. Click **Site Actions -> New Site**.
3. From the list of site templates, locate **Blog**.
4. Provide the title of the site and URL and click **Create**.

Once the site has been created, you will be taken right to the list view of the blog post page. Click on the title **Welcome to your Blog** and you will see a list item detail view for posting list items. The web part in the center is a view of the list item detail page transformed with an XSL. To verify that fact, click **Site Actions -> Edit Page**. From the edit page, click **Edit Web Part** as shown on the screenshot below.

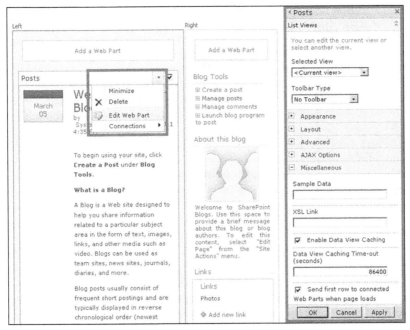

Figure 9-2 Editing web part properties

One of the great new features available in SharePoint is the ability to easily assign a new XSL rendering template to the **List View** web part that hosts all of the views in SharePoint. Scroll down to the bottom of your web part properties window on the right of the screen and locate the **Miscellaneous** section. Expand the section and locate the **XSL link** property. This property allows you to specify the location of the XSL that will transform the look of the rendering template for this view.

As you can imagine, this particular list view already has its own custom template defined somewhere in the list schema. In fact, we will be using this very template to make a copy of it to build up our own modification. First, let's take a look at how we can make ad-hoc modifications through the **Miscellaneous** web part property.

1. Open the following folder in your SharePoint root: *[Drive]:\ Program Files\Common Files\Microsoft Shared\Web Server Extensions\14\TEMPLATE\LAYOUTS\XSL.*
   This is where SharePoint keeps all of its XSL templates.

2. Open **blog.xsl** in a Visual Studio and copy its entire content to the clipboard.

3. Use an existing Visual Studio project or create a new **Empty SharePoint 2010 project**. Assign a debug URL as http:// intranet.contoso.com and chose **Farm solution** as the deployment option.

4. Right click on the project name to **Add -> Layouts mapped folder**.

5. Right click on the folder and create a new subfolder in it called **XSL**.

6. Right click on the XSL folder to add a new item. The item will be located under the **Data** category; the template will be called **XSLT file**. Give your new file a name like **MyXSLSheet. xsl**.

7. Open the newly created **MyXSLSheet.xsl** and paste the contents of the clipboard you have copied from **blog.xsl**.

8. You will see a lot of XSL transformation code since this template holds the code for several lists and item detail pages for the **Blog** site template. To make it easier in your Visual Studio, you can collapse the code into nodes (**CTRL+M +L**) and expand the root node.

9. Search for the following string in the file:
   <!-- BaseViewID='0' and TemplateType='301' is Home Page view for Blog's posts list -->.
   The comment above suggests that we're working with the template for blog posts. However, there is a more certain way to find out which exact template we're working with— we'll take a look at it further down.

10. Expand the structure under the comment in the above step and locate the following section:
    <xsl:if test="$ShowBody=1">.
    This is the part which is going to render various blog post body parts. Let's see how we can add show/ hide links right before the body content is rendered so viewers can hide or show the post body.

Place the following code right after the code section from above:

LISTING 9-2

```
<a href='#' id='ExpandLink{$thisNode/@ID}'
onclick='javascript:ToggleBlogPost(PostBodyVisible,
"{$thisNode/@ID}")' style='display:none'>
<img src='/_layouts/images/plus.gif' style='border:
none;'/> Show details
</a>
<a href='#' id='CollapseLink{$thisNode/@ID}' onclick='j
avascript:ToggleBlogPost(PostBodyVisible, "{$thisNode/@
ID}")'>
<img src='/_layouts/images/minus.gif' style='border:
none;'/> Hide details
</a>
```

11. Place the following script which will facilitate showing and hiding of the post body right before the <xsl:if test="$ShowBody=1">:

LISTING 9-3

```
<script type="text/javascript">
var PostBodyVisible=true;
function ToggleBlogPost(toggleOff, postId)
{
if (PostBodyVisible)
{
$get("PostBody"+postId).style.display="none";
$get("PostBody"+postId).style.height="0px";
$get("ExpandLink"+postId).style.display="";
$get("CollapseLink"+postId).style.display="none";
}else
{
$get("PostBody"+postId).style.display="";
```

```
$get("PostBody"+postId).style.height="";
$get("ExpandLink"+postId).style.display="none";
$get("CollapseLink"+postId).style.display="";
}
PostBodyVisible = !toggleOff;
}
</script>
```

12. Finally, locate the area containing the body of the post *<div class="ms-PostBody">* and add the **ID** attribute to the *<div>* so it looks like this:
    <div id="PostBody{$thisNode/@ID}" class="ms-PostBody">. This way we add an **ID** of the post so that our javascript can consume it to hide or show the specific post body which was selected.
13. Save the file and deploy your solution from Visual Studio.
14. Go back to your newly created blog site and click **Site Actions -> Edit Page** to open the **Edit Web Part** panel of the last sequence of steps from above.
15. Scroll down to the **Miscellaneous** section and enter the following relative URL in the **XSL link** property: */_layouts/ xsl/MyXSLSheet.xslt*. Ensure the file name and extension is exactly as in Visual Studio, otherwise you will get a rendering error when saving the properties of the web part.
16. Click OK on the **Edit Web Part** panel and the **Stop Editing** button on the ribbon.

You will see how now we have the ability to show and hide post body of the default post. You can also create couple of more posts to test those too. This solution might be handy if you want to keep the site clean and allow users to manage which post they want to see. Mainly, this solution demonstrates how to work with XSL driven list views and as you can see there is a lot of flexibility on how you can change the look and feel of the rendered markup.

Figure 9-3 Enhancement added to the blog list to show/hide post detail

The same approach can be applied to any list view in SharePoint since all **ListView** Web Parts support custom XSL transformations.

Defining list view look and feel in your custom list schema

In the last example, we looked at how you can define the look of your list view using the XSL of the blog post template. In this example, we'll take a look at how you can take any list you create from the custom list definition in Visual Studio and make it render however you want with custom XSL.

If you're working in a team of back-end developers, they will take care of the list provisioning for you and you will just need to add a required branding piece, which is going to take care of SharePoint list rendering. However, I will go over the steps required to create a custom list so that you can try things out in your environment and see the changes for yourself.

Let's start with creating a custom list definition in Visual Studio.

1. Right click the project name in your Visual Studio structure and add a new item of type: **List Definition**.
2. The type of list definition we will be inheriting is a **Custom List**.
3. Also choose to **create a list instance** with our list definition. Once the list definition module is created, open the **schema.xml** file. The file has very basic markup and we have only two views; views are defined with the <View/> node:

LISTING 9-4

```
<View BaseViewID="0" Type="HTML"
    MobileView="TRUE" TabularView="FALSE">
```

and

LISTING 9-5

```
<View BaseViewID="1" Type="HTML"
WebPartZoneID="Main"
CssStyleSheet="blog.css"
DisplayName="$Resources:core,objectiv_schema_
mwsidcamlidC24;"
DefaultView="TRUE"
```

```
MobileView="TRUE"
MobileDefaultView="TRUE"
SetupPath="pages\viewpage.aspx"
ImageUrl="/_layouts/images/generic.png"
Url="AllItems.aspx">
```

You will also notice that one of the properties in the view is the **XSL link** you're familiar from the last example; the value of it is **main.xsl**: *<XslLink Default="TRUE">main.xsl</XslLink>*.

You guessed right, there is a **main.xsl** in *[Drive]:\Program Files\ Common Files\Microsoft Shared\Web Server Extensions\14\ TEMPLATE\LAYOUTS\XSL* defining how your list items are going to look.

Next, let's create a new XSL file for this list to inherit the look from.

1. Navigate to the **Layouts** folder you mapped earlier in your Visual Studio solution and create an **XSL** folder in it, unless you have it from the previous example.
2. Add an **XSLT** type of a document from the **Data** category just like in the last example; let's call it **CustomListXSL.xslt**.
3. Replace the content of the newly created **MyXSLSheet.xsl** with the following code:

LISTING 9-6

```
<xsl:stylesheet xmlns:x="http://www.w3.org/2001/
XMLSchema" xmlns:d="http://schemas.microsoft.com/
sharepoint/dsp"
version="1.0" exclude-result-prefixes="xsl msxsl
ddwrt" xmlns:ddwrt="http://schemas.microsoft.com/Web
Parts/v2/DataView/runtime" xmlns:asp="http://schemas.
microsoft.com/ASPNET/20" xmlns:__designer="http://
schemas.microsoft.com/Web Parts/v2/DataView/designer"
xmlns:xsl="http://www.w3.org/1999/XSL/Transform"
xmlns:msxsl="urn:schemas-microsoft-com:xslt"
xmlns:SharePoint="Microsoft.SharePoint.WebControls"
```

```
xmlns:ddwrt2="urn:frontpage:internal" ddwrt:oob="true">
<xsl:import href="/_layouts/xsl/main.xsl"/>
<xsl:output method="html" indent="no"/>
<xsl:param name="NoAJAX" select="1"/>
<xsl:template mode="Item" match="Row[../../@
BaseViewID='1']">
<xsl:param name="Fields" select="."/>
<xsl:param name="Collapse" select="."/>
<xsl:param name="Position" select="1"/>
<xsl:param name="Last" select="1"/>
<xsl:variable name="thisNode" select="."/>
<table width="100%" border="0" cellspacing="0"
cellpadding="0" dir="None">
<tr>
<td width="690">
<h4>
<xsl:apply-templates select="$Fields[@Name='LinkTitle']"
mode="PrintField">
<xsl:with-param name="thisNode" select="."/>
<xsl:with-param name="Position" select="$Position"/>
</xsl:apply-templates>
</h4>
</td>
<xsl:if test="($thisNode/../@value.listpermission.
EditListItems = '1') and
   ($thisNode/../@value.listpermission.ManageLists  =
'1') ">
<td align="right" class="ms-blogedit">
<a href="javascript:"
  onclick='ShowPopupDialog("{$HttpVDir}/Lists/Platform-
  ListInstance1/EditForm.aspx?ID={$thisNode/@ID}&amp;
  Source={$HttpVDir}/Lists/PlatformListInstance1/
  EditItem.aspx?ID={$thisNode/@ID}");return false;'>
  Edit Item
</a>
</td>
</xsl:if>
</tr>
</table>
```

```
<div class="ms-CommentBody">
<div dir="">
If you had more than one field - this is where you can
output their values..
</div>
</div>
</xsl:template>
</xsl:stylesheet>
```

The above **TemplateType='10000'** will depend on the **Template ID** you have assigned in your list definition **Elements.xml** file. Also, references to **/Lists/Branding-ListInstance1** will depend on the URL attribute in the **Elements.xml** of your list definition. Take a look at the template to see how the logic is constructed; we'll see how it works in a moment.

4. Navigate to your list definition **schema.xml** file, and for the *BaseViewID="1"* set the value of the **XSL link** to be the following: *<XslLink Default="TRUE">CustomListXSL.xslt</XslLink>*.
5. Deploy the solution from Visual Studio and navigate to the root URL of your test site: http://intranet.contoso.com.
6. Open the list instance, which is going to be automatically provisioned by Visual Studio, the default name is **Branding-ListInstance1**. Create a new item or two in the newly created list instance and observe the look of how those items are placed in the list view.

The XSL template we defined above will render the title of the item and a link to its edit form if the user has permissions to edit items in a list. Also, if we had any other fields in our list, we could render them just like the title field, but instead we just display a hardcoded message.

Here is how my list is going to look after I add a few items into it:

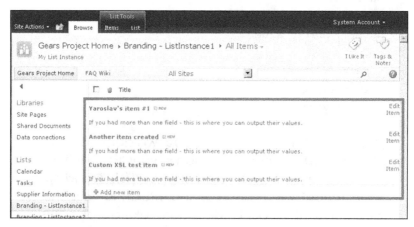

Figure 9-4 Custom list with few items in it, rendered with custom XSL

As you can see, we have completely transformed what the out-of-the-box list view looks like. Those changes are local changes only; none of the other lists' presentation will be affected. Customizations like the one above can really make a difference when you're considering changes to your user interface. The approach in this sample demonstrated how you could use extension points to make desired changes without rewriting the out-of-the-box functionality that exists in SharePoint already.

Creating custom list item detail forms

As your users work with SharePoint, they get used to the idea of creating list instances with fields in them that drive the way those list instances look. When you add a new field to your list, your field gets rendered in a predefined way, depending on the template that has been specified in SharePoint. When you create a new column in your list, you have a set of radio buttons allowing you to choose the kind of field you want to create and some basic settings around it. For example, if you choose a choice field, you can define choices available to users when they create new items. After a while your users will exhaust the list of available choices; that's when you will be asked to incorporate custom user experience elements and possibly the behavior from third-party components into list item forms. Whether its custom rendering they are after or they require some logic around when to display the field and when not, this can be achieved by creating your own list item details template. You and your back-end developers will work closely together to coordinate efforts around getting such customization brought to life.

As you have seen from working with SharePoint, there are three types of templates:

1. **New** form—used to create new items. Users can enter values into fields that get saved.
2. **Edit** form—used to edit existing items. Users can edit values in fields and save them.
3. **View** form—used when the item is viewed and all fields are in read-only mode.

By default, SharePoint implies that you're going to be using default templates for all of those forms, but you don't really have to. Let's see how you can define your own. Just as we did before with publishing pages, we need to create a content type for your items first. This is, again, something your back-end developer will do for you, but essentially the task boils down to the following steps:

1. Right click on the project name in your Visual Studio solution to add the new item of type **Content Type**; the content type will have **Item** as a parent, we'll give it a name **MyListItem**.
2. Open the **Elements.xml** file of the new content type.
3. Locate the </FieldRefs> element in the XML document; right after it, place the following code:

LISTING 9-7

```
<XmlDocuments>
<XmlDocument
NamespaceURI="http://schemas.microsoft.com/sharepoint/v3/
contenttype/forms">
```

```
<FormTemplates
    xmlns="http://schemas.microsoft.com/sharepoint/v3/
contenttype/forms">
    <Display>MyTemplate</Display>
    <Edit>MyTemplate</Edit>
    <New>MyTemplate</New>
</FormTemplates>
</XmlDocument>
</XmlDocuments>
```

Notice how there are three types of templates defined (**New**, **Edit**, and **View**), and the corresponding form value for each. We will be using the same template for each of the forms and you will see why in a moment.

4. In your Visual Studio add a new item of type **List Definition from Content Type**, when asked for the content type, pick *MyListItem*, which we created earlier. Let's call our list definition *MyCustomList*.

5. Open the *schema.xml* file of the newly created list definition and locate the *<ContentTypes>* section.

6. Replace the contents of the section inside *<ContentTypes>* with the reference below:
   <ContentTypeRef ID="ID" />
   Replace the ID value in brackets with the corresponding automatically generated ID in your content type's (*MyListItem*) *Elements.xml* file.

7. In your *Features* folder in the Visual Studio structure, you will have a feature created that will provision all of your components. Open the feature item (*Feature 1*) by double clicking on it; when the feature properties form opens, ensure *MyListItem (Branding)* is not one of the items in the feature.

8. Right click on the *Features* folder and choose to add a new feature with a default name; change its **Scope** to **Site**; add a content type definition *MyListItem (Branding)* to that feature.
   By now, you're probably wondering, what does this all have to do with modifying the look of the list item form?

Remember the **MyTemplate** we have defined in the listing above; we're about to create it and make it render the list item form in any fashion we want. SharePoint keeps its default rendering templates in the following file: *[Drive]:\ Program Files\Common Files\Microsoft Shared\Web Server Extensions\14\TEMPLATE\CONTROLTEMPLATES\ DefaultTemplates.ascx.*

We're not going to make any changes to the **DefaultTemplates. ascx** file. Any changes to that file will take effect on all of the instances in your server farm. Changing the look of all the forms is not what we want; we need to change the look of only one specific list item form. What we will do is make a copy of the default template and make a few tweaks to it to match our requirements.

1. In your Visual Studio solution structure, right click on the project name to add the following mapped folder: CONTROLTEMPLATES. It's capitalized by default in SharePoint.
2. Right click on the folder to create new item of type **User Control**. This is where our template will be defined.
3. Give the newly created template a nice name, like **MyRenderingTemplate.ascx**. The file name here doesn't make a difference as long as it is not the same as other files in *[Drive]:\Program Files\Common Files\Microsoft Shared\ Web Server Extensions\14\TEMPLATE\CONTROLTEMPLATES*
4. Ensure your **ASCX** file has the new name within its control definition just like mine here:

LISTING 9-8

```
<%@ Control Language="C#"
AutoEventWireup="true"
CodeBehind=" MyRenderingTemplate.ascx.cs"
Inherits="Chapter9.Branding.CONTROLTEMPLATES.
MyRenderingTemplate " %>
```

5. Open the default templates file ([Drive]:\Program Files\Common Files\Microsoft Shared\Web Server Extensions\14\TEMPLATE\CONTROLTEMPLATES\ DefaultTemplates.ascx) and ensure you have copied all of the SharePoint control references from the header of **DefaultTemplates.ascx** to the header section of your **MyRenderingTemplate.ascx** custom control. Your custom control **ASCX** file will look similar to this:

LISTING 9-9

```
<%@ Assembly Name="$SharePoint.Project.
AssemblyFullName$" %>
<%@ Control Language="C#" AutoEventWireup="true"
CodeBehind=" MyRenderingTemplate.ascx.cs"
Inherits="Chapter9.Branding.CONTROLTEMPLATES.
MyRenderingTemplate" %>
<%@Assembly Name="Microsoft.SharePoint, Version=14.0.0.0,
Culture=neutral, PublicKeyToken=71e9bce111e9429c" %>
<%@Register TagPrefix="SharePoint" Assembly="Microsoft.
SharePoint, Version=14.0.0.0, Culture=neutral, PublicKey
Token=71e9bce111e9429c" namespace="Microsoft.SharePoint.
WebControls"%>
<%@Register TagPrefix="ApplicationPages"
Assembly="Microsoft.SharePoint, Version=14.0.0.0,
Culture=neutral, PublicKeyToken=71e9bce111e9429c"
namespace="Microsoft.SharePoint.ApplicationPages.
WebControls"%>
<%@Register TagPrefix="SPHttpUtility"
Assembly="Microsoft.SharePoint, Version=14.0.0.0,
Culture=neutral, PublicKeyToken=71e9bce111e9429c"
namespace="Microsoft.SharePoint.Utilities"%>
<%@ Register TagPrefix="wssuc" TagName="ToolBar" src="~/_
controltemplates/ToolBar.ascx" %>
<%@ Register TagPrefix="wssuc" TagName="ToolBarButton"
src="~/_controltemplates/ToolBarButton.ascx" %>
```

6. Next, we're going to copy the SharePoint default rendering template for list items. Find the following line of code in your **DefaultTemplates.ascx**:
   <SharePoint:RenderingTemplate id="ListForm" runat="server">

7. Copy the entire content of the *ListForm* rendering template from **DefaultTemplates.ascx** to your custom **MyRenderingTemplate.ascx**.

8. Inside the **MyRenderingTemplate.ascx** replace the value of the **ID** initlally set to **ListForm** to your custom name you defined earlier in content type **MyTemplate**.

What we have now is a custom rendering template that mimics an out-of-the-box list form template with out-of-the-box controls, fields, and buttons. Almost all of the controls you see in the template are built right in the **DefaultTemplates.ascx** file, and you can explore their structure, add new items, and modify markup if necessary.

The part which renders all the fields according to their type (lookup as drop-down box, text as a text box, etc.) is this: *<SharePoint:ListFieldIterator runat="server"/>*. This declaration represents a control that will go through each of the fields in SharePoint list and display them as appropriate control in a proper state (read only, edit, new).

In our **MyRenderingTemplate .ascx**, let's add below code right before the *<SharePoint:ListFieldIterator runat="server"/>*:

<img src='/PublishingImages/Gear%20Still.PNG' />
</br>
Form fields are rendered below:

Now let's deploy our Visual Studio solution; when you open the list instance **Branding-ListInstance2** on your http://intranet. contoso.com site and try to edit, view, or create a new item, you will be presented with the message and an image you placed.

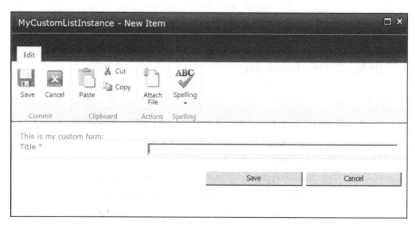

Figure 9-5 Custom List Item form with sample text added

Combining this example with some of the previous samples, this provides a technique with a significant potential. Not only you can use the technique above to modify your list item forms, your back-end developers may use this technique to modify the behavior of the controls on the form. You can help your users with the data entry into the form by supplying them with information from other sources or incorporating user interface elements into the form which are particular to your scenario and yet tied to SharePoint as a platform. In a next sample we'll take a look at how you can conditionally manage the state controls on a list form.

Conditionally displaying user interface elements in SharePoint list forms

As you can see, adding your content to the list item forms brings a lot of value to the table. One of the examples we will look at is how you can display or hide a control or markup based on the security context of currently logged-in users. As we saw with the rendering template of a list form from the last sample, SharePoint forms contain fields, and their behavior is described in a general field control know as **Composite Field**. Essentially, this field is a template that will render a control (text box, drop-down, text area) depending on the type of the field in the current mode (read, edit, new).

In some cases you may be required to display controls on the form depending on a given condition. For example, a condition can be a cascading option of a parent item. We looked at how this can be achieved earlier with one of the free community extension. Another condition can be dependent on a more complex situation; for example, on a context of a currently logged-in user.

Let's see how we can control the state of the field based on a group of which currently logged-in user belongs to.

This task is considered more of an advanced user experience development, and techniques here can be used by both advanced user experience developers and back-end developers.

Let's go ahead and extend the behavior of the current **Composite Field** to also render the field if the current user has required permissions to see it.

We will start by creating a custom control based on **Composite Field** in our Visual Studio solution structure.

1. Right click on the Visual Studio solution structure and add new folder to it called **Controls**.
2. In your newly created folder, right click to **Add -> Class**.
3. Let's call the class *SecurityAwareCompositeField*.
4. Add the following namespace references to your class by using references folder in the Visual Studio solution structure:
    - *using Microsoft.SharePoint.WebControls.*
    - *using Microsoft.SharePoint;.*
5. Replace the class definition with the following code:

LISTING 9-10

```
public class SecurityAwareCompositeField :
CompositeField
{
public string RequiredGroup
{ get; set; }
```

```
protected override void CreateChildControls()
{
base.CreateChildControls();
int groupID = SPContext.Current.Web.
Groups[RequiredGroup].ID;
if (SPContext.Current.Web.IsCurrentUserMemberOfGroup(gr
oupID))
{
    base.Visible = true;
}
else
{
    base.Visible = false;
}
}}
```

Above, we get a hold of the group that will be passed in our rendering template and determine whether the current user belongs to the group. If a user doesn't belong to the group, we hide the new control; otherwise, we show it.

6. Now, we'll add the reference to our new control from the rendering template you created earlier called **MyRenderingTemplate.ascx**. Add the following item to the header of your rendering template:

LISTING 9-11

```
<%@ Register TagPrefix="mycontrols"
Assembly="Chapter9.Branding, Version=1.0.0.0,
Culture=neutral, PublicKeyToken=2652984327752174"
Namespace="Chapter9.Branding.Controls" %>
```

Here **mycontrols** is an arbitrary name and assembly name, and the rest of the assembly information is taken from *[Drive]:\windows\assembly*, the properties of your assembly.

7. Add the instance of your custom control to the rendering
    template replacing the *<SharePoint:ListFieldIterator
    runat="server"/>*.

LISTING 9-12

```
<tr>
<mycontrols:SecurityAwareCompositeField ID="TitleField"
RequiredGroup="Viewers" runat="server"
FieldName="Title" />
</tr>
```

By replacing the field control iterator, you set your own logic for
iterating your fields. Here, we create an instance of the control
and assign it to use the **Title** field, and our **Required Group**
is **Viewers**, meaning that whoever does not belong to the
Viewers SharePoint security group will not see the title control,
even if you have the site collection administrator logged in.

Your user control will end up with the following rendering
template code:

LISTING 9-13

```
<SharePoint:RenderingTemplate id="MyTemplate"
runat="server">
<Template>
<span id='part1'>
<SharePoint:InformationBar runat="server"/>
<div id="listFormToolBarTop">
<wssuc:ToolBar CssClass="ms-formtoolbar"
id="toolBarTbltop" RightButtonSeparator=" "
runat="server">
<Template_RightButtons>
<SharePoint:NextPageButton runat="server"/>
<SharePoint:SaveButton runat="server"/>
```

```
<SharePoint:GoBackButton runat="server"/>
</Template_RightButtons>
</wssuc:ToolBar>
</div>
<SharePoint:FormToolBar runat="server"/>
<SharePoint:ItemValidationFailedMessage runat="server"/>
<table class="ms-formtable" border="0" width="100%">
<SharePoint:ChangeContentType runat="server"/>
<SharePoint:FolderFormFields runat="server"/>
<tr>
<mycontrols:SecurityAwareCompositeField ID="TitleField"
RequiredGroup="Viewers" runat="server"
FieldName="Title" />
</tr>
This is my custom form:
<SharePoint:ApprovalStatus runat="server"/>
<SharePoint:FormComponent TemplateName="AttachmentRows"
runat="server"/>
</table>
<table cellpadding="0" cellspacing="0" width="100%">
<tr><td class="ms-formline">
<img src="/_layouts/images/blank.gif" width='1'
height='1' alt="" /></td></tr>
</table>
<table cellpadding="0" cellspacing="0" width="100%"
style="padding-top: 7px"><tr><td width="100%">
<SharePoint:ItemHiddenVersion runat="server"/>
<SharePoint:ParentInformationField runat="server"/>
<SharePoint:InitContentType runat="server"/>
<wssuc:ToolBar CssClass="ms-formtoolbar" id="toolBarTbl"
RightButtonSeparator=" " runat="server">
<Template_Buttons>
<SharePoint:CreatedModifiedInfo runat="server"/>
</Template_Buttons>
<Template_RightButtons>
<SharePoint:SaveButton runat="server"/>
<SharePoint:GoBackButton runat="server"/>
</Template_RightButtons>
</wssuc:ToolBar>
```

```
</td></tr></table>
</span>
<SharePoint:AttachmentUpload runat="server"/>
</Template>
</SharePoint:RenderingTemplate>
```

To test the logic, **deploy** your solution with Visual Studio and navigate to the list instance based on a custom content type we used in last sample. When you choose to add a new item, you will see that no fields are rendered, though there is only one anyway. Add your username to the **Viewers** group on a portal.

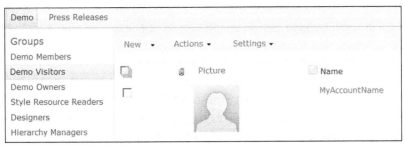

Figure 9-6 Account name added to the group required by the security aware field

Now, when you try adding a new item, you will be recognized as a valid user by the control and the field will be rendered.

Important part to remember is that since we have removed the list field iterator control, we are now responsible for rendering all of our fields manually and new fields added to the list will not be rendered automatically. In your scenario you would probably want to add your custom logic below the iterator control rather than replacing it. This way you get your fields rendered automatically and then custom logic or controls rendered right after.

This simple example shows that it's pretty easy to define your custom look and feel on item detail forms, and you can piggyback on SharePoint list forms to implement your custom and complex functionality.

Dynamically changing SharePoint 2010 list form rendering templates

If you've noticed, every time we performed the replacement of our rendering template of a list, it resulted in solution deployment and complete loss of any test data we had in the list. It's not a problem when it happens in your development environment, but what if you want to implement a new rendering template on a production environment? Fortunately, there is a solution where you can assign a new rendering template, providing it has been deployed to the server file system before ([Drive]:\Program Files\ Common Files\Microsoft Shared\Web Server Extensions\14\ TEMPLATE\CONTROLTEMPLATES\DefaultTemplates.ascx). Having a rendering template on a server is as simple as copying it to the **ControlTemplates** folder.

In this example, we will be using SharePoint Designer 2010, which you already used in past examples and have installed on the virtual machine image. You're not required to have SharePoint Designer installed on the server computer; you need to have sufficient permissions to access your server from SharePoint Designer installed on a client computer. You also must have sufficient username and password credentials to edit your site—we will be using **contoso\administrator** as a username for editing the site with SharePoint Designer.

Here is how to assign the template to your custom list.

1. Open SharePoint Designer and open the URL of the site where your target list instance is located.
2. Once the site is open, on the right hand side of the SharePoint Designer navigation, select **Lists and Libraries**.
3. Select the list that you would like to change the rendering template for; the list information page will open in the main window.
4. Locate the **Forms** section in the main area of the SharePoint Designer and click on the name of the form for which you would like to change the rendering template. If you like

to change it for all **New/View/Edit** forms, you will have to perform a switch on each form individually.

5. SharePoint Designer will load the selected view and the item detail view that is currently used. At the bottom of SharePoint Designer window, locate three display options: **Design**, **Split**, and **Code**. Click the **Split** option.

6. SharePoint Designer will split the screen, part of it being code and part of it being a user interface with your form. Click anywhere on the form view that is currently used.

7. In the code view, you will see a part of the code highlighted; that's the area that represents the current list view form. Scroll down to the bottom of the highlighted code until you locate the **TemplateName** node.

8. The default value of the **TemplateName** is **ListForm**. Replace the **ListForm** with the rendering template name that you provisioned earlier to the **ControlTemplates** folder.

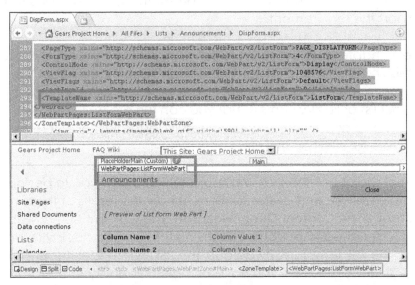

Figure 9-7 Switching the list view template to another template in SharePoint Designer

9. This concludes the switch. Save your changed form in SharePoint Designer. The form will be swapped for everyone else using it after you save it.

Now you can repeat the steps starting with Step 4 to make changes to the remaining forms if required.

Branding aggregated content within lists and rollups

As previously mentioned, SharePoint lists are used to build many out-of-the-box and custom features in SharePoint. One of the most common tasks developers are asked on nearly every SharePoint project is to roll up data stored in one list on a dashboard of the main site, or aggregate content from multiple lists on the site and display it in a custom view on a home page of the portal. Since all of the list information in SharePoint is stored as database records, SharePoint natively supports rollup operations, and those remain very popular requests among users. In fact, those are so popular that SharePoint comes with several out-of-the-box web parts that support this requirement.

A few chapter ago, when we created individual content types for publishing pages and list items, this wasn't just to make your life difficult; one of the advantages of having a custom content type for your list or library items is that you can run site-wide queries against the content type and get results regardless of where the items are located on the site.

One of the out-of-the-box web parts which allows you to perform complex rollups and customizations of how the results of those roll ups look is the **Content Query web part**. The Content Query web part is designed to perform queries on the site and display results using the XSL template. By default, the XSLT will render items with links to them; however, you have complete flexibility to customize the look and feel of the result set.

Let's take a look at what is involved in setting up a rollup with the Content Query web part:

1. Navigate to your publishing site, in our case www.contoso. com, and click **Site Actions -> Edit Page**.

2. Locate the *Header* web part zone and click **Add a Web Part**. From the ribbon **Categories** select **Content Rollup** and same for the **Web Part**. Click **Add**.

3. Click on **open tool pane** to configure the web part. In the properties of the web part, you will see quite a few options allowing you to configure various aspects of the web part query and presentation. Most of them are clear to many advanced users and definitely developers.

4. Open the **Query** category under **Content Query Tool Part** to ensure **Pages Library** is selected for the **List Type**. This is the list which our items will be queried from. As you can see, there are a few other options related to item filtering and other grouping options. All of those options are driven by the XSL template we're about to take a look at in a moment.

5. Under **Presentation** group, check out the **Fields** to display. Those are fields that will be rendered on the page for the **Pages** type of item. Click **OK** on the web part properties. When the page reloads, you should see few of the pages rolled up in the web part; if not, feel free to create a page or two using the **Site Actions** -> **New Page** command.

Before changing the look and feel of the default view of the rollup, let's see what is out there in out-of-the-box options:

1. From the publishing site, click **Site Actions** -> **View All Site Content**.

2. Click **Style Library** under Libraries, then open **XSL Style Sheets** folder. Among others, there are three style sheets related to Content Query web part:

ContentQueryMain.xsl—logic with calls to the **Header** and **Item** templates for each item, those also help user interface developers to modify the **Item** and **Header** XSLT transforms.

ItemStyle.xsl—templates defining how to display an item by receiving and processing one row at a time. Some of the templates included (as described on technet http://msdn. microsoft.com/en-us/library/bb447557.aspx):

Default
LinkImage is on the left.
LinkTitle is at the top.
Description is below.

NoImage
LinkTitle is at the top.
Description is below.

TitleOnly
Item contains only the LinkTitle.

Bullets
Item contains the LinkTitle pre-pended by a bullet.

ImageRight
LinkImage is on the right.
LinkTitle is at the top.
Description is below.

ImageTop
LinkImage is above.
LinkTitle is in the middle.
Description is below.

ImageTopCentered
LinkImage is above and centered.

LinkTitle is in the middle.
Description is below.

LargeTitle
LinkImage is on the left.
LargeLinkTitle is at the top.
Description is below.

ClickableImage
Contains only the LinkImage.

NotClickableImage
Contains only Image, without a link.

FixedImageSize
LinkImage with a size constraint on the left.
LinkTitle is at the top.
Description is below.

TitleWithBackground
Contains the LinkTitle with a background color

Header.xsl—templates that manage the display of a header.

Here are few of the out-of-the-box templates:

DefaultHeader
Displays the Group Header in medium font size.

LargeText
Displays the Group Header in large font size.

SmallText
Displays the Group Header in small font size.

Band
Displays the Group Header with a squared background color.

Centered
Centers the Group Header.

Separator
Inserts a line between the Group Header and content below.

Whitespace
Inserts white space between the Group Header and content below.

Let's download the *ItemStyle.XSL* from **XSL Style Sheets** and open it in Visual Studio to make some changes. The reason why we're using Visual Studio to edit this XSL is to take advantage of the editing capabilities, including the ability to collapse the outlining of the XSLT to see its high level structure. To collapse the tree of the XSL use **CTRL+M+L** shortcut.

1. Locate the following *XSL:Template* below:
   <xsl:template name="Default" match="*" mode="itemstyle">.
2. Since it's already collapsed, copy the entire contents of the above *XSL:Template* and paste them below the definition so both templates are siblings.
3. Rename the header part of the copied template to something like this, in my case:
   <xsl:template name="YaroslavsTemplate" match="Row[@Style='YaroslavsTemplate']" mode="itemstyle">.
4. Before we start modifying the template, let's see how this newly added template will show in the Content Query web part on our site. First, go back to the **XSL Style Sheets** folder and upload the newly edited instance of *ItemStyle.XSL*.
5. Overwrite the existing file and ensure you also publish the file by using **Publish a Major Version** command from the context menu of the item.
6. Then navigate back to the Content Query web part properties on your home page, and access the web part properties by editing the page.
7. You will see the new template name showing up as an option in the **web part properties** -> **Presentation** -> **Styles** -> **Item Style** drop-down. See how there are also few text boxes under the group of **Fields to display**? We'll add a new one as a parameter for our template to consume it in our XSL.
8. In your <xsl:template name="YaroslavsTemplate" match="Row[@Style='YaroslavsTemplate']" mode="itemstyle"> right under <xsl:variable name="DisplayTitle">...</xsl:variable> add the following code:

LISTING 9-14

```
<xsl:variable name="PageBody">
<xsl:call-template name="cleanupHtml">
<xsl:with-param name="string" select="@
PublishingPageContent"/>
</xsl:call-template>
</xsl:variable>
```

The above code will declare a new variable which will be populated each time the new item is constructed (since this XSL gets called for each item rendered). The variable will access the **PublishingPageContent** field of the item, which is the page in our case. **PublishingPageContent** is the page's actual content for publishing pages. We also call *cleanupHtml* template we're about to declare which will remove HTML markup from the **PublishingPageContent** field.

9. Right below our *<xsl:template name="YaroslavsTemplate" match="Row[@Style='YaroslavsTemplate']" mode="itemstyle">...</xsl:template>*
    We'll define *cleanupHtml* template as below:

LISTING 9-15

```
<xsl:template name="cleanupHtml">
<xsl:param name="string" />
<xsl:choose>
<xsl:when test="contains($string, '&lt;')">
<xsl:variable name="nextString">
<xsl:call-template name="cleanupHtml">
<xsl:with-param name="string" select="substring-
after($string, '&gt;')" />
</xsl:call-template>
</xsl:variable>
<xsl:value-of select="concat(substring-before($string,
'&lt;'), $nextString)" />
</xsl:when>
```

```
<xsl:otherwise>
<xsl:value-of select="$string" />
</xsl:otherwise>
</xsl:choose>
</xsl:template>
```

Here, we just iterate through the HTML and remove the encoded characters.

10. The final task is to render the result on the page. The rendering is done within
    <div class="item">...</div>.
    Locate the *<div class="description">...</div>*.
    Copy its contents and paste it right under the original declaration. Inside the copied markup, replace the value within *<div class="description">...</div>* as below:

LISTING 9-16

```
<xsl:value-of select="substring($PageBody,1,50)"/>
(<a href="{$SafeLinkUrl}"
mce_href="{$SafeLinkUrl}"
target="_blank"
title="{@LinkToolTip}">Read more ...
</a>)
```

The code above will call the link to the page but only will display first fifty characters and link to *Read more*.

11. Now, it's time to test. Go back to the **XSL Style Sheets** folder, and upload the newly edited instance of *ItemStyle.XSL*.

12. Overwrite the existing file and ensure you also publish the file by using **Publish a Major Version** command from the context menu of the item. Then navigate back to the Content Query web part properties on your home page, and access the web part properties.

13. Since we already have our new template name showing up as an option in **web part properties** -> **Presentation** -> **Styles** -> **Item Style** drop-down, all we need to do is, under **Fields to display** -> **PublishingPageContent** enter the value *PublishingPageContent*. Then, click OK.

If you have content within your publishing pages, and if it exceeds our limit of fifty, you will see the first fifty only and the *Read more* link to the page. Try it out.

Also, if you're wondering how I found the name of the field **PublishingPageContent**, here is how to track such field names down:

1. On your site, under **Site Actions** -> **Site Settings** -> **Site Content types** -> under **Page Layout Content Types** ->, click **Article Page**.
2. Here, under **Columns**, you will find **Page Content**. Click on this field.
3. Since we need to get the internal name of the field, we'll extract it from the query string parameter of the page as a **Field** parameter. In our case it's *PublishingPageContent*. Yes, this is not very straighforward—but SharePoint allows display names to be different from internal names, and one of the easiest ways to find out the internal name is using the method we used here.
   The main goal of this chapter was to demonstrate how to modify and enhance the look and feel of the ou-of-the-box user interface elements in lists, forms, rollups etc. Lots of those deal with XSL which can initially be a barrier. The key to keep in mind is that by modifying the XSL of some of the components above you are able to achieve the presentation goal in your solution without building out the back-end functionality in custom controls, which already exists in SharePoint.

CHAPTER 10

Client-Side Interaction with External and Local Web Services

When adding interaction to your solution, you will encounter cases where you need to call external or internal web services and return data from the call to the client side UI. An example of such an application can be a text box which allows users to search within SharePoint lists and autocomplete their search query with a list of options. This will be an example where your developers will set up a search mechanism as a local SharePoint web service and you will interact with it on a client side. Another example of using SharePoint out-of-the-box web services can be a requirement where users must be able to interact with your custom UI based on the data stored in a list item. An example of external web service call can be a call to an external system where your custom client UI will fetch the data and render it in your SharePoint solution.

As we're going through each of the scenarios, I will point you to some of the open source components available for download which will come quite handy. From there you can decide whether to take the open source component further and either extend it or use it to get started with a new concept.

Working with external SharePoint 2010 web service calls

Since SharePoint is commonly used on the intranet, which is now believed to be a users' desktop – quite often you will be asked to integrate external dynamic data onto the page. Let's take a look at how you can use a custom Visual Web Part to integrate something simple and something that everyone can try - a twitter status updates into your SharePoint page.

1. Create a new Visual Studio project of **Visual Web Part** template, specify the debug URL to be www.contoso.com.
2. Right click project name to **Add -> SharePoint "Layouts" Mapped Folder.** This folder is a globally accessible virtual folder which is going to be relative to the site where we deployed the solution. Files and folders placed within the **Layouts** folder are accessible with the following URL: www.contoso.com/_layouts/[foldername]/[filename]. There the *[foldername]* is usually the name of the project.
3. Download a JQuery library which will be used by one of the open source components here. There are few sources you can download the JQuery from. Here is one of them: http://ajax.microsoft.com/ajax/jquery/jquery-1.3.2.min.js.
4. Add downloaded JQuery file to the mapped **Layouts** folder.
5. Now, let's switch to our custom Visual Web Part. If you have accepted the default name **VisualWebPart1**, double click on the Visual Web Part work item to open the design view of the Visual Web Part. Essentially it's an ASP.NET user control which will be compiled and run as a web part. Place the following HTML into the web part, right after :
    <%@ Control Language="C#" AutoEventWireup="true" CodeBehind="VisualWebPart1UserControl.ascx.cs" Inherits="SharePointProject1.VisualWebPart1.VisualWebPart1UserControl" %>.

LISTING 10-1

```
<script src="http://ajax.microsoft.com/ajax/jquery/
jquery-1.3.2.min.js" type="text/javascript"></script>
<script src="/_layouts/SharePointProject1/tweet.js"
type="text/javascript"></script>
<style type="text/css">
body {
font: 12px Arial;
color: #555;
}
.progress {
background:
url('http://www.contoso.com/_layouts/images/PROGRESS-
CIRCLE-24.gif')
no-repeat;
}
</style>
<div id="tweet">
<div class="progress"></div>
</div>
```

Above, we're performing a basic setup, defining a few areas where our tweets are going to appear as well as referencing **progress** image to load JQuery library. We also reference our main **tweet.js** file, which is responsible for calling the Twitter web service and getting a hold of the JSON object representing our tweets. This object is then being iterated through, and each tweet is being extracted. Results appear in **tweet** DIV.

6. Let's add the **tweet.js**. Expand the **Layouts** mapped folder from the solution structure and right click on the **SharePointProject1** (if you kept the project name as default) to **Add** -> **New Item....**

7. Pick **Web** from the installed templates on the left side and select **JScript** file.
8. Give it the file name **tweet.js** and add it to the solution, then add the following code to the body of the newly created file:

LISTING 10-2

```
function twitterCallback2(twitters) {
var statusList = [];
for (var i=0; i<twitters.length; i++){
var twittername = twitters[i].user.screen_name;
var status = twitters[i].text;
statusList.push('<p>&ldquo;'+status+'&rdquo;</p>');
}

$('.progress').fadeOut(750, function() {
$('#tweet').append($(statusList.join('')).hide().
fadeIn(750));
});
}

$(document).ready(function() {
var twittername = 'spentsarsky';
$.getScript('http://twitter.com/statuses/user_timeline/'
+ twittername + '.json?callback=twitterCallback2&cou
nt=10');
});
```

Above, the highlighted piece of code shows the call to the Twitter service, where I pass my username. The function which is going to handle processing of results, **twitterResult**, does extracting of the tweet and adding it to the DIV in our web part. The number of items displayed is going to be ten as we specified in the parameter call in the Twitter service. When our results are ready to be displayed, the progress graphic is going to fade away and results will appear on the screen.

9. Hit F5 to **deploy** your solution with Visual Studio; this will create a **SharePointProject1** folder in the **Layouts** mapped folder with the **tweet.js** file in it. Also, the web part user control will be copied to the CONTROLTEMPLATES folder (*C:\Program Files\Common Files\Microsoft Shared\Web Server Extensions\14\TEMPLATE\CONTROLTEMPLATES\ SharePointProject1\VisualWebPart1*). The user control in this location will have your custom HTML added.

10. Once deployment is complete, the site home page will open.

11. Edit the page: **Site Actions** -> **Edit Page**. Scroll down to the page and click **Add a Web Part**. From the area below the ribbon, select **Custom** as a category and **VisualWebPart1** as a web part, and click **Add**.

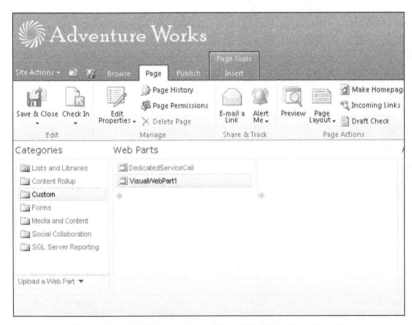

Figure 10-1 Adding custom VisualWebPart1 to the site

12. Save the page and you will see how items from your Twitter feed will display in the web part.

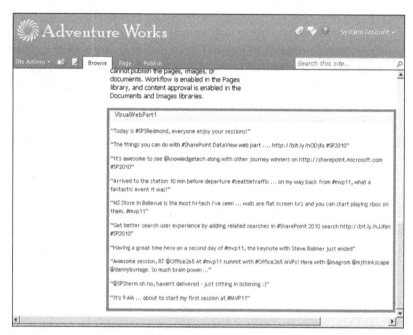

Figure 10-2 Twitter feed web part added to the site

Whether you are actually going to make the twitter timeline available on your intranet or you will apply the technique above to communicate with another external web service, the steps here will come quite handy and applicable across variety of the integration scenarios. Next, let's take a look at what's involved in executing SharePoint internal web service calls and rendering dynamic UI based on the results.

Working with internal SharePoint 2010 web service calls

As you're working with SharePoint, you will notice users often asking you to bring functionality they see on the web to SharePoint. This usually involves manipulating data on the site visually, re-arranging and re-sorting items in lists and libraries on the fly and other UI functionality not currently available in SharePoint out-of-the-box. When working with SharePoint lists in your client UI, you will make use of SharePoint ListData Service. ListData Service is an out-of-the-box service allowing you to list any lists available on the current web and access items within those lists using web service calls. The service is hosted in SharePoint and performs behind-the-scenes operations in the context of the current user. Let's take a look at how we can query items in the list using the service and a simple web part.

1. Navigate to http://intranet.contoso.com as administrator and ensureyou're using an existing instance of the site.
2. Let's create a custom list in this site. Click **Site Actions** -> **More Options** -> and select **Custom List** option ->, then provide the name of the list and create it.
3. Add a few items to the newly created list.
4. Let's now use ListData Service to see the list we created. In your browser navigate to: http://intranet.contoso.com/_vti_bin/ListData.svc/.
   You should see the XML listing available lists and libraries on the site:

LISTING 10-3

```xml
<?xml version="1.0" encoding="utf-8" standalone="yes" ?>
<service xml:base="http://www.contoso.com/_vti_bin/
listdata.svc/" xmlns:atom="http://www.w3.org/2005/Atom"
xmlns:app="http://www.w3.org/2007/app" xmlns="http://www.
w3.org/2007/app">
<workspace>
<atom:title>Default</atom:title>
<collection href="Attachments">
<atom:title>Attachments</atom:title>
</collection>
<collection href="CacheProfiles">
<atom:title>CacheProfiles</atom:title>
</collection>
...
</collection>
</workspace>
</service>
```

5. Now, let's target the list we have just created by calling the following URL: http://intranet.contoso.com/_vti_bin/ListData.svc/NewList. This will return an XML with SharePoint item properties, and if you're using IE it will appears as an RSS feed.

Now, let's see how we can create a custom web part in Visual Studio and implement our client-side logic in it.

1. Create a new Visual Studio project of **Visual Web Part** template; specify the debug URL to be intranet.contoso.com.

2. Since we will be using JQuery in our client-side script, if you haven't already, download the latest version of JQuery from here (or another reliable source): http://ajax.microsoft.com/ajax/jquery/jquery-1.3.2.min.js.

3. Right click project name to **Add -> SharePoint "Layouts" Mapped Folder.**

4. Now, let's switch to our custom Visual Web Part.If you have accepted the default name *VisualWebPart1*, double click on the Visual WebPart work item to open the design view of the Visual Web Part.
   Place the following HTML into the web part, right after :
   <%@ Control Language="C#" AutoEventWireup="true" CodeBehind="VisualWebPart1UserControl.ascx.cs" Inherits="SharePointProject1.VisualWebPart1.VisualWebPart1UserControl" %>.

LISTING 10-4

```
<script src="/_layouts/SharePointProject1/jquery-
1.3.2.min.js"
type="text/javascript">
</script>
<script type="text/javascript">
$(document).ready(function() {
$.getJSON("/_vti_bin/ListData.svc/
Calendar",function(data) {
var count = 0;
```

```
$.each(data.d.results, function(i,result) {
var title = result.Title;
html = "<table><tr><td>" + title +"</td></tr></table>";
$('#resultarea').append($(html));
});
});
});
</script>
<div id="resultarea">
</div>
```

The highlighted code parts are the relative location of the JQuery and then a call to a SharePoint ListData Service. We then get a hold of the JSON object returned and iterate through each of the items, extracting the title of the item. We then output the result into a **resultarea**.

The best part is that this code will be able to retrieve list data from external URLs (some external online site running SharePoint) if you have access to the list on that external URL. To test, you could point the ListData Service URL to the calendar list of the http://intranet.contoso.com like this: *http://intranet.contoso.com/_vti_bin/ListData.svc/Calendar* and if there was data in the calendar list, you would receive results, too.

5. Hit F5 to **deploy** your solution with Visual Studio. During this deployment, the **SharePointProject1** folder will be created in mapped **Layouts** folder with the JQuery file in it.
6. Once deployment is complete, the site home page will open.
7. Edit the page: **Site Actions -> Edit Page**. Scroll down to the page and click **Add a Web Part**, from the area below the ribbon select **Custom** as a Category and **VisualWebPart1** as a web part and click **Add**.
8. Save the page and you will see how items from your custom list are displayed in the web part.

Figure 10-3 Extracting items from local Calendar list using web service call

As you can see, we work quite a lot with JQuery in our solution. You might be thinking, why can't we use Silverlight in our solution to get even better interaction? The answer is—it depends. In some cases, using client-side JQuery might be more feasible in situations where you need to extend an existing solution without doing heavy deployment and scheduling a down time for it. The next example will illustrate a situation just like that.

Using JQuery and additional extensions to enhance interaction of SharePoint forms

As mentioned in the last example, sometimes we can't afford to make complex changes to an existing system due to solution complexity or down time associated with deployment of our customizations. Another case—you're using cloud hosted SharePoint and have no permission to deploy custom code. In this example, I would like to show you we can enhance functionality on any SharePoint out-of-the-box form to add functionalitywhich is not available by default. This type of customization will require nothing but some JavaScript in your solution.

We'll take a look at how we can make such a change just by using SharePoint UI, and then we'll quickly touch on how customization like this can be deployed to the server using a deployment script.

Let's open our http://intranet.contoso.com; there is no difference whether we're using the collaboration or publishing site template when it comes to this customization. Let's open the Team Discussions list from the quick launch on the left. When you click the **Add new discussion** link, we get a form which allows us to add a new discussion topic. Let's enhance this functionality so that the new discussion **Subject** line will autocomplete from the **Title** in the **Announcememts** list also located in this site.

1. While in the Team Discussions list (http://intranet.contoso. com/Lists/Team Discussion/AllItems.aspx), replace the last part of the URL containing **AllItems.aspx** with **NewForm. aspx**. This is the page you have seen in the modal dialog to add new discussion, but in the modal dialog view we can not modify the page and add new web parts, which is why we open the page directly.
2. Click **Site Actions** -> **Edit Page** to edit the New Discussion page.
3. In the **Main** web part zone, click **Add a Web Part**.
4. Below the ribbon, you will see choices for web parts; pick **Media and Content** as a **Category** and **Content Editor** as a web part.
5. Click **Add**. The web part we added will contain content we'll enter in it. In our case we'll add JavaScript to it, which will manipulate the form below.
6. When the Content Editor is added to the page, click **Click here to add new content**. Then, from the ribbon, under

Markup group, pick the **HTML** flyout and select **Edit HTML source**.

7. The modal will open for you to edit the source of the web part. Enter the following **HTML**:

LISTING 10-5

```
<script language="javascript"
src="/SiteAssets/jquery-1.3.2.min.js"
type="text/javascript"></script>

<script language="javascript"
src="/SiteAssets/jquery.SPServices-0.5.8.min.js"
type="text/javascript"></script>

<script language="javascript">
$(document).ready(function() {
$().SPServices.SPAutocomplete({
sourceList: "Announcements",
sourceColumn: "Title",
columnName: "Subject",
ignoreCase: true,
numChars: 3,
slideDownSpeed: 100,
debug: true
});
});
</script>
```

Above we reference the JQuery library and community JQuery extension for SharePoint, which I will explain how to download in a moment. Then we call one of the methods in the community extension, which connects to the **Announcements** list and uses the **Title** of the announcement to allow autocomplete of the **Subject** column in our Team Disucssion form.

8. Click OK and, on the ribbon **Page** tab, click **Stop Editing**.
9. Let's add all of the referenced libraries.

jquery-1.4.2.min.js—can be downloaded from here: http:// code.jquery.com/jquery-1.4.2.min.js . Alternatively you can search for the file name and you will get one of the versions widely available for download. Keep in mind that the version you might be downloading now might be higher than the version available when this book was written. *jquery.SPServices-0.5.8P1.min.js*—can be downloaded from here: http://spservices.codeplex.com/SourceControl/list/ changesets

Open the archive and extract the necessary file to disc.

10. Once you have both JavaScript files. Upload them both to the **Site Assets** library on the Contoso intranet site (http:// intranet.contoso.com/SiteAssets/Forms/AllItems.aspx).
11. Now, that all of the components are in place, let's test the functionality. Open the Team Discussions library and click **Add new discussion**.
12. Start typing the **Subject** of the discussion, and after three letters you will get an autocomplete suggestion for the item which exists in the announcements library.

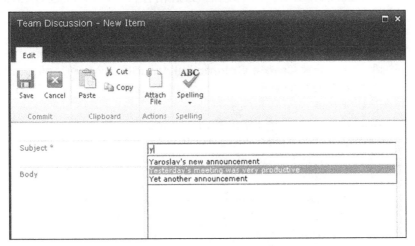

Figure 10-4 Autocomplete for Discussion list based on items from the Announcements list

This is all that's required to enhance your new form. Keep in mind that the **New Item Form,** although it looks similar to the **Edit Item Form**, is not the same instance. If you want the same functionality when users are editing the form, you will need to add Content Editor web part with all of the JavaScript to the Edit Form here: http://intranet.contoso.com/Lists/Team Discussion/ EditForm.aspx.

Let's take a look at another example of leveraging JQuery on your list item form to enhance interaction between the user interface— **cascading drop-downs**.

The requirement around cascading drop-down is quite simple. You have two lists: the main list (parent) and supporting list (child). The main list contains two drop-down boxes; the value of the second drop-down box will depend on what choice was made in the first box.

Let's set up an example using our Team Discussion list at http:// intranet.contoso.com/.

1. Create a new **Custom List**. Click **Site Actions -> More options ->**. Pick **List** from **Categories** and **Custom List** from the list of available templates.
2. Give your custom list the name **Categories**.
3. Open the Categories list and from the **List Settings** on the ribbon, click **Create Column** link to add another column to the list. We'll give it the name *SubCategory* and set **Single line of text** as the type.
4. Add the following three items to the list:
   Title: *Choice 1 SubCategory: Sub 1*
   Title: *Choice 1 SubCategory: Sub 2*
   Title: *Choice 2 SubCategory: Sub 1*
5. Now let's go back tour **Team Discussion** and access list settings from the ribbon. Click the **Create Column** link to add another few columns to the list just like we did with **Categories**.
6. Give the first column the name *Category* with the type **Lookup**. For **Get information from** select **Categories**. For **In this column** leave **Title**. For **Add a column to show each of these additional fields** pick **Title** and **SubCategory**. Leave other options as default and click OK to add this column.

7. Now, let's add another column. Give the column the name *SubCategory* with the type **Lookup**. For **Get information from** select **Categories**. For **In this column** leave **SubCategory**. For **Add a column to show each of these additional fields** pick **Title** and **SubCategory**. Leave other options as default and click OK to add the second column.

8. Navigate to the New Item form just like we did before by accessing it using direct URL: http://intranet.contoso.com/Lists/Team Discussion/ NewForm.aspx.

9. Click **Site Actions** -> **Edit Page**. The Content Editor should be already there. Click the editing area in the content editor. Then, from the ribbon, under **Markup** group, pick the **HTML** flyout and select **Edit HTML source**.

10. In the modal enter the following **HTML**:

LISTING 10-6

```
<script language="javascript" type="text/javascript"
src="/SiteAssets/jquery-1.4.2.min.js">
</script>

<script language="javascript" type="text/javascript"
src="/SiteAssets/jquery.SPServices-0.5.8P1.min.js"></
script>

<script language="javascript" type="text/javascript">
$(document).ready(function() {
$().SPServices.SPCascadeDropdowns({
relationshipList: "Categories",
relationshipListParentColumn: "Title",
relationshipListChildColumn: "SubCategory",
parentColumn: "Category",
childColumn: "SubCategory",
debug: true
});
});
</script>
```

Just like in the last example, we reference JQuery library and community JQuery extension for SharePoint. Then we call one of the methods in the community extension, which will connect to the **Categories** list and extract our subcategories based on the selection on the form from the parent category.

11. Save the JavaScript code and test the functionality by opening the **Team Discussions** library and clicking **Add new discussion**. When you pick main categories, the choices for subcategories will change based on the values you provided in the **Categories** list.

I encourage you to take a look at other functions available in this open source projects at http://spservices.codeplex.com/. Functionality often requested by users is implemented in the SPServices project using techniques we looked at here, which dramatically reduce complexities related to modifying SharePoint user interface functionality.

Also, this type of customization is ad-hoc since we're modifying the page directly and not retaining the previous version, and typically in your business you want to keep track of changes to page instances. This can cause complexities during SharePoint upgrade in the future and tracing back problems with site functionality when they start occurring.

As you noticed, we uploaded our JQuery library and extension files to the document library on a SharePoint site. If you wanted to allow another site to use the same functionality, you might need to duplicate files, which is also not the best approach.

The recommended approach for both cases above is to deploy your changes as a Visual Studio solution so it sits in the solution store. This way administrators or site collection owners are aware of the customization and can enhance it in the feature. Your JavaScript files are best to be deployed into a centralized location on a site, unless you're deploying in a cloud hosted scenario—then you can't store files in a virtual directory on a file system.

Let's see how we can leverage Visual Studio to deploy one of the customizations from above:

1. Create a new Visual Studio 2010 Empty SharePoint project, and set the project to be deployed as a **sandbox solution** with http://inranet.contoso.com as a debug URL.
2. Right click on the solution name to **Add** -> **New Item**.... From the SharePoint 2010 category of installed templates, pick **Module** and give it the name *JSResources*.
3. Delete the *Sample.txt* file and add our existing *jquery-1.4.2.min.js* and *jquery.SPServices-0.5.8P1.min.js*.
4. We're also going to keep the JavaScript code of the autocomplete example from *listing 10-5*, which actually performs calls, in a separate file called *AutoComplete.js*. This will allow us to reference it more easily further down the road.

   Add new *AutoComplete.js* to the *JSResources* module and add the following code to it:

LISTING 10-7

```
$(document).ready(function() {
$().SPServices.SPAutocomplete({
sourceList: "Announcements",
sourceColumn: "Title",
columnName: "Subject",
ignoreCase: true,
numChars: 3,
slideDownSpeed: 100,
debug: true
});
});
```

5. Add the following XML to the *Elements.xml* located in the *JSResource* module:

LISTING 10-8

```xml
<?xml version="1.0" encoding="utf-8"?>
<Elements xmlns="http://schemas.microsoft.com/
sharepoint/">
<Module Name="JSResources" Url="SiteAssets">

<File Path="JSResources\jquery-1.3.2.min.js"
Type="GhostableInLibrary" Url="jquery-1.3.2.min.js" />

<File Path="JSResources\jquery.SPServices-0.5.8.min.js"
Type="GhostableInLibrary" Url="jquery.SPServices-
0.5.8.min.js" />

<File Path="JSResources\AutoComplete.js"
Type="GhostableInLibrary" Url="AutoComplete.js" />

</Module>
</Elements>
```

This part will provision all files into the Site Asset library.

Now, from here you can go a few ways. In essence, you need to ensure the JavaScript is emitted to the page when
you need it. We can inject it right to the Masterpage if it's required for most of the forms on the site. In this example I will demonstrate how you can inject the JavaScript onto a page using the content editor web part; the only thing is, this time we're going to provision the web part and the content automatically.

6. Locate the **Features** folder and **Feature1** folder in it, which was created for us by Visual Studio while provisioning the module. Right click on the **Feature1** to **Add Event Receiver**. This will add a .NET code to the feature.
7. Replace the commented out **FeatureActivated** section with the code below:

LISTING 10-9

```
public override void FeatureActivated(SPFeatureReceiver
Properties properties)
{
SPWeb web = properties.Feature.Parent as SPWeb;
SPFile file = web.GetFile(web.Lists["Team Discussion"].
DefaultNewFormUrl);
web.AllowUnsafeUpdates = true;

Microsoft.SharePoint.WebPartPages.
SPLimitedWebPartManager partManager =
file.GetLimitedWebPartManager(
System.Web.UI.WebControls.WebParts.PersonalizationScope.
Shared);

Microsoft.SharePoint.WebPartPages.ContentEditorWebPart
contentEditor = new Microsoft.SharePoint.WebPartPages.
ContentEditorWebPart();

XmlDocument xmlDoc = new XmlDocument();
XmlElement xmlElement = xmlDoc.CreateElement("Root");
xmlElement.InnerText =
"<script language='javascript' src='/SiteAssets/jquery-
1.3.2.min.js'></script>"
+ "<script language='javascript' src='/SiteAssets/jquery.
SPServices-0.5.8.min.js'></script>"
+ "<script language='javascript' src='/SiteAssets/
AutoComplete.js'></script>";
contentEditor.Content = xmlElement;

partManager.AddWebPart(contentEditor, "Main", 0);
partManager.SaveChanges(contentEditor);

}
```

In the code above, we're getting a hold of the current site and the list called **Team Discussion** on the site. We then get a hold of the **NewForm.aspx** page and add a new instance of **Content Editor** web part to it. We assign the same JavaScript code we used last in our autocomplete example. One difference you will notice is this time we moved the actual JavaScript of the function call to the separate file **AutoComplete.js** provisioned in the same library as other JavaScript resources.

8. That's it. Deploy the solution using Visual Studio and navigate to http://intranet.contoso.com . Open the **Team Discussion** and verify whether you have the autocomplete functionality on the title field pulling items from the Announcements list.
If you have added the content editor web part for the last two examples, you will have at least two web parts added to the **NewForm.aspx** page. Our feature receiver code does not validate whether there is an existing web part before adding it to the page. You're welcome to drop me a note on my blog for more details.

Working with custom web services in SharePoint 2010

Below is a scenario in which you might be involved partially from the user interface development front and partially the back-end developer on your team will help you with.

There are cases when you need to perform more complex manipulations in your solution, and results of those manipulations will have to be consumed by a dynamic UI. For example, assume you're creating a slick UI for user registration on a public site hosted in SharePoint. You have your registration form, which interacts with the user, and as a result of this interaction, you need to provision new sites or create list items or maybe trigger workflows. You want your UI to be as smooth as possible and decide to add client-side JavaScript to your registration form. This client-side script will need to interact with the back-end system and perform custom actions. To achieve this, you will need to ensure you have a web service running to perform those custom actions. The results of web service execution will be returned back to the UI involved in interacting with the user.

Since SharePoint 2010 is also a Windows Communication Foundation (WCF) host, you can create WCF services, and those can be hosted by SharePoint. Let's see how we go about creating our custom WCF service and then wire it to our UI.

1. Create a new Visual Studio Empty SharePoint 2010 project, then set the project to be deployed as a **farm solution** with www.contoso.com as a debug URL.

2. Right click on the solution name to **Add -> SharePoint Mapped Folder**. From the list of folders select **ISAPI** folder. That's where our Service definition is going to live.

3. Add a new Text file in the newly mapped ISAPI folder. Right click the newly mapped ISAPI folder and click **Add -> New Item....**

4. From the **Installed Templates** select **General** and pick **Text File**. Rename the text file to *SharePointProject1.SVC* extension and add the following code to it:

LISTING 10-10

```
<% @ServiceHost Language="C#" Debug="true"
Service="SharePointProject1.Service1,
SharePointProject1, Version=1.0.0.0, Culture=neutral,
PublicKeyToken=<we'll insert this value later>"
Factory="Microsoft.SharePoint.Client.Services.
MultipleBaseAddressWebServiceHostFactory,
Microsoft.SharePoint.Client.ServerRuntime,
Version=14.0.0.0,
Culture=neutral,
PublicKeyToken=71e9bce111e9429c" %>
```

5. Right click **References** and to add a new reference. Click the **.NET** tab and locate the following libraries: *Microsoft.SharePoint.Client.Runtime.DLL*—make sure you pick the one from here: *C:\Windows\assembly\GAC_MSIL*

Microsoft.SharePoint.Client.ServerRuntime\14.0.0.0__71e9bc
e111e9429c\Microsoft.SharePoint.Client.ServerRuntime.dll
System.ServiceModel.DLL
System.ServiceModel.Web.DLL

6. Add a new folder to your solution called WCF Service. This is where we're going to place our service classes and contract.

7. Right click on the newly created WCF Service folder and **Add** -> **New Item....** From the **Installed Templates** select **Code** and pick **Interface** as an item. Give a file a name *IService1.cs*.

8. Replace the body of the newly created *IService1.cs* with the following code:

LISTING 10-11

```
using System;
using System.Collections.Generic;
using System.Linq;
using System.Runtime.Serialization;
using System.ServiceModel;
using System.Text;
using System.ServiceModel.Web;
namespace SharePointProject1
{
[ServiceContract]
public interface IService1
{
[OperationContract]
[WebGet(UriTemplate = "/MyCall?message={message}",
BodyStyle = WebMessageBodyStyle.Bare,
ResponseFormat = WebMessageFormat.Xml)]
string GetData(string message);
}
}
```

Above, we're creating a service contract describing the syntax the service will be called with.

9. Add another code file just like you did in step 7, name the
    file **Service1.cs**, and add the following code to replace the
    body of the file:

```
using System;
using System.Collections.Generic;
using System.Linq;
using System.Runtime.Serialization;
using System.ServiceModel;
using System.Text;
using System.ServiceModel.Activation;
using Microsoft.SharePoint.Client.Services;
namespace SharePointProject1
{
[BasicHttpBindingServiceMetadataExchangeEndpointAttribute]
[AspNetCompatibilityRequirements(RequirementsMode =
AspNetCompatibilityRequirementsMode.Required)]
public class Service1 : IService1
{
public string GetData(string message)
{
return string.Format("You entered: {0}, Entered on: {1}",
message, DateTime.Now.ToString());
}
}
}
```

Above, we implement the method we referenced earlier.
In this case it'll just display the message we have passed as
a parameter. Obviously, in your case, you may receive an
XML back, or other result format such as JSON.

10. Now we need to grab the public key of the custom DLL we
    will deploy. Right click on the project name and **deploy** the
    solution.

11. Open *C:\Windows\Assembly* and locate the assembly named **SharePointProject1**—the name we have specified for our output assembly name. Access the properties of the assembly and copy down the **Public Key Token** value.

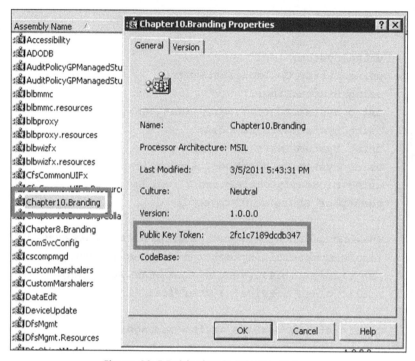

Figure 10-5 Retrieving Public Key Token

12. In your Visual Studio solution, open **SharePointProject1. svc**, which you created earlier in **ISAPI** folder. Replace the value of the **PublicKeyToken** we have identified in **bold** in the listing of step 4 with the value you copied from the **assembly** folder.

13. Deploy the solution again so that new version of our updated **SharePointProject1.svc** is provisioned to the server.

14. Open the browser and try to hit your web service: http:// www.contoso.com/_vti_bin/SharePointProject1.svc/ MyCall?message=Some Text.

You should see the following result:
<string xmlns="http://schemas.microsoft.com/2003/10/ Serialization/">You entered: Some Text, Entered on: 1/22/2011 10:17:54 AM</string>

Now let's consume our service in a custom script, which is something you as a user interface developer will be more involved with:

1. Just like in the example with internal SharePoint 2010 web service calls, we will be using JQuery in our client-side script. If you haven't already, download the latest version of JQuery: http://ajax.microsoft.com/ajax/jquery/jquery-1.3.2.min.js.
2. Right click project name to **Add -> SharePoint "Layouts" Mapped Folder.**
3. Right click on the project name to **Add -> New Item ...** and pick **Visual Web Part.**
4. In the design view of the Visual Web Part place the following HTML into the web part, right after:
<%@ Control Language="C#" AutoEventWireup="true" CodeBehind="VisualWebPart1UserControl.ascx. cs" Inherits="SharePointProject1.VisualWebPart1. VisualWebPart1UserControl" %>

LISTING 10-13

```
<script src="/_layouts/SharePointProject1/jquery-
1.3.2.min.js"
type="text/javascript">
</script>
<script type="text/javascript">
$(document).ready(function() {
$.getJSON("http://www.contoso.com/
    _vti_bin/SharePointProject1.svc/MyCall?message=Some
    Text",
function(data) {
var count = 0;
$.each(data.d.results, function(i,result) {
html = "<div>" + result +"</div>";
```

```
$('#resultarea').append($(html));
});
});
});
</script>
<div id="resultarea">
</div>
```

The highlighted code part is the URL of our custom web service. We get a hold of the JSON object, which holds results returned by the service, extracting the result, which gets output to **resultarea**.

I didn't go too elaborate and colorful on this example—I trust your requirements will supply a way better scenario which you can practice with.

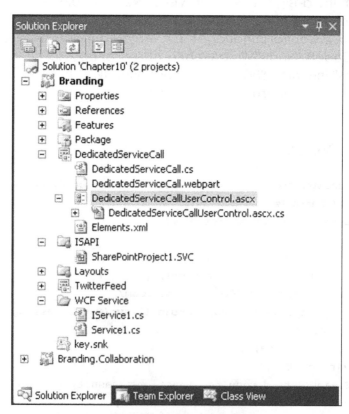

Figure 10-6 Final Visual Studio solution structure

5. Hit F5 to deploy your solution with Visual Studio.
6. Once deployment is complete, the site home page will open.
7. Edit the page: **Site Actions** -> **Edit Page**. Scroll down to the page and click **Add a Web Part**. From the area below the ribbon select **Custom** as a Category and **VisualWebPart1** as a web part and click **Add**.

Save the page and observe how data from the custom web service gets displayed in your web part using a web service call.

This scenario is very typical when you need to interact with a web service which is a proxy to another mechanism which works with actual data. In a real situation you and your team might face the scenario where data gets extracted by a third-party system and with a predefined period of time, and gets saved into a file on another server. This data might be stock information, for example, which is not usually supplied real time due to the associated cost per request. Then, this data will be read by multiple other systems, including your intranet site. If you want to do proxy reading of the data to perform some additional processing and expose the result to other systems, you might want to use a proxy service just like the one we created here before consuming the result in your web part. This way if you have other web parts using the results, they will hit your service directly rather then performing yet another processing on their own.

CHAPTER 11

Creating SharePoint 2010 Ribbon Components and Managing Existing Eibbon Elements

SharePoint ribbon interface is one of the new features in SharePoint 2010 user interface. Although ribbon has been implemented in past versions of other Microsoft applications, we can really see now that with SharePoint, the ribbon is here to stay. In this chapter, we'll take a detailed look at how to create your own custom ribbon controls which will interact with site users.

Creating basic SharePoint ribbon controls

By now, you probably had many chances to take a look at the ribbon; after all, you have to use it every time you need to call up any function in SharePoint. At the time of the writing this chapter, there were no publicly accessible tools that would let you generate ribbon markup on the fly by dragging and dropping controls. That is not to say that something like this won't be released soon. Maybe you're thinking about creating a tool like that as you read this chapter. Despite all of the complexities that might be involved in ribbon authoring, you will be able to create any control that you see on the out-of-the-box ribbon.

Another important part of the ribbon architecture is that its controls, such as buttons, drop-down boxes, and other controls, reside in the context of the current page or element that has a ribbon context. This means that if you want to add a new button to the ribbon, you have to specify whether that button will appear in the document library, and, if so, what type of library. Along with the library, you will have to specify what tab the ribbon appears on and in what group.

The easiest way to get started with this concept is to create a sample, so let's go ahead and create a ribbon button that will reside in the **Shared Documents** library on your team site. I assume you have a team site already created as a root of your site collection http://intranet.contoso.com.

1. In your Visual Studio project structure, create a new folder in the root of the solution called Ribbon.
2. Right click on the folder to add a new item of type: **Empty Element**, and give the instance the name **RibbonButton**.
3. Open the **Elements.xml** file you have just created and replace the contents of it with the following code:

LISTING 11-1

```xml
<?xml version="1.0" encoding="utf-8"?>
  <Elements xmlns="http://schemas.microsoft.com/
  sharepoint/"/>
  <CustomAction
     Id="Ribbon.Library.Share.ButtonSample"
     Location="CommandUI.Ribbon"
     RegistrationId="101"
     RegistrationType="List"
     Title="Using Button">
  <CommandUIExtension>
  <CommandUIDefinitions>
  <CommandUIDefinition
     Location="Ribbon.Library.Share.Controls._children">
  <Button
```

```
        Id="Ribbon.Library.Share.Button"
        Sequence="20"
        LabelText="My Button"
        Image16by16="/_layouts/images/QuickTagILikeIt_16.png"
        TemplateAlias="o1"
        Command="NewRibbonButtonCommand"/>
    </CommandUIDefinition>
    </CommandUIDefinitions>
    <CommandUIHandlers>
    <CommandUIHandler
        Command="NewRibbonButtonCommand"
        CommandAction="javascript:alert('Button clicked');" />
    </CommandUIHandlers>
    </CommandUIExtension>
    </CustomAction>
    </Elements>
```

I should mention a few things about the code above:

1. The **ID** of the custom action can be user defined.
2. The **Location** attribute has to match a subset of defined locations in this case.
3. **Registration ID** and **Registration type** are optional attributes and are required only if you plan on attaching the ribbon button to the list or library. In our case, we want to attach our button to the list with the template number **101**, which is a generic document library. To find out what other registration type IDs are available, refer to the features folder and extract the template ID from the respective feature. For example, the custom list feature is located here: *[Drive]:\Program Files\Common Files\Microsoft Shared\ Web Server Extensions\14\TEMPLATE\FEATURES\CustomList.* The **ID** of the list is specified in here: *ListTemplates\ CustomList.xml,* as a **Type** attribute.
4. The remaining required structure defines the nested nature of ribbon where we specify our custom control *<Button/>*.
5. Besides attributes that define the style of the button, there is an attribute that defines action when the button is clicked: *NewRibbonButtonCommand*.

Now let's deploy the solution using Visual Studio and open a **Shared Documents** library on the root of your team site site. Make sure that you click on the **Library** tab since that's where we defined our button in the **Location** attribute: *Ribbon.Library.Share.Controls*.

If your deployment succeeded, you should see a ribbon button as shown below.

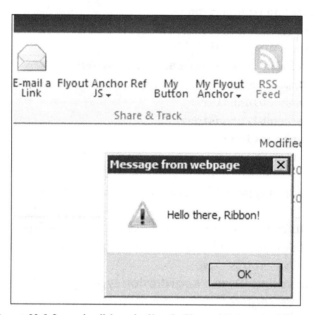

Figure 11-1 Sample ribbon button in Shared Document library

Now that we know how to create the simplest version of a control, let's go ahead and try creating something more complex.

Creating a flyout anchor on your ribbon

A flyout anchor is a type of a button, except when you click on it, you get additional options as buttons. Flyout anchors are used frequently in SharePoint—for example, in the document library workflow options.

Let's reuse the same Visual Studio item we used in the previous example, but this time, replace the **<Button>** control in the **Elemnets.xml** structure with the **<FlyoutAnchor>**.

1. Open the **Elements.xml** in your ribbon elements file you created in the last sample.
2. Locate the section where you defined button controls.

LISTING 11-2

```
<Button
    Id="Ribbon.Library.Share.Button"
    Sequence="20"
    LabelText="My Button"
    Image16by16="/_layouts/images/QuickTagILikeIt_16.png"
    TemplateAlias="o1"
    Command="NewRibbonButtonCommand"/>
```

3. Replace the button definition from Step 2 with the following code of the fly out anchor:

LISTING 11-3

```
<FlyoutAnchor
    Id="Ribbon.Library.Share.FlyoutAnchor"
    Sequence="20"
    LabelText="My Flyout Anchor"
    Image16by16="/_layouts/images/QuickTagILikeIt_16.png"
    TemplateAlias="o1">
<Menu Id="Ribbon.Library.Share.FlyoutAnchor.Menu">
<MenuSection Id="Ribbon.Library.Share.FlyoutAnchor.Menu.
MenuSection"
    Sequence="10" DisplayMode="Menu16">
<Controls Id="Ribbon.Library.Share.FlyoutAnchor.Menu.
MenuSection.Controls">
```

```
<Button
    Id="Ribbon.Library.Share.FlyoutAnchor.Menu.
MenuSection.MyButton"
    Sequence="10"
    Command="NewRibbonButtonCommand"
    LabelText="MyButton"
    Image16by16="/_layouts/images/QuickTagILikeIt_16.png"
    TemplateAlias="o2" />
</Controls>
</MenuSection>
<MenuSection Id="Ribbon.Library.Share.FlyoutAnchor.Menu.
MenuSection1"
    Sequence="20" DisplayMode="Menu16">
<Controls Id="Ribbon.Library.FlyoutAnchor.Menu.
MenuSection1.Controls">
<Button
    Id="Ribbon.Library.FlyoutAnchor.Menu.MenuSection1.
MyButton1"
    Sequence="10"
    Command="NewRibbonButtonCommand"
    LabelText="MyButton1"
    Image16by16="/_layouts/images/QuickTagILikeIt_16.png"
    TemplateAlias="o3"
    />
</Controls>
</MenuSection>
</Menu>
</FlyoutAnchor>
```

One difference you will notice is that the flyout anchor
defines its own structure of controls, which in our case are
buttons just like from the previous sample. Also, a flyout
anchor doesn't have a JavaScript handler to handle
clicks since it has a default one that unfolds dependent
buttons. Since our buttons all reference the same JavaScript
function, the message that we will get when any of them is
clicked will be the same.

4. Let's deploy our solution and navigate to the same **Shared
Documents** library we used in the previous example.

If your ribbon got deployed with no problems, you will see two buttons when clicking on the drop-down-looking button in the Shared section of the document library.

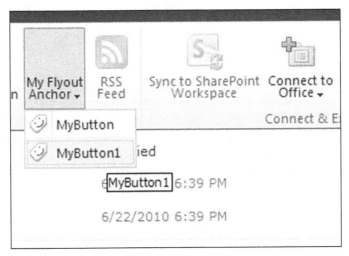

Figure 11-2 Flyout anchor in the SharePoint ribbon

What if your ribbon JavaScript is too large for one file?

In the last two examples, our JavaScript was a one-line piece of code, and in reality your JavaScript, whatever you end up doing with it, will be larger, and it's harder to maintain it all in one place.

One of the approaches to creating ribbon items using a large piece of JavaScript is to define it in a separate **CustomAction**. You have already seen how our entire ribbon is defined in **CustomAction**, but you can also define any helper elements or other ribbon elements all in one **Elements.xml** file.

Let's take a look at the last example, where we provisioned a flyout anchor; but this time, the JavaScript will be defined with our new method.

1. Locate the **Elements.xml** file you have been using to define your custom ribbons.
2. Open the file and replace the contents of it with the following code:

LISTING 11-4

```xml
<?xml version="1.0" encoding="utf-8"?>
<Elements xmlns="http://schemas.microsoft.com/
sharepoint/">
<CustomAction
    Id="Ribbon.Library.Share.ButtonSample"
    Location="CommandUI.Ribbon"
    RegistrationId="101"
    RegistrationType="List"
    Title="Using Button">
<CommandUIExtension>
<CommandUIDefinitions>
<CommandUIDefinition
    Location="Ribbon.Library.Share.Controls._children">
<FlyoutAnchor
    Id="Ribbon.Library.Share.FlyoutAnchor"
    Sequence="20"
    LabelText="My Flyout Anchor"
    Image16by16="/_layouts/images/QuickTagILikeIt_16.png"
    TemplateAlias="o1">
<Menu Id="Ribbon.Library.Share.FlyoutAnchor.Menu">
<MenuSection Id="Ribbon.Library.Share.FlyoutAnchor.
Menu.MenuSection"
Sequence="10" DisplayMode="Menu16">
<Controls Id="Ribbon.Library.Share.FlyoutAnchor.Menu.
MenuSection.Controls">
<Button
    Id="Ribbon.Library.Share.FlyoutAnchor.Menu.
    MenuSection.MyButton"
    Sequence="10"
    Command="NewRibbonButtonCommand"
    LabelText="MyButton"
    Image16by16="/_layouts/images/QuickTagILikeIt_16.png"
```

```
        TemplateAlias="o2" />
    </Controls>
</MenuSection>
<MenuSection Id="Ribbon.Library.Share.FlyoutAnchor.Menu.
MenuSection1"
    Sequence="20" DisplayMode="Menu16">
<Controls Id="Ribbon.Library.FlyoutAnchor.Menu.
MenuSection1.Controls">
<Button
    Id="Ribbon.Library.FlyoutAnchor.Menu.MenuSection1.
    MyButton1"
    Sequence="10"
    Command="NewRibbonButtonCommand"
    LabelText="MyButton1"
    Image16by16="/_layouts/images/QuickTagILikeIt_16.png"
    TemplateAlias="o3"
    />
</Controls>
</MenuSection>
</Menu>
</FlyoutAnchor>
</CommandUIDefinition>
</CommandUIDefinitions>
<CommandUIHandlers>
<CommandUIHandler
    Command="NewRibbonButtonCommand"
    CommandAction="javascript:HelloRibbon();" />
</CommandUIHandlers>
</CommandUIExtension>
</CustomAction>
<CustomAction Id="Ribbon.Library.Share.
FlyoutAnchorSample.Script"
    Location="ScriptLink"
    ScriptBlock="
    function HelloRibbon()
    {
    alert('Hello there, Ribbon!');
    }" />
</Elements>
```

3. Now, deploy the solution with Visual Studio and take a look at the results.

You will see a different message indicating that a different JavaScript function was called.

In simple cases, this might address the problem. In cases where you create a large ribbon library with multiple controls to handle your custom application built on SharePoint, you will probably have user interaction developers giving you a large file or a few where all of the JavaScript is stored.

In the scenario described above, you can use our **CustomAction** to reference a JavaScript file like this:

LISTING 11-5

```
<CustomAction
Id="Ribbon.Library.Share.FlyoutAnchorSample.Script"
Location="ScriptLink"
ScriptSrc="/_layouts/SharePointProject1/RibbonActions.js" />
```

Assuming you're using our solution structure and have a mapped **Layouts** folder in your solution, that's where you would place your custom JavaScript file, which will be deployed to the SharePoint root once the solution is deployed.

All of the functions defined in the external JavaScript file will be available to ribbon control if the file is referenced with the method above.

Working with ribbon groups and tabs

So far, we've been looking at how to create buttons and a few other controls and how to handle actions when those controls are clicked. Now is the time to take a look at how you can position your controls in the different containers available, such as groups and tabs.

In last few samples, we created a button in the **Share** group of a **Library** tab. Let's now create a new tab and group similar to **Share**, and place a simple button in it.

1. Locate the ***Elements.xml*** you've been using to make changes to your ribbon.
2. Replace the code in the ***Elements.xml*** with the following:

LISTING 11-6

```xml
<?xml version="1.0" encoding="utf-8"?>
<Elements xmlns="http://schemas.microsoft.com/
sharepoint/">
<CustomAction
    Id="MyProject.RibbonButton"
    Location="CommandUI.Ribbon.ListView"
    RegistrationId="101"
    RegistrationType="List">
<CommandUIExtension>
<CommandUIDefinitions>
<CommandUIDefinition
    Location="Ribbon.Tabs._children">
<Tab
    Id="MyProject.Ribbon.HelloTab"
    Title="Custom Tab Title">
<Scaling
    Id="MyProject.Ribbon.HelloTab.Scaling">
<MaxSize
    Id="MyProject.Ribbon.HelloTab.MaxSize"
    GroupId="MyProject.Ribbon.HelloTab.HelloGroup"
    Size="OneLargeButton"/>
<Scale
    Id="MyProject.Ribbon.HelloTab.Scaling.TabScaling"
    GroupId="MyProject.Ribbon.HelloTab.HelloGroup"
    Size="OneLargeButton" />
```

```
</Scaling>
<Groups Id="MyProject.Ribbon.HelloTab.Groups">
<Group
    Id="MyProject.Ribbon.HelloTab.HelloGroup"
    Title="Custom Group Title"
    Template="MyProject.Ribbon.Templates.HelloTemplate">
<Controls Id="MyProject.Ribbon.HelloTab.HelloGroup.
Controls">
<Button
    Id="MyProject.Ribbon.HelloTab.HelloGroup.HelloButton"
    Command="MyProject.Scripts.HelloCommand"
    LabelText="Button Text!"
    TemplateAlias="CutomHelloTemplate"/>
</Controls>
</Group>
</Groups>
</Tab>
</CommandUIDefinition>
<CommandUIDefinition Location="Ribbon.Templates._
children">
<GroupTemplate Id="MyProject.Ribbon.Templates.
HelloTemplate">
<Layout
    Title="OneLargeButton"
    LayoutTitle="OneLargeButton">
<Section Alignment="Top" Type="OneRow">
<Row>
<ControlRef DisplayMode="Large" TemplateAlias="CutomHel
loTemplate" />
</Row>
</Section>
</Layout>
</GroupTemplate>
</CommandUIDefinition>
</CommandUIDefinitions>
<CommandUIHandlers>
<CommandUIHandler
    Command="MyProject.Scripts.HelloCommand"
    CommandAction="javascript:alert('New button
    clicked!');" />
```

```
</CommandUIHandlers>
</CommandUIExtension>
</CustomAction>
</Elements>
```

Above, we used the following new definitions:

- **<Tab>** - to define a tab.
- **<Scaling>** - to define how your control will render, depending on whether the page is resized; in our example, we use the same size. This definition is optional.
- **<Groups>** - defines groups under the **<Tab>**; purely a container.
- **<Group>** - defines individual group under **<Groups>**. **Template** attribute inside your **<Group>** - will define how your group is displayed. The definition is in **<GroupTemplate>**.
- **<Controls>** - will contain your controls; in our case, we just use **<Button>**.
  Command inside your **<Button>** will carry the name of the command that will execute when the button is clicked—defined in **<CommandUIHandler>**.
- **TemplateAlias** - contains the name of the template according to which your button will be displayed.

3. Deploy the solution, and if the deployment was successful, you will see your custom tab and button rendered as shown below.

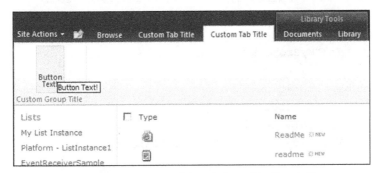

Figure 11-3 Sample ribbon tab and button in it

Creating site-level ribbon tabs

Until now, we have been looking at how to create ribbon buttons that are bound to a particular list type's context. In other words, we created ribbon buttons and tabs that will show up only when you navigate to the library of your choice. In this sample, we'll take a look at how to create ribbon tabs that will be displayed on a site-level ribbon.

Remember at the beginning of this chapter, I mentioned how ribbon is contextual and doesn't float around by itself? In this sample, in order for our ribbon tab to work, we not only will need to provision the XML markup for its structure elements, we will also need to activate the tab. Since SharePoint doesn't have enough information on the context of our tab—because we won't supply it—it will be hidden until instructed to show up.

Let's start with defining our ribbon elements.

1. In your Visual Studio, locate the **Ribbon** folder we created earlier and add a new item of type: **Empty Element**.
2. Open the *Element.xml* file and replace the contents of it with the following code:

LISTING 11-7

```
<?xml version="1.0" encoding="utf-8"?>
<Elements xmlns="http://schemas.microsoft.com/
sharepoint/">
<CustomAction
    Id="MyProject.RibbonButton"
    Location="CommandUI.Ribbon">
<CommandUIExtension>
<CommandUIDefinitions>
<CommandUIDefinition
    Location="Ribbon.Tabs._children">
<Tab
```

```
        Id="MyProject.Ribbon.HelloTab"
        Title="Custom Tab Title">
<Scaling Id="Ribbon.Read.Scaling">
</Scaling>
<Groups Id="Ribbon.Read.Groups">
<Group
        Id="MyProject.Ribbon.HelloTab.HelloGroup"
        Title="Custom Group Title"
        Template="MyProject.Ribbon.Templates.HelloTemplate">
<Controls Id="MyProject.Ribbon.HelloTab.HelloGroup.
Controls">
<Button
        Id="MyProject.Ribbon.HelloTab.HelloGroup.HelloButton"
        Command="MyProject.Scripts.HelloCommand"
        LabelText="Button Text!"
        TemplateAlias="CutomHelloTemplate"/>
</Controls>
</Group>
</Groups>
</Tab>
</CommandUIDefinition>
<CommandUIDefinition Location="Ribbon.Templates._
children">
<GroupTemplate Id="MyProject.Ribbon.Templates.
HelloTemplate">
<Layout
        Title="OneLargeButton"
        LayoutTitle="OneLargeButton">
<Section Alignment="Top" Type="OneRow">
<Row>
<ControlRef DisplayMode="Large" TemplateAlias="CutomHel
loTemplate" />
</Row>
</Section>
</Layout>
</GroupTemplate>
</CommandUIDefinition>
</CommandUIDefinitions>
<CommandUIHandlers>
```

```
<CommandUIHandler
    Command="MyProject.Scripts.HelloCommand"
    CommandAction="javascript:alert('New button
clicked!');" />
</CommandUIHandlers>
</CommandUIExtension>
</CustomAction>
</Elements>
```

Above, we define our **CommandUIExtension** to be referenced the following location attribute ***Ribbon.Tabs._ children***, meaning that we place a new tab right in the root of the ribbon structure. The rest of the structure, such as groups and buttons, is similar to what we have used in the previous example.

3. Now that we have our structure defined, we need to activate the ribbon on the context where we need it. Remember, just because you defined the structure of the ribbon, that doesn't mean the ribbon knows when to activate itself. The activation is done using a .NET code and, therefore, can be defined in the user control that later is referenced in your Masterpage or in any other .NET components, such as a web part. By definition, your ribbon activation code in a web part will be responsible for ensuring your web part is placed on a page you need and runs; otherwise, users won't see your custom tab activated.

4. Create a new folder called ***Web Parts*** in your Visual Studio solution structure and add a new instance **Visual Web Part** to it.

5. In your project references, add a new referenced DLL located here:
   [Drive]:\Program Files\Common Files\Microsoft Shared\ Web Server Extensions\14\ISAPI Microsoft.Web.CommandUI. dll.

6. Switch to code behind file of your control, ***VisualWebPart1. ascx.cs***.

7. Add the following namespace reference in to your code:
   ■ *using Microsoft.SharePoint.WebControls;.*

8. Replace the **Page_Load** method in your code with the following:

LISTING 11-8

```
protected void Page_Load(object sender, EventArgs e)
{

SPRibbon.GetCurrent(this.Page)
    .MakeTabAvailable("MyProject.Ribbon.HelloTab");
}
```

In here, we activate the tab by the **ID** we have defined in the **Elements.xml** file.

9. Deploy the solution and navigate to the root of your SharePoint test site.

10. You will not see a ribbon tab on the page; you will need to edit the page and add a new custom web part you have just created. As soon as the web part is added to the page, the custom ribbon tab will appear. You can save the page and click on the tab to test the button functionality.

Determining the state of ribbon tabs and hiding ribbon

Assuming your SharePoint test site is of part a **Team Site** template, you see the ribbon all the time. Since Team Site is a collaboration site template, just like most site templates in SharePoint, it will include the ribbon by default. Publishing site template doesn't show the ribbon by default. After all, you don't want your public site users being able to see a ribbon; this will remind them of Microsoft Office too much. You can turn the ribbon on and off when you're working with the publishing site template.

In this sample, we will take a look at how you can turn off ribbon on any site you're working with, as well as check the status of individual tabs on the ribbon and turn them off, too.

Similar to the previous example, where we created new site-level ribbon tabs, the state of tabs and the entire ribbon is a contextual property depending on where you are on the site. This means that you will have to run .NET code to determine the state of the ribbon at that particular state and see whether you still need to perform ribbon action.

As a suggestion, I recommend not turning off ribbon for the entire site by default, even when you think it's not necessary. If you need to turn off ribbon user interface, ensure that in your code you verify your ribbon is turned on if the current user is an administrator. A lot of administrative functions are available through the ribbon, and if you remove it for everyone, your administrators will lose a lot of good functionality—for example, functionality to add new users or groups to the site.

In fact, let's create a piece of functionality that verifies if the user is a site administrator and disables the ribbon if not.

Let's reuse the same web part you created in the previous sample.

1. Locate the web part you created in the last sample and switch to the code behind the web part control **VisualWebPart1.ascx.cs**.
2. Add the following namespace reference to your **Visual Web Part** code:
   - *using Microsoft.SharePoint;*.
3. Replace the **Page_Load** method content with the following code:

LISTING 11-9

```
protected void Page_Load(object sender, EventArgs e)
{
    if (!SPContext.Current.Web.UserIsSiteAdmin)
    {
    SPRibbon.GetCurrent(this.Page).CommandUIVisible =
    false;
    }
}
```

This code will verify whether the current user is an administrator and turn off the ribbon if the user isn't.

4. Deploy the solution and navigate to the root of your SharePoint test site. If you reused the web part from the last sample, it will be already added to the page, but the ribbon still shows up. Chances are that you run as a **contoso\administrator**, and to test the scenario when you're not an administrator, you will need to log in with a user that has lower privileges. For http://intranet.contoso.com you can use the user account of **contoso\brads** with the same password as administrator. Alternatively, you can remove the administrator privileges checking in the **Page_Load** method of the code behind in your web part.

Where is SharePoint out-of-the-box ribbon defined?

From the moment we started experimenting with ribbon and adding buttons to tabs, you probably began thinking how nice it would be to be able to have a sample for each individual ribbon control that SharePoint uses for its own out-of-the-box ribbon control rendering. After all, by having access to the code of out-of-the-box functionality and definitions, you would be able to build your own definitions much easier. Also, you would be able to define ribbon buttons and other controls not just within lists and libraries, but also in other types of containers that we didn't cover here.

Well, here is where you can find SharePoint ribbon definitions: *[Drive]:\Program Files\Common Files\Microsoft Shared\Web Server Extensions\14\TEMPLATE\GLOBAL\XML\ CMDUI.XML.*

The file is quite large, but if you open it in Visual Studio and collapse all outlining (**CTRL+M+L**), you will see how groups, tabs, and controls are structured. You will also see the default templates for controls, which you can use in your code. Also, check out this video below as a bonus guide to starting your ribbon development.

```
<Tabs Id="Ribbon.Tabs">
    <Tab Id="Ribbon.Read" Sequence="100" Command="ReadTab" Desc
        <Tab Id="Ribbon.BDCAdmin"
            Sequence="1600"
            Command="BDCAdminTab"
            Description=""
            Title="$Resources:core, cui BDCAdminTabTitle;">
    <Tab Id="Ribbon.DocLibListForm.Edit" Sequence="200" Command
    <Tab Id="Ribbon.ListForm.Display" Sequence="300" Command="R
    <Tab Id="Ribbon.ListForm.Edit" Sequence="400" Command="Ribb
    <Tab Id="Ribbon.PostListForm.Edit" Sequence="500" Command="
    <Tab Id="Ribbon.SvcApp"
        Sequence="700"
        Command="SvcAppTab"
        Title="$Resources:core,cui_SvcAppTitle;"
        Description="$Resources:core,cui_SvcAppDescription;">
    <Tab Id="Ribbon.Solution" Sequence="800" Command="SolutionT
    <Tab Id="Ribbon.UsageReport" Sequence="900" Command="UsageRep
    <Tab Id="Ribbon.WikiPageTab" Sequence="1000" Command="WikiP
        <Tab Id="Ribbon.PublishTab" Sequence="2000" Command="Publ
<Tab Id="Ribbon.WebPartPage" Sequence="1100" Command="Ribbon.WebP
    <Tab Id="Ribbon.WebApp"
        Sequence="1300"
        Command="WebAppTab"
        Title="$Resources:core,cui_WebAppTitle;"
        Description="$Resources:core,cui_WebAppDescription;">
    <Tab Id="Ribbon.SiteCollections" Sequence="1400" Command="S
    <Tab Id="Ribbon.ManageTrust"
        Command="ManageTrustTab"
        Sequence="800"
        Title="$Resources:core,cui_TrustTitle;"
        Description="$Resources:core,cui_TrustDescription;">
    <Tab Id="Ribbon.CustomCommands" Sequence="1700" Command="Cu
```

Figure 11-4 Collapsed version of ribbon definitions

LEARN MORE:

Video screencast: Tips & Tricks: Creating Complex SharePoint 2010 Ribbon Elements http://vimeo.com/10685740

Working with SharePoint application pages and their relation to ribbon

When users usually interact with SharePoint ribbon UI, they call a modal dialog box where they are asked to perform some of the additional configurations or fill in choices. In a sample just after this, we'll see just how that can be achieved. In this sample, I would like to touch on important concept of application pages and their role in SharePoint solutions.

Thus far we have looked at various scenarios to customize different parts of SharePoint user interface. In most cases, we utilized out-of-the-box components, since SharePoint had enough flexibility to let us extend some of its functionality and saved us from rewriting existing features. There are some other scenarios where you may be migrating custom .NET applications to be hosted within SharePoint and, for one reason or another, you just cannot break down the functionality into separate web parts to be provisioned on the page. In other cases, you may need to work on provisioning user interface for administrative functionality on the site which lives in application pages, just like in the case of out-of-the-box SharePoint. In this case, SharePoint has a nice ability for you to create what is known as application pages. Whether you know it or not, you have been using out-of-the-box application pages quite often to interact with your SharePoint site. All of the application pages are located in the _**Layouts**_ virtual directory and are relative to the site from which you're calling them. Most commonly used ones are pages available when you navigate to **Site Settings** and access various options related to site administration.

Application pages are simply **ASPX** pages that allow you to write your custom code behind them and place controls on them. The benefit is that they run within a context of SharePoint, and if you need access to SharePoint objects, you can retrieve the content and identify whether the page was called from one subsite as opposed to another. In this chapter, we're not going to take a granular look at custom application pages; after all we're only discussing their relation when working with ribbon. We will cover a few interesting features and extensions you can take advantage of.

First, let's create a typical application page using Visual Studio and see what it's all about.

1. Open Visual Studio and create a new project using the **SharePoint 2010 Empty Project** template.
2. Specify http://intranet.contoso.com/ as your debug URL and choose **Deploy as farm solution** for your deployment method.
3. Right click project name to **Add -> SharePoint "Lyouts" Mapped Folder**. This is where all of our application pages live. Visual Studio will create a child folder with the same name as your project name, in my case *SharePointProject1*.
4. Right click on the folder name *SharePointProject1*and select **Add -> New Item....** From Installed templates pick **SharePoint -> 2010** and for the template type pick **Application Page**; give it a name *MyCustomPage.aspx*.
5. The page and code behind will be created for you in the solution. Let's take a look at its structure and what some of the elements mean.

LISTING 11-10

```
<!--Since our application page has a code behind, this
references current assembly which will potentially
execute custom code running behind the application
page-->
<%@ Assembly Name="$SharePoint.Project.
AssemblyFullName$" %>
<%@ Import Namespace="Microsoft.SharePoint.
ApplicationPages" %>

<!--References to classes representing standard
SharePoint controls and other utility resources; if you
```

have third party controls you would like to use — this
is an example how you register them-->

```
<%@ Register Tagprefix="SharePoint"
Namespace="Microsoft.SharePoint.WebControls"
Assembly="Microsoft.SharePoint, Version=14.0.0.0,
Culture=neutral, PublicKeyToken=71e9bce111e9429c" %>
<%@ Register Tagprefix="Utilities" Namespace="Microsoft.
SharePoint.Utilities" Assembly="Microsoft.SharePoint,
Version=14.0.0.0, Culture=neutral, PublicKeyToken=71e9bce
111e9429c" %>
<%@ Register Tagprefix="asp" Namespace="System.Web.
UI" Assembly="System.Web.Extensions, Version=3.5.0.0,
Culture=neutral, PublicKeyToken=31bf3856ad364e35" %>

<%@ Import Namespace="Microsoft.SharePoint" %>
```

<!--This reference facilitates ribbon UI -->

```
<%@ Assembly Name="Microsoft.Web.CommandUI,
Version=14.0.0.0, Culture=neutral, PublicKeyToken=71e9bce
111e9429c" %>
```

<!--Application page is declared here with reference
to a masterpage, if you're planning to use custom
masterpage ensure it's been placed in the masterpage
gallery and content placeholders in this application
page do exist in the masterpage you'er referencing-->

```
<%@ Page Language="C#" AutoEventWireup="true"
CodeBehind="ApplicationPage1.aspx.cs"
Inherits="SharePointProject1.Layouts.SharePointProject1.
ApplicationPage1" DynamicMasterPageFile="~masterurl/
default.master" %>
```

<! -- Place holder for additional header information,
ex. custom style sheets -->

```
<asp:Content ID="PageHead" ContentPlaceHolderID="PlaceHo
lderAdditionalPageHead" runat="server">
</asp:Content>
```

<!--Main part of the page where all the content is
rendered -->

```
<asp:Content ID="Main" ContentPlaceHolderID="PlaceHolder
Main" runat="server">
</asp:Content>

<! -- Placeholder  to populate page title-->
<asp:Content ID="PageTitle" ContentPlaceHolderID="PlaceH
olderPageTitle" runat="server">
Application Page
</asp:Content>

<! --Used by SharePoint to render title and description
of the site-->
<asp:Content ID="PageTitleInTitleArea" ContentPlaceHolde
rID="PlaceHolderPageTitleInTitleArea" runat="server" >
My Application Page
</asp:Content>
```

As you can see, the structure of the page is simpler than publishing or collaboration page, for example. Content within **PlaceHolderMain** is the key player here. All the content will be placed into this placeholder, and this is where you build any additional markup you may want to include, just like you do in page layouts.

Since you're familiar with most of the sections of the application page from the previous experience with page layouts in earlier chapters, let's see how we can use our application page when working with ribbon.

Opening modal windows upon ribbon control clicked

One of the most common SharePoint out-of-the-box actions that happen when you click a ribbon button, is opening a modal dialog. There are two components you will need to get your custom page opening upon ribbon button click: a ribbon definition and an application page.

Let's go ahead and create sample that will open a custom page in a modal when the ribbon is clicked.

1. In your Visual Studio structure, create a new instance of the item of type **Empty Element**.
2. Open the *Element.xml* file of the newly created element definition and replace the content of the file with the following code:

LISTING 11-11

```
<Elements xmlns="http://schemas.microsoft.com/
sharepoint/">
<CustomAction
    Id="Ribbon.MyTab"
    Title="Adds a new Ribbon tab to Generic List"
    RegistrationType="List"
    RegistrationId="100" Location="CommandUI.Ribbon.
    ListView">
<CommandUIExtension>
<CommandUIDefinitions>
<CommandUIDefinition
    Location="Ribbon.Tabs._children">
<Tab Id="Ribbon.MyTab" Sequence="110" Title="My Tab
Name">
<Scaling Id="Ribbon.MyTab.Scaling">
<MaxSize
    Id="Ribbon.MyTab.Scaling.MyGroup.MaxSize"
    Sequence="15" GroupId="Ribbon.MyTab.MyGroup"
    Size="LargeMedium"/>
</Scaling>
<Groups Id="Ribbon.MyTab.Groups">
<Group
    Id="Ribbon.MyTab.MyGroup"
    Sequence="15" Title="My Group Name"
    Template="Ribbon.Templates.MyTab.MyGroup.
CustomTemplate">
<Controls Id="Ribbon.MyTab.MyGroup.Controls">
<Button
```

```xml
        Id="Ribbon.MyTab.MyGroup.Button"
        Alt="Ribbon.MyTab.MyGroup.Button"
        Command="Ribbon.MyTab.MyGroup.Button_CMD"
        Image16by16="/_layouts/images/siteIcon.png"
        Image32by32="/_layouts/images/siteIcon.png"
        LabelText="Button"
        Sequence="10" TemplateAlias="o1"
        ToolTipTitle="Button"
        ToolTipDescription="Shows a dialog" />
    </Controls>
    </Group>
    </Groups>
    </Tab>
    </CommandUIDefinition>
    <CommandUIDefinition
        Location="Ribbon.Templates._children">
    <GroupTemplate Id="Ribbon.Templates.MyTab.MyGroup.
    CustomTemplate">
    <Layout Title="LargeMedium">
    <OverflowSection Type="OneRow"
        TemplateAlias="o1" DisplayMode="Large"/>
    <OverflowSection Type="ThreeRow"
        TemplateAlias="o2" DisplayMode="Medium"/>
    </Layout>
    </GroupTemplate>
    </CommandUIDefinition>
    </CommandUIDefinitions>
    <CommandUIHandlers>
    <CommandUIHandler
        Command="Ribbon.MyTab.MyGroup.Button_CMD"
        CommandAction="javascript:RibbonButtonHandler();" />
    </CommandUIHandlers>
    </CommandUIExtension>
    </CustomAction>
    <CustomAction Id="Ribbon.Library.Actions.Scripts"
        Location ="ScriptLink"
        ScriptSrc="/_layouts/Chapter11/RibbonActions.js" />
    </Elements>
```

Here, our ribbon will be defined on the list view of a custom list with the list definition of type: **100**. Our ribbon tab and its button will call a script command, **RibbonButtonHandler**, which is defined in an external file: **RibbonActions.js**. This file will be located in the **Layouts** mapped folder we're about to create next.

3. Locate the **Layouts** mapped folder in your solution and create a new folder within it called **Chapter11** just to keep things separate. If you name it some other name, remember to update the reference in the ribbon definition in step 2.
4. Add a new item to the **Chapter11** folder of type **JScript File** from the **Web** category in Visual Studio dialog to **add new item**. Give your file the following name: **RibbonActions.js**.
5. Open the newly created file and replace its content with the following code:

LISTING 11-12

```
function RibbonButtonHandler()
{
    var options = {
    url: "/_layouts/Chapter11/MyCustomPage.aspx",
    width: 500,
    height: 600
    };

    SP.UI.ModalDialog.showModalDialog(options);
}
```
Here we open a new modal dialog using the out-of-the-box command: *SP.UI.ModalDialog.showModalDialog*.

6. Within the **Layouts/Chapter11** folder, I assume you already have the **MyCustomPage.aspx** created from the previous sample, if not, add a new item of type: **Application Page**, and give it a name: **MyCustomPage.aspx**.
7. Open your newly created application page and locate the following code within its content:

LISTING 11-13

```
<asp:Content ID="Main" ContentPlaceHolderID="PlaceHolder
Main" runat="server">
</asp:Content>
```

8. Replace the content found in the last step with the following:

LISTING 11-14

```
<asp:Content ID="Main" ContentPlaceHolderID="PlaceHolder
Main" runat="server">
This is the content of my custom page
</asp:Content>
```

9. Deploy your solution from Visual Studio and navigate to the root of your SharePoint test site, http://intranet.contoso.com. As you remember, our custom ribbon button is bound to a list view of a custom list. This means you need to create a custom list of your site and navigate to its view.
10. Locate and click our custom ribbon tab called **My Tab Name** and click on the button there; you will see a dialog with the content of the page we created.

Although in this example we created our custom application page so that we could add new functionality to its code, you can reference any SharePoint page in your ***RibbonActions.js*** event if it's a complex page with web parts on it. Give it a try!

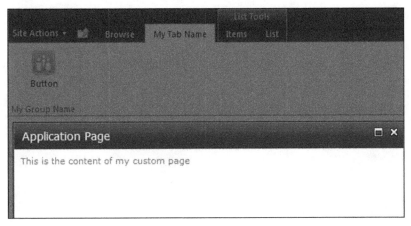

Figure 11-5 Modal window opened when custom ribbon button is clicked

Over the last few samples, you've been going through quite a lot that has to do with ribbon. You learned how to create simple and a bit more complex ribbon elements and how to find out the structure of out-of-the-box ribbon items to create your own. It's definitely a new approach to referencing your custom applications.

...ETC.

Here we are...if you've been good, you're reading this after you read the entire book. Hopefully you have gotten a complete overview of what branding for SharePoint 2010 is all about. If you haven't already, be sure to check out the source code for each chapter at www.sharemuch.com. That's where you can also reach me and tell me what you liked and didn't like about the book. I do hope you found this book resourceful and complete with examples that closely resemble your scenarios, and that everything actually worked from the first time.

If you find this book worth sharing with your peers or colleagues, please do so; you can also make me very happy by posting your review on Amazon. Authors like me read reviews religiously and you won't believe how warm it makes me feel to read a good review about my work ☺.

Thank you!

Yaroslav

www.ingramcontent.com/pod-product-compliance
Lightning Source LLC
Chambersburg PA
CBHW071405050326
40689CB00010B/1762